# Creativity
and the Imagination

*Also Published in This Series*

*The Culture of Biomedicine*
Edited by D. Heyward Brock

*The Languages of Creativity*
  *Models, Problem-Solving, Discourse*
Edited by Mark Amsler

# Creativity and the Imagination

## Case Studies from the Classical Age to the Twentieth Century

Studies in Science and Culture, Volume 3

*Edited by Mark Amsler*

D. Heyward Brock, General Editor
Center for Science and Culture
University of Delaware

DELAWARE

Newark: University of Delaware Press
London and Toronto: Associated University Presses

Associated University Presses
440 Forsgate Drive
Cranbury, NJ 08512

Associated University Presses
25 Sicilian Avenue
London WC1A 2QH, England

Associated University Presses
2133 Royal Windsor Drive
Unit 1
Mississauga, Ontario
Canada L5J 1K5

The paper used in this publication meets the
requirements of the American National
Standard for Permanence of Paper for Printed
Library Materials Z39.48-1984.

**Library of Congress Cataloging-in-Publication Data**

Creativity and the imagination.

(Studies in science and culture ; v. 3)
Includes bibliographies and index.
Contents: Seming and being / Glenn W. Most—History,
technical style, and Chaucer's Treatise on the
astrolabe / George Ovitt—Creation and responsibility in
science / Leonard Isaacs— [etc.]
1. Creative ability—Case studies. 2. Creation
(Literary, artistic, etc.)—Case studies. I. Amsler, Mark,
1949–     . II. Series.
BF408.C7546   1987        153.3        85-41031
ISBN 0-87413-296-7 (alk. paper)

Printed in the United States of America

# Contents

Preface   7

Seming and Being: Sign and Metaphor in Aristotle   11
  GLENN W. MOST

History, Technical Style, and Chaucer's *Treatise on the Astrolabe*   34
  GEORGE OVITT, JR.

Creation and Responsibility in Science: Some Lessons from
the Modern Prometheus   59
  LEONARD ISAACS

History and Geology as Ways of Studying the Past   105
  STEPHEN BRUSH

Science's Fictions: The Problem of Language and Creativity   134
  STUART PETERFREUND

Creative Problem-solving in Physics, Philosophy, and
Painting: Three Case Studies   168
  DONALD A. CROSBY and RON G. WILLIAMS

Notes on Contributors   215

Index   217

# Preface

This collection of essays on creativity and the imagination complements the second volume in this series *(The Languages of Creativity: Models, Problem-Solving, Discourse)* by offering in-depth critical accounts of creative problem-solving and discursive strategies from Plato and Aristotle to Rauschenberg and Einstein. The writers focus on sociological and historical issues in understanding how human beings have produced coherent or persuasive interpretations of their world, or better, how human beings have produced their world though constructions of reality.

One of the themes dominating the essays is the role of metaphor in both scientific and aesthetic work. Glenn Most details how metaphor is the ground of Aristotle's theory of cognition, while Leonard Isaacs elaborates on metaphor as the basis for the romantic approach to intuition and knowledge. In addition, Most and Isaacs link metaphor to those cultural schemata or poetic frames that Mark Johnson and George Lakoff have called "metaphors we live by." The other writers take up the problems of metaphoricity in scientific discourse and demonstrate in specific cases how science is discursive knowledge in a particular frame.

The dominance of metaphor in these essays may be related to the fact that all the writers are affiliated with traditional humanities departments (English, history, classics, philosophy). But to associate metaphor with the humanities alone would be to deny the very argument these essays collectively put forth—that metaphor, frames, scenarios, and schemata are crucial to all human cognition, not just to poetry or aesthetic play, and that one of the strongest links between the sciences and the humanities, as Mary Hesse has argued in *Models and Analogies in Science*, is that metaphor and discourse are the basis of the kinds of knowledge both disciplines produce. In this sense, the essays in Volume 2 of this series (especially those by William Frawley, James Dye, Stephen Barker, and W. H.

Bossart) provide the theoretical prologue to the historical case studies presented here.

Metaphoricity, where remoteness persists in proximity and difference in similarity, has also been a principal component of the work of Hans–Georg Gadamer and Paul Ricoeur. What Gadamer and Ricoeur demonstrate is that language in its metaphoricity is a "seeing-as" rather than a juxtaposition of images. Again, poetry, history, and science are kinds of discourse, ways of seeing-as, which constitute as much their alienation from the world they interpret as their adequacy to that world. Metaphor in science and art marks the place in discourse where concept formation is interrupted by the perception of difference and contingency. And in that place the relation between the sciences and the humanities is spelled out in the alphabet of knowledge.

# Creativity
# and the Imagination

# Seming and Being: Sign and Metaphor in Aristotle

GLENN W. MOST

*Princeton University*

Profound apologies for the pun in my title. Originally I had planned a more neutral and straight-forward announcement of my topic, but I must confess that later, in a moment of weakness, I succumbed to the blandishments of my φαντασία, by which, as we all know, we are often led into error. Yet what if it turns out, upon closer inspection, that the processes of appearing and of signifying, of seeming and of seming, have so much in common for Aristotle that the change of a single letter can almost appear insignificant? If so, then I shall perhaps not owe the reader an apology; but I shall still owe one to Aristotle, the first thinker to have attempted to provide the conceptual foundations for a systematic theory of the sign and someone whose ghost inevitably haunts volumes such as this one. Aristotle himself, of course, refers to puns of the sort I have inflicted upon the title of this essay, but he praises them with faint damns. Thus in the *Rhetoric*, in a discussion of urbanity (τὰ ἀστεῖα):

> This also comes about when something unexpected happens, and, as he [scil. Theodorus] says, not according to the previous expectation, but rather like slight alterations of words among jokesters (this can also be achieved by jokes which change a few letters, for they deceive) and among poets. For example, "He marched, bearing under his feet chilblains" does not end as the listener supposed it would, for he thought the poet would say "sandals." As soon as this is said it must be clear . . . In all these cases, success is attained when the word is applied appropriately by homonymy or by metaphor.[1]

11

We need not be surprised that Aristotle associates these wit-
ticisms with metaphor, even though the description he gives
does not require the association, and none of his examples
involves metaphor. The association may be understood as a
result of the many features such jokes share with metaphors in
Aristotle's account of the latter: both are brief, both teach something new, both are produced by a faculty that is not shared
equally by all people and both produce pleasure in the listener.
I will say more about metaphor shortly; but at the moment
Aristotle's correlation of urbanity with homonymy is worth
lingering over briefly, for it is to this latter phenomenon that he
devotes most of his analysis and almost all his examples in the
*Rhetoric*. Homonymy, by which one word has at least two
different meanings,[2] is clearly going to be more closely involved in any account of puns than is metaphor. But for the
reader of the *Rhetoric*, by this point in the third book the term
*homonymy* has become so univocally specified that its brief
mention here is enough to put him on his guard. In the second
chapter of this same book Aristotle had written, "Among
nouns, it is homonyms that are useful to the sophist, for by
means of them he uses unfair arguments" (*Rhet.* 3.2.1404b37–
39), and, a few chapters later, he had given as one of the five
rules for attaining grammatical correctness the avoidance of the
closely related phenomenon of ἀμφιβολία or ambiguity[3]:

> The third rule is not to speak in ambiguous terms. But these
> can be used if this is just what is sought, as is done whenever
> people in fact have nothing to say but pretend to be saying
> something. . . . All such things are alike; hence they are to
> be avoided, unless for some such reason [as deliberately
> intending to deceive]. (*Rhet.* 3.5.1407a32–34, 1407b5–6)

And in Aristotle's list of the false enthymemes in the second
book, those based upon homonymy are awarded the dubious
distinction of the second place (*Rhet.* 2.24.1401a13–25).
    My punning title was designed to call attention to the dis-
quieting collocation, at this point in Aristotle's thought, of metaphor and homonymy—disquieting because, while metaphor
is almost always accorded by Aristotle a position of considerable honor (and one practically unparalleled in ancient
thought[4]), he almost never has kind words for homonymy.
Aristotle is a central figure in that most basic tradition of West-

ern philosophy that begins with Hesiod's distinction between the two kinds of 'Ἔρις [5] and continues well beyond Frege, Russell, and Austin,[6] and locates one of the greatest handicaps to clarity of thought in the ability of words to mean different things. This tendency of Aristotle is expressed particularly in two well-known and interrelated strategies in his writings. On the one hand, he consistently attributes to sophists, charlatans, fools, predecessors, and other low types the habit of arguing on the basis of homonymy.[7] To these people may be applied what Aristotle writes at the beginning of the *Sophistical Refutations*:

> Some reasonings do not do this [scil. achieve rigorous proof or refutation] but seem to do so for many reasons; of these the single most natural and common field is the one by means of words. For since it is not possible to converse and simultaneously bring in the things themselves, but instead we use words in place of things as their symbols, we suppose that what follows in the case of words follows too in that of things, just as those do who reckon with counters. But this is not the same. For the number of words and the quantity of discourses are limited, while things are unlimited in number. Hence the same discourse and a single word must necessarily signify more than one thing. Just as then in counting those who are not skilled at using the counters are cheated by those who have this skill, so in the same way in the case of discourses as well those who are inexperienced in the meaning of words reason falsely, both when they themselves are conversing and when they listen to others.[8] . . . Now since for some people it is preferable to seem to be wise rather than to be wise without so seeming (for sophistry is a seeming wisdom which is not in fact so, and the sophist makes money from a seeming wisdom which is not in fact one), clearly it is necessary that for these people it is likewise preferable to seem to do the job of a wise man rather than in fact to do it but not to seem to do so. . . . Hence those who wish to practice sophistry must of necessity investigate the aforementioned type of discourses. (*Soph. Elench.* 1.1.165a3–17, 19–24, 28–29)

Had we only been given the chance, I suspect that most of us would in fact have preferred really to be wise rather than merely to seem so; and there is no doubt where Aristotle's own sympathies lie. For symmetrical with this first strategy is a second one by which he assigns principally to the philosopher the task of discriminating among the various meanings of words. Much of Aristotle's actual philosophical practice consists in precisely such discriminations.[9] A theoretical justification for this practice is supplied in the *Topics:*

> It is useful to examine how many meanings a word has, with a view both towards clarity (for one would likelier know what one is proposing if it were previously made clear how many meanings a word has) and towards its coming about that the reasonings are in accordance with the thing itself and not directed towards the words. For if it is unclear how many meanings a word has, it is possible that the answerer and the questioner are not directing their thought to the same thing; but if it is made clear how many meanings a word has and with regard to which one he proposes it, the questioner would seem ridiculous if he did not direct his discourse to this one. It is also useful with a view both towards not being misled by fallacious reasoning and towards misleading others in this way. . . . But this mode of argumentation does not belong properly to dialectic; for this reason dialecticians should be thoroughly wary of this kind of thing, arguing with regard only to the words, unless one is quite incapable of arguing about the matter proposed in any other way. (*Top.* 1.18.108a18–27, 33–37)

In other words, even a philosopher can get caught short sometimes and must weasel his way out of a tight situation by throwing in an opponent's eyes the sand of homonymy. But in doing so, he will not be arguing *qua* philosopher, but *qua* weasel.

Clearly, a prejudice and a hope underlie these twin strategies. The prejudice is that our lives would be much easier if words did not mean more than one thing. But why should it cause us trouble that words can have multiple meanings? Why could not the partners in a philosophical interchange regard the polysemantic quality of their terms as an enrichment? The answer is obvious: the trouble is caused by the fact that people naively assume that words *are* monovalent and that the meaning that occurs to them must therefore be the only possible one and must be what their interlocutor has in mind. It is only because they take this monovalence for granted without having examined the words in question that they can be misled by the unscrupulous and that the sophists can make money. One may term this first principle *naive* monovalence. Aristotle's hope is that people can be brought to move beyond this unreflective acceptance of words to a recognition of the plurality of meanings they may conceal. But that is not all—if it were, his enterprise would ultimately be skeptical or pessimistic. Instead, he harbors the hope that the various meanings of terms can be so carefully discriminated and clarified that each of them will become thoroughly disambiguated. The word $x$ may have $n$ meanings, but Aristotle holds it to be possible so to analyze $x$ that, by means of suitable qualifications or definitions, it will be broken down into the $n$ varieties $x_1$, $x_2$, $x_3$, . . . $x_n$, each of which will be unmistakable and univocal. That is, the word $x$ will turn out to be a covering term that can be unpacked into $n$ unambiguously defined or qualified $x$'s, and true agreement and progress will thereby be made possible. One may term this second principle that of *sophisticated* monovalence; in this regard, Aristotle's goal is to retain—in fact, to secure and strengthen—monovalence by discarding pennies on the naive level so as to recoup dollars on a sophisticated one.

This strategy must be borne is mind when we consider Aristotle's most extensive analysis of the material of language, in chapters 20 and following of the *Poetics*, for it is presupposed by that analysis.[10] Aristotle begins by distinguishing the eight parts of speech (λέξις): elements, syllable, connective, joint, name, verb, case, and proposition (*Poet.* 20.1456b20ff.). What Aristotle means by some of these terms is far from clear, and I shall set aside here the interesting but perhaps insoluble question of how they are to be correlated with other Greek analyses of the parts of speech, let alone with modern ones.[11] Instead, I should like to emphasize the fundamental structure of his analysis, which is tabulated in table 1.

Aristotle's analysis (from *Poet.* 20) is obviously organized around two pairs of oppositions: a basic one of signifying versus nonsignifying and a subsidiary one of divisible versus indivisible; this latter is modified in the case of signifying units to become divisible into signifying parts versus indivisible into signifying parts. The only partial exception is case (πτῶσις, 1457a18–23), which is in fact not itself a separate part of speech but instead assists names and verbs in signifying when they

| Non-signifying ἄσημος | | Signifying σημαντικός | |
|---|---|---|---|
| indivisible ἀδιαίρετος | divisible συνθετή | parts do not signify | parts signify |
| element στοιχεῖον | syllable συλλαβή<br><br>connective σύνδεσμος<br><br>joint ἄρθρον | name ὄνομα<br><br>verb ῥῆμα<br><br>(case) πτῶσις | proposition λόγος |

Table 1. Aristotle's analysis of the parts of speech (*Poet.* 20).

become parts of propositions; and even here the emphasis upon signification is unmistakable. For Aristotle, the essential feature of language is that it signifies: there is no part of language that does not contribute to this function, either by itself signifying or by being entirely taken up as a part, in itself nonsignifying, into a larger whole that does signify. Thus, for example, the element is a nonsignifying indivisible sound (1456b22), but not just any such sound: rather it is only one out of which, by its nature, a composite intelligible sound can be constituted. The brute animals utter nonsignifying indivisible sounds, too, but none of these is an element in Aristotle's sense, as he himself explicitly asserts (1456b22–25). From the very beginning, therefore, Aristotle's account of language is placed under the aegis of signification.

But what *is* signification? Aristotle does not bother to tell us here: he presupposes that we already know so clearly what signification signifies that we will be able without difficulty to follow his cursory sketch. To find out what signification is, we must detour for a moment to the beginning of Aristotle's *De Interpretatione:*[12]

Things that are spoken are symbols of experiences in the soul, and things that are written are symbols of those that are spoken. And just as letters are not the same for all men, the elements of speech are not the same either; but the experiences of the soul, of which first these are the signs, are the same for all men, and the things, of which these experiences are the likenesses, are also the same. (*De Interp.* 1.16a3–8)

A closed system of equivalences is constructed here. Written words are the symbols of spoken ones, spoken words are the symbols of mental experiences, and mental experiences are the symbols of external objects.[13] It may look at first as though Aristotle is operating with a three-part account of the total phenomenon of language: words (whether written or spoken would be indifferent here), mental images, and things. If that were so, we could directly correlate Aristotle's analysis with the basically triadic structure that characterizes most modern accounts of the linguistic sign. Whether we think of Peirce's triad of representamen, interpretant, and object, or of Saussure's triad of *signifiant, signifié,* and *referent,* or of Frege's triad of *Zeichen, Sinn,* and *Bedeutung*[14]—to name only a few—we could add Aristotle to the ranks of those who analyze language into a signifying material substrate, a concept or mental process that would provide the meaning of that substrate, and an independent and nonlinguistic phenomenon to which in some way the sign would refer.[15] But to do so would represent a serious misunderstanding of Aristotle's position. Why does he claim, in the passage just cited, that the mental experiences and the things of which those experiences are the likenesses are the *same* for all people? A moment's consideration will reveal that both claims are empirically quite false.[16] We all use the word *pizza,* but the mental experience I associate with the word is by no means identical with anyone else's, as a brief conversation on the subject will readily disclose; just so, the thousands of pizzas upon which my mental image and other people's are based are not the same for all of us. The difficulties become even greater for words such as *honorable* or *nonexistence.*

A claim so clearly counterfactual is usually strongly motivated not by the examination of the way things are but rather by the internal economy of an argument: the claim is often put forth largely because the consequences that would follow from its being the case are convenient for the author's interests rather than because it is true. I suggest that this is the case here. Aristotle himself was not unaware of the obstacles reality interposes in the path of such a theory as he outlines in *De Interpreta-*

*tione,* as is made clear by his many discussions of ambiguity and by such passages as the one from the *Sophistical Refutations* quoted above. What advantage, then, may he be suspected to have derived from such a bizarre claim? The postulated identity of all mental experiences permits those experiences to become a transparent medium through which words can point directly to objects; for if we did not all share identical mental experiences, the process of communication would require us to compare, and, if possible, try to reconcile our varying mental images so that we could make ourselves understood to one another when we ordered a pizza. As it is, on Aristotle's account, the significa-tion of *pizza* passes through our mental experience of pizzas without let or hindrance and comes to rest at the object *pizza* upon which all those experiences are based. And the postu-lated identity of those objects means that, from the point of view of language's signifying capability, the enormous dif-ferences among the many empirical pizzas in the world are of no account.

Clearly, more is at stake here than lunch. Though Aristotle invokes the three terms of words, mental experiences, and objects, his analysis is designed to reduce their relations from triadic to dyadic. Words are subsumed entirely into mental images, and mental images are subsumed in turn into objects. The middle term can be short-circuited and then words will turn out to be subsumable without residue into objects. These objects are not so much the concrete particulars themselves (which we would have expected to function as the source of our mental experiences) as their essence, which permits the right word to be properly applied to them. It need not be pointed out how unsatisfactory, from a modern perspective, such an ac-count is, nor how many difficulties—ontological, epis-temological, linguistic—it suppresses. But Aristotle should not be judged too unkindly for having failed to develop a triadic model of language of the sort that was not established systemat-ically (albeit imperfectly) until the Stoics.[17]

With this in mind we may return to the *Poetics.* Having concluded his catalogue of the parts of speech in chapter 20, Aristotle turns in chapter 21 to a closer consideration of names. After establishing that names can be either simple or com-pound (a continuation, admittedly a trifle inconsistent, of his use of the opposition divisible versus indivisible from the pre-ceding chapter), Aristotle asserts that all names are either standard (κύριον), dialect (γλῶττα), metaphor, or ornament (κόσμος); these last are further subdivided into words that are coined, lengthened, shortened, or altered (*Poet.* 21.1457a31ff.). While Aristotle does not revert explicitly in this chapter to the vocabulary of signification so conspicuous in the preceding section, it is easy to show that his treatment of the kinds of nouns presupposes the same conception of signification we found premised there and elaborated in the *De Interpretatione*. *Standard* and *dialect* are complementary terms: the former refers to words that, under normal circumstances in a particular linguistic community at a particular time, are used univocally to designate some object, while the latter refers to those words that, from the point of view of this same community, designate the object with equal monovalence but under abnormal circumstances (e.g., it is used by other communities or by the same community at an earlier period). In this pair of terms, the nonsemantic value of a word is qualified by considerations of concrete linguistic usage, but semantic monovalence is in no way affected. The four categories of ornamental names represent different ways in which the phonic materiality of the word can be altered without affecting its signification: that materiality can be lengthened or shortened by the addition or suppression of syllables in the second or third cases, or some or all of the syllables can be substituted for in the fourth or first cases, but again the word designates its proper object without causing confusion.

The great exception, of course, is metaphor, and it is to this phenomenon that Aristotle devotes the greater part of this chapter.[18] "Metaphor," according to Aristotle, "is the transfer to one thing of a name belonging to something else, either from the genus to the species or from the species to the genus or from the species to the species or according to analogy" (*Poet.* 21.1457b6–9). Aristotle's analysis is summarized in figure 1.

By far the greater part of his analysis is devoted to metaphors by analogy, and elsewhere Aristotle repeatedly adverts to such metaphors as the best or most popular kind.[19] I suggest that the privilege he bestows upon analogical metaphors is due to the fact that these provide the clearest case of the fundamental structure underlying all metaphors,—that is, that the other three kinds of metaphor can be reduced to special cases of metaphors by analogy. How this reduction can be performed is indicated clearly enough in figure 1; a more interesting ques-

4. $\kappa\alpha\tau\grave{\alpha}$ $\tau\grave{o}$ $\overset{\backprime}{\alpha}\nu\acute{\alpha}\lambda o\gamma o\nu$ :

$$\frac{A}{B} = \left[\frac{X}{Y}\right] = \frac{C}{D} \quad < \quad \begin{array}{l} A = \dfrac{CB}{D} \\[2mm] C = \dfrac{AD}{B} \end{array}$$

where X ≡ genus of A and C    CB ≡ figure apparent in text ≡ AD
      Y ≡ genus of B and D    A ≡ absent meaning ≡ C
                              D ≡ suppressed to allow metaphor ≡ B

3. $\overset{\backprime}{\alpha}\pi\grave{o}$ $\tau o\hat{v}$ $\overset{\prime\prime}{\epsilon}\iota\delta o\upsilon\varsigma$ $\overset{\backprime}{\epsilon}\pi\grave{\iota}$ $\overset{3}{\epsilon}\iota\delta o\varsigma$ :

   identical to 4, with possible difference
   that X and Y are more strictly generic

1. $\overset{\backprime}{\alpha}\pi\grave{o}$ $\tau o\hat{v}$ $\gamma\acute{\epsilon}\nu o\upsilon\varsigma$ $\overset{\backprime}{\epsilon}\pi\grave{\iota}$ $\overset{3}{\epsilon}\iota\delta o\varsigma$ :

$$\frac{A}{B} = \left[\frac{X}{Y}\right] = \frac{C}{D} \longrightarrow A = \frac{CB}{D}$$

   where X = C = genus of A
         Y = D = genus of B

2. $\overset{\backprime}{\alpha}\pi\grave{o}$ $\tau o\hat{v}$ $\overset{\prime\prime}{\epsilon}\iota\delta o\upsilon\varsigma$ $\overset{\backprime}{\epsilon}\pi\grave{\iota}$ $\tau\grave{o}$ $\gamma\acute{\epsilon}\nu o\varsigma$ :

$$\frac{A}{B} = \left[\frac{X}{Y}\right] = \frac{C}{D} \longrightarrow A = \frac{CB}{D}$$

   where X = A = genus of C
         Y = B = genus of D

Fig. 1. Aristotle's analysis of the kinds of metaphor (*Poet.* 21).

tion, and one deserving of closer examination, is how, according to Aristotle, metaphor fundamentally operates.

"I speak of the analogical variety," says Aristotle, "whenever a second term bears the same relation to a first term as a fourth term bears to a third one; for it will say the fourth instead of the second or the second instead of the fourth" (*Poet.* 21.1457b16–19). There are thus two stages that must be performed if metaphor is to come about, both equally indispensable: first a set of ratios must be constructed; then the metaphor itself is created by an act of substitution. As Aristotle makes clear in his analysis of analogy in his discussion of distributive justice in the *Nicomachean Ethics*,[20] his use of the concept in such passages represents a (metaphorical) transference of a technique from the domain of mathematics, where it has its source and more properly belongs, to another domain, one in which the elements that enter into ratios with one another are not numerical. We may take this mathematical hint to diagram as follows the examples Aristotle himself provides, "the cup is the shield of Dionysus" and "the shield is the cup of Ares" (*Poet.* 21.1457b20–22):

$$\frac{A}{B} = \frac{C}{D} = \left(\frac{E}{F}\right) \cdots \left[\frac{X}{Y}\right]$$

$$\frac{\text{cup}}{\text{Dionysus}} = \frac{\text{shield}}{\text{Ares}} = \left(\frac{\text{winnowing-basket}}{\text{Demeter}}\right)$$

$$\cdots \left[\frac{\text{round, flat attribute}}{\text{god}}\right]$$

The construction of this ratio is the indispensable preliminary step; it is governed by the generic terms indicated as X and Y, and in principle may be extended further by other examples (here E and F). The metaphor itself is created by moving up one of the terms to the other side of the equation:

$$A = \frac{CB}{D}$$

$$\text{cup} = \frac{\text{shield of Dionysus}}{\text{Ares}}$$

Here C designates the word that is the metaphorical term itself, and A the meaning of the metaphor, which would normally be absent, unexpressed in the text but understood by the reader. B, on the other hand, symbolizes the context within which the metaphor occurs: it can of course be explicitly supplied as in the phrase "shield *of Dionysus*," but it need not be; it is only necessary that the general context evidently refer to Dionysus for the word *shield* to be understood in this case as signifying not a shield, but a cup. But that means that the normal meaning of *shield* must be forgotten by the reader if he is to arrive at the figural meaning of a cup. There are obviously very many situations, for example on the battlefield, where if *shield* does not mean a shield somebody is going to be in big trouble.[21] This necessary forgetting is symbolized here by the bar that separates D and puts it in the denominator: this is Lacan's bar of suppression, indicating that D must be repressed into the unconscious if the metaphor is to work.[22]

Viewed in this way, Aristotle's discussion, which may at first glance seem dishearteningly formalist, takes on a new richness and psychological complexity—as is only appropriate, for metaphors are only metaphors insofar as they are recognized to be such by human writers and readers. Every metaphor is shown thereby to depend upon a determinate context and a specific kind of forgetting, both of which must be given if the substitution of terms involved is to be recognized as such. Aristotle implies by his examples here, and makes the explicit claim elsewhere (*Rhet.* 3.4.1407a15–18), that every analogical metaphor should be reversible. In principle this is certainly true, but no literary tradition is required to give equal prominence to both possibilities, and hence it can happen that one possible substitution becomes more familiar than the other. Thus, the proportion

$$\frac{\text{evening}}{\text{day}} = \frac{\text{old age}}{\text{life}} = \frac{\text{autumn}}{\text{year}} \cdots \left[\frac{\text{last, golden part}}{\text{period of time}}\right]$$

can generate such perfectly intelligible metaphors as "the evening of life" or "the old age of the day," to stay with Aristotle's own examples (*Poet.* 21.1457b22–25), or, to add one from Shakespeare's Sonnet 73,

> That time of year thou mayst in me behold
> When yellow leaves, or none, or few, do hang

Upon those boughs which shake against the cold,
Bare ruin'd choirs, where late the sweet birds sang.
In me thou see'st the twilight of such day
As after sunset fadeth in the West;
Which by and by black night doth take away,
Death's second self, that seals up all the rest.

But readers in every literary tradition are not always prepared equally to accept all such conversions. Consider the analogy

$$\frac{\text{camel}}{\text{desert}} = \frac{\text{ship}}{\text{sea}} \cdots \begin{bmatrix} \text{swaying conveyance} \\ \text{wavy trackless waste} \end{bmatrix}$$

The trope "ship of the desert" is very familiar, but, despite the frequency of such related Old English kennings as *brimhengest*, *merehengest*, and *lagumearh*(sea-horse, ship), the modern English-speaking reader is likely to find the converted metaphor "camel of the sea" for "ship" faintly ridiculous.[23]

To stay with this last example for a moment, we can see how Aristotle's account of metaphor can be fruitfully applied to the interpretation of literary texts by considering a celebrated passage from Wordsworth, the dream of the Arab in Book 5 of the *Prelude*. Wordsworth, reading *Don Quixote* and pondering the internal perfection and hence putative immortality of poetry and geometry, falls asleep after having read the first few pages of Part I, Book II, Chapter 1 of the text,[24] and has a curious and deeply unsettling dream:

I saw before me stretched a boundless plain
Of sandy wilderness, all black and void,
And as I looked around, distress and fear
Came creeping over me, when at my side,
Close at my side, an uncouth shape appeared
Upon a dromedary, mounted high.
He seemed an Arab of the Bedouin tribes:
A lance he bore, and underneath one arm
A stone, and in the opposite hand, a shell
Of a surpassing brightness. At the sight
Much I rejoiced, not doubting but a guide
Was present, one who with unerring skill
Would through the desert lead me; and while yet
I looked and looked, self-questioned what this freight
Which the new-comer carried through the waste

Could mean, the Arab told me that the stone
(To give it in the language of the dream)
Was "Euclid's Elements"; and "This," said he,
"Is something of more worth"; and at the word
Stretched forth the shell, so beautiful in shape,
In colour so resplendent, with command
That I should hold it to my ear. I did so,
And heard that instant in an unknown tongue,
Which yet I understood, articulate sounds,
A long prophetic blast of harmony;
An Ode, in passion uttered, which foretold
Destruction to the children of the earth
By deluge, now at hand. No sooner ceased
The song, than the Arab with calm look declared
That all would come to pass of which the voice
Had given forewarning, and that he himself
Was going then to bury those two books . . .[25]

Wordsworth follows the Arab, who "to my fancy, had become the knight / Whose tale Cervantes tells; yet not the knight, / But was an Arab of the desert too; / Of these was neither, and was both at once" (5.122–25), until both notice behind them

A bed of glittering light: I asked the cause:
"It is," said he, "the waters of the deep
Gathering upon us"; quickening then the pace
Of the unwieldy creature he bestrode,
He left me: I called after him aloud;
He heeded not; but, with his twofold charge
Still in his grasp, before me, full in view,
Went hurrying o'er the illimitable waste,
With the fleet waters of a drowning world
In chase of him; whereat I waked in terror . . .
(5.129–38)

Many features of this dream are odd, not the least of which is the role of the sea. Why should the sea pose such a threat within the dream that its approach can lend it an atmosphere of such desperate urgency and its imminent arrival can cause Wordsworth to awaken in terror? Wordsworth, to be sure, does not explicitly employ the metaphor "ship of the desert" in this passage, though there can be no doubt that he was familiar with it;[26] but he does describe the dromedary in terms appropriate for a ship,[27] and it is at least worth suggesting that this dream can be interpreted as the narrative of Wordsworth's failed attempt to construct the metaphor

$$\text{camel} = \frac{\text{ship of the desert}}{\text{sea}}$$

We have the camel (in the form of a dromedary), and we have more than enough desert. We even have one kind of metaphor in the conflation of the Arab and Don Quixote: both are similar in being creations of Cervantes's imagination, in being mounted on high and equipped with a lance, and in being engaged in noble, futile, and ludicrous pursuits. But if the Arab's conflation with Don Quixote aligns him with the creative vitality of Cervantes's poetic genius, Wordsworth's stance with regard to the Arab must remind us of Sancho Panza, with all the latter's earth-bound realism and lack of imagination. Such a correlation puts Wordsworth's own poetic genius implicitly into question; at issue is whether Wordsworth is as great a poet as Cervantes, and this issue becomes in a very real sense a matter of life and death, both in the immediate context of the question of the survival of great poetry and before the larger background of Wordsworth's persistent doubts about his own poetic capabilities. For a poet, the proof of his vitality is his ability to make metaphors:[28] underlying the narrative is the urgent question whether Wordsworth will succeed in creating the metaphor "ship of the desert" and proving himself as a poet. The reason that the metaphorical substitution fails, the reason that we never attain this trope, is that the fourth term in the ratio, *sea*, cannot be adequately suppressed. At the very horizon of consciousness, it arises as a threat to the activity of metaphorization and therefore as a terrifying danger to the poet whose stock in trade is metaphors; when the sea can no longer be held back, the attempt to create the metaphor that is narrated here must end prematurely in failure. Wordworth had the dream, as he tells us,

> While I was seated in a rocky cave
> By the sea-side, perusing, so it chanced,
> The famous history of the errant knight
> Recorded by Cervantes . . .

> While listlessly I sate, and, having closed
> The book, had turned my eyes toward the wide sea.
>                                             (5.58–61, 63–64)

The first thing he sees when he wakes in terror is the sea in front of him (5.139). Hence we can redescribe Wordsworth's situation psychologically: the sea is the object of his conscious, wakeful mind; only if he forgets it can he fall asleep and dream; but he fails to do so entirely and hence wakefulness, in the form of the sea before him, threatens his sleep and his dream; when he can no longer suppress his subliminal awareness of the sea, he awakens. This psychological redescription is possible and indeed in some sense obviously right; but I think that the deep-seated horror the dream inspires in Wordsworth becomes more comprehensible if we also analyze it rhetorically along the lines I have suggested.

With Wordsworth we have moved not only from a theoretical description of metaphorization to its practical enactment, but also from an ancient philosopher for whom metaphor, all things considered, is still a relatively minor and controllable phenomenon to a modern poet for whom the ability to create metaphors is a matter, not only figuratively, of life and death. For Wordsworth, the rhetorical theory of figural language has intimate and important links with an epistemological notion of the creative imagination he shares with other romantics: the poet's direct access to that fundamentally human capability enables him to speak a poetic language that can be simultaneously both powerfully original and thoroughly shareable with other members of his linguistic community. We may well feel that Aristotle, however sympathetically we may wish to interpret his remarks on metaphor, has a less profound understanding of it than Wordsworth does. To find out whether or not this is in fact the case, however, we must inquire whether there are connections also in Aristotle between linguistics and epistemology—more specifically, between metaphor and imagination.

The first point is that, with the exception of the kind of metaphor to which no literal term corresponds,[29] which functions here as a unique and possibly disruptive violation, Aristotle's linguistic theory is organized by a conceptual model of considerable power and simplicity, presented in schematic form in figure 2. As this diagram indicates, Aristotle's notion of language involves, under normal, literal circumstances, a one-to-one correspondence between words and their referents. Only in the case of metaphor does a word designate not its own referent but another word's: only here does *cup* mean not a cup but a shield. Thus metaphorical substitution represents a kind of disruption of the normal functioning of language, but a disruption that is strictly limited, highly organized, and (unless one is Wordsworth) easily controlled. For the rules whereby one word is permitted to signify the object of a different word are clearly defined: *cup* may mean, under certain determinate conditions, not a cup but a shield, but the competent reader will have no difficulty in understanding that, in this context, it is a shield and not a cup that is at issue.

When we turn to Aristotle's theories of sense perception and imagination (φαντασία), as presented in the *De Anima* and the *Parva Naturalia*,[30] we find that they are organized in terms of a structure that evinces a fundamental homology with that just outlined. (See figure 2).

For Aristotle, sense perception is always a binary relationship, involving a one-to-one correspondence between an

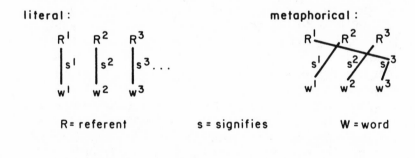

Fig. 2. Linguistics and Epistemology in Aristotle.

external object and an internal sensation. That object is always a concrete particular existing independent of the subject, and it actively exerts a stimulus upon him that he passively receives.[31] The monovalence of this relationship takes several forms. First, an object only presents itself to a particular sense-organ in the appropriate mode: as visible to sight, as tactile to touch, and so on.[32] But experience teaches that we very often apprehend a sense object by more than one faculty. This rather elementary observation evidently seems highly problematic to Aristotle, and he examines it at length in his discussion of common sensibles in De Anima 3.1. Presumably this phenomenon would not pose such difficulties for him if he were less attached to a very strict version of this binary model for perception, for it is only on such a version of this model that objects apprehended by the sensations of the various sense-organs must be provisionally theorized as being atomized into discrete, disparate units, so that the inevitable question of their integration into a single unified object capable of affecting different sense-organs in different ways can become particularly urgent. And second, each act of sensation occupies a unique and indivisible moment of time; as Aristotle says, perception refers only to the present, not to the past or future.[33] But again, experience teaches that we can perceive two different things simultaneously, and the question how this might be possible provokes a lengthy and elaborately artificial analysis in chapter 7 of De Sensu.[34] Again, it may be suggested that Aristotle's strict adherence to his binary model for sense-perception leads him to treat this simple fact as so problematic.

There is only one variety of sense-perception that Aristotle dispenses from this strict correlation of a single passive sensation and a single active copresent sensible object, and that is φαντασία, imagination, to which Aristotle devotes De Anima 3.3[35] Unlike Plato, for whom φαντασία is a faculty whereby sensations are interpreted,[36] Aristotle tends to define it as a kind of sensation: like sensation, it is directed to particulars rather than to generals and provides only individual images without combining or dividing, affirming or denying them.[37] But there is a crucial difference between imagination and perception, for imagination does not depend passively upon the simultaneous presence of an active sensible object, but is instead itself active and provides an image in the absence of the object to which it belongs.[38] Just as there is no perception of the past or future, so too, symmetrically, there should be no imagination, strictly speaking, of the present.[39] Hence we must ascribe to imagination all those forms of mental activity that provide us with the appearances of absent objects: the production of mental images accompanying concepts in *De Anima*, of memories in *De Memoria*, and of dreams and after-images in *De Insomniis*.[40]

In other words, imagination gives us an image of an object that had belonged to a different sensation, and, as indicated in figure 2b, it operates within the binary structure of sense-perception in precisely the same way as metaphor operates within the binary structure of literal language. It is quite true that what Aristotle calls φαντασία does not have the same degree of absolutely creative capability that some modern theories of the imagination, particularly various romantic theories of the poetic imagination, ascribe to that faculty, and we can readily understand why interpreters of Aristotle frequently warn us not to think of his φαντασία as poetic imagination.[41] But to stop here is to remain on the surface of his doctrine, and I would like to close with two questions that might suggest more fruitful, and more penetrating, lines for further discussion. First, the structural homology between metaphor and φαντασία may well indicate that there is a deeper justice in correlating these two terms within Aristotle's thought than the surface level of his texts might seem to warrant; if we remind ourselves of the essential role that metaphor plays in Aristotle's account of poetry, might we not be able to establish a covert connection between imagination and poetry in Aristotle's thought which we would otherwise have to go to Longinus and even later authors to find?[42] And second, it is admitted that Aristotle nowhere claims that imagination supplies us with images of objects that have never been perceived by some sensation. But this, translated onto the linguistic level, corresponds to the privilege Aristotle accords to metaphors for objects for which there is a literal equivalent. Might not that other variety of metaphor, those to which no literal expression corresponds and which a later tradition learned to call catachreses, provide, if translated back into the epistemological register, that eye of the needle through which, into Aristotle's seemingly closed system, could pass the idea of an imagination providing images to which no object of sensation could ever correspond, and thereby supply us with an implicit ancient precursor for romantic theories of the creative imagination?[43]

# NOTES

1. Aristotle, *Rhetoric* 3.11.1412a26–33, 1412b11–12. Here and in subsequent passages I have identified quotations by title, book (when relevant), chapter, and Bekker page, column, and line numbers. All translations are my own.

2. On this general phenomenon in Aristotle, see Jaakko Hintikka, *Time and Necessity: Studies in Aristotle's Theory of Modality* (Oxford: Clarendon Press, 1973), 1–26 ("Aristotle and the Ambiguity of Ambiguity,"), and Walter Leszl, *Logic and Metaphysics in Aristotle: Aristotle's Treatment of Types of Equivocity and Its Relevance to His Metaphysical Theories* (Padua: Antenore, 1970), 85ff.

3. For the connection between ὁμωνυμία and ἀμφιβολία in Aristotle, see *Soph. Elench.* 1.4.166a14f., 22f.; 1.17.175a36f., 40f., 175b7f., 39f.; 1.19.177a9f.

4. Cf. George Whalley, "Metaphor," in *Princeton Encyclopedia of Poetry and Poetics*, ed. Alex Preminger (Princeton: Princeton University Press, 1974).

5. Hesiod, *Works and Days*, 11–26.

6. Gottlob Frege, "Ueber die wissenschaftliche Berechtigung einer Begriffsschrift," in *Begriffsschrift und andere Aufsätze*, ed. I. Angelelli (Hildesheim: Georg Olms, 1964), 106ff.; Bertrand Russell, *The Philosophy of Logical Atomism* (Department of Philosophy, University of Minnesota, n.d.), 11ff, and *The Monist* 28 (1918): 517ff. (Russell's ironic plea in defense of the ambiguity of natural language is of course at the same time a justification for the development of a nonambiguous, philosophically satisfactory ideal language.) Also see J. L. Austin, *Philosophical Papers*, 2d ed., ed. J. O. Urmson and G. J. Warnock (Oxford: Clarendon Press, 1970), 69ff.

7. For example, *Top.* 6.10.148a23ff.; *Soph. Elench.* 4.165b30ff., 33.182b13; *De Part. An.* 1.1.641a1; *Metaph.* 1.9.991a6, 10.10.1059a14; *Eth. Nic.* 5.1.1129a27; *Rhet.* 2.24.1401a13, 3.2.1404b38.

8. There is an odd asymmetry to this analogy: in the case of counters the deceivers are the experts, in that of discourses the inexpert.

9. Cf. Hintikka, *Time and Necessity*, 4ff. in general; for analyses of several such passages, see Leszl, *Logic and Metaphysics*, 387ff.

10. The classic study of this chapter is H. Steinthal, *Geschichte der Sprachwissenschaft bei den Griechen und Römern*, 2 vols. (1890; reprint, Hildesheim ᴊeorg Olms, 1971), 1:253ff. The standard modern commentary is Aristotle, *Poetics*, ed. D. W. Lucas (Oxford: Clarendon Press, 1968), 198ff.

11. See A. Gudeman, "Grammatik," *Paulys Real-Encyclopädie der Classischen Altertumswissenschaft*, rev. ed., 7:1786f.

12. Cf. Leszl, *Logic and Metaphysics*, pp. 25ff., and Wolfgang Wieland, *Die aristotelische Physik* (Göttingen: Vandenhoeck u. Ruprecht, 1970), 162ff. A useful recent translation and commentary are provided by J. L. Ackrill in *Aristotle's Categories and De Interpretatione* (Oxford: Clarendon Press, 1963).

13. In fact, Aristotle uses three different terms to cover what I have indicated in this sentence with the single word *symbols*: σύμβολα (16a4) for the relation of spoken words to mental experiences and of written words to spoken ones; σημεῖα (16a6) for the relation of spoken words to mental experiences; and ὁμοιώματα (16a7) for the relation of mental experiences to external objects. But there is no clear systematic

distinction between these three terms in this passage, and they seem to be used interchangeably.

14. C. S. Peirce, *Elements of Logic*, in *Collected Papers*, ed. C. Hartshorne and P. Weiss, 8 vols. (Cambridge: Harvard University Press, 1932), 2:135ff.; F. de Saussure, *Cours de linguistique générale*, ed. T. de Mauro (Paris: Payot, 1972), 97ff.; Gottlob Frege, *Kleine Schriften*, ed. I. Angelelli (Darmstadt: Wissenschaftliche Buchgesellschaft, 1967), 143–62. To be sure, the theories of all three of these authors are too complicated for this triadic structure to be immediately apparent in any of them. Thus Peirce introduces additionally a ground of the representamen, "a sort of idea" in reference to which the sign stands for its object; it is not Saussure himself but his followers who have introduced the term *referent* (he himself excludes the object designated by a sign from the domain of linguistics); and Frege introduces as the purely subjective component of the sign a *Vorstellung*, between which and the *Bedeutung* the *Sinn* assumes an intermediary position. But it can be shown nevertheless that in essence all three theories are triadic in the sense described; for the purposes of the present argument, the differences introduced by the modifications added to this fundamental basis can be set aside as superficial.

15. It may be suggested that this triadic analysis of the sign is the distinguishing feature of all modern semiotic theories, and that it goes back to Kant; I hope to return to this question on another occasion.

16. Cf. Ackrill, *Aristotle's Categories and De Interpretatione*, 113f.

17. Cf. Steinthal, *Geschichte der Sprachwissenschaft*, 286ff., and Benson Mates, *Stoic Logic* (Berkeley and Los Angeles: University of California Press, 1961), 11ff.

18. A guide to the enormous secondary literature on this subject is provided by W. A. Shibles, *Metaphor: An Annotated Bibliography and History* (Whitewater, Wisc.: Language Press, 1971); the ancient material is conveniently collected by Heinrich Lausberg, *Handbuch der literarischen Rhetorik: Die Grundlegung der Literaturwissenschaft*, 2 vols. (Munich: Hueber, 1973), 1:285ff. Among recent studies, the most important include Jacques Derrida, "La mythologie blanche," in *Marges de la philosophie* (Paris: Minuit, 1972), 247–324; Marsh H. McCall, Jr., *Ancient Rhetorical Theories of Simile and Comparison* (Cambridge: Harvard University Press, 1969), 24ff.; Paul Ricoeur, *La métaphore vive* (Paris: Seuil, 1975); and W. Bedell Stanford, *Greek Metaphor: Studies in Theory and Practice* (1936; reprint, New York: Johnson Reprint, 1972), 6ff.

19. For example, *Rhet.* 3.2.1405a10f.; 10.1411a1f.; 11.1411b22f., 1412a5, 1412b34f.

20. *Eth. Nic.* 5.3.1131a29–32.

21. This act of forgetting on the part of the reader, without which metaphor is impossible, is usually neglected by authors writing on the subject; for an exception, see Hedwig Konrad, *Etude sur la métaphore*, 2d ed. (Paris: J. Vrin, 1958), 85ff. This is one crucial difference (but not the only one) between metaphor and the really quite disparate phenomenon of simile. A peculiar tendency to conflate the two by defining metaphor as an abbreviated simile has greatly hampered the development of an adequate theory of metaphor. The tendency begins already with Aristotle (*Rhet.* 3.14.1406b20ff.), is canonized by Cicero (*De Oratore* 3.39.157) and Quintilian (8.6.8), and largely determines the Renaissance reception of Aristotle (see Gerd Breitenbürger, *Metaphora: Die Rezeption des aristotelischen Begriffs in den Poetiken des Cinquecento* [Kronberg/Ts: Scriptor-Verlag, 1975], 18f, 84, 114, 133) and thereafter most modern theories of metaphor.

22. I adopt this use of the bar from Jacques Lacan, *Ecrits* (Paris: Seuil, 1966), 497ff. Of course, the bar does not function in this way in the preliminary ratio A/B-C/D, but that is because there no substitution and hence no psychic activity has as yet taken place.

23. Cf. B. Kliban, *Never Eat Anything Bigger Than Your Head* (New York: Work-man, 1976), "Transportation."

24. For a justification of these last words and for an interpretation of the relationships between the texts of Wordsworth and Cervantes, see my forthcoming "Wordsworth's 'Dream of the Arab' and Cervantes." To be sure, Wordsworth's dream is a highly complex, multifaceted, lengthy text, and I do not intend the remarks that follow as a global interpretation of it; instead they are to be understood as tentative, necessarily somewhat reductive suggestions, designed to suggest the utility of this analysis of Aristotle's view of metaphor by showing how it may be used to bring out otherwise hidden aspects of a celebrated but problematic poetic text. On my interpretation, Wordsworth's poem is a marginal case in the present context, if only because it seems to fail to construct a metaphor rather than realizing one. The same kind of analysis could more easily have been performed upon a short and simple poem organized around a single successful metaphor—for example, Anacreon 417 *PMG*, with the metaphorical ratio: $\dfrac{\text{girl}}{\text{humans}} = \dfrac{\text{filly}}{\text{horses}},$ yielding the metaphor girl $= \dfrac{\text{human filly}}{\text{horses}},$ in which the erotic context of the symposiastic performance makes the suppression of horses quite easy. But this would have been rather less interesting.

25. William Wordsworth, *The Prelude or Growth of a Poet's Mind,* ed. Ernest de Selincourt, rev. Helen Darbishire, 2d ed. (Oxford: Clarendon Press, 1959), Bk. 5, ll. 71–102. Here and below I cite from this edition, the 1850 version, indicating the passages in question by book and line numbers.

26. Cf. *OED* 3.240, s.v. "Desert," sb[2] 1 and 5c, and 9.704, s.v. "Ship," 4c.

27. So, for example, in terming the stone and the shell *freight* (5.84). Cf. *OED* s.v. "Freight," sb 2, where it is pointed out that the extension to land usages is an Americanism. To be sure, the *OED* itself includes the present passage under 2b (*transf.* A load, burden), but this is not necessary.

28. Wordsworth, *The Prose Works,* ed. W. J. B. Owen and Jane Worthington Smyser, 3 vols. (Oxford: Clarendon Press, 1974), 1:148–49 (preface to *Lyrical Ballads:* "the pleasure which the mind derives from the perception of similitude in dissimilitude"); 1:160 (Appendix on Poetic Diction: the earliest poetry was largely figural); and especially 3:31ff (1815 preface: all the examples of poetic imagination Wordsworth provides turn out upon inspection to be metaphors).

29. Cf. Derrida, "La mythologie blanche," 289ff, 304ff.

30. On φαντασία in Aristotle, J. Freudenthal, *Ueber den Begriff des Wortes* ΦΑΝΤΑΣΙΑ *bei Aristoteles* (Göttingen: A Rente, 1863), remains useful. More recent studies include W. D. Ross, *Aristotle,* 5th ed. (London: Methuen, 1949), 142–45; D. A. Rees, "Aristotle's Treatment of φαντασία, " in *Essays in Ancient Greek Philosophy,* ed. John P. Anton and George L. Kustas (Albany: State University of New York Press, 1971), 491–504; J. Engmann, "Imagination and Truth in Aristotle," *Journal of the History of Philosophy* 14 (1976): 259–65; Malcolm Schofield, "Aristotle on the Imagination," in *Aristotle on Mind and the Senses,* ed. G. E. R. Lloyd and G. E. L. Owen (Cambridge: At the University Press, 1978), 99–129, and *Articles on Aristotle. 4: Psychology and Aesthetics,* ed. Jonathan Barnes, Malcolm Schofield, and Richard Sorabji (London: Duckworth, 1979), 103–32; and Gerard Watson, "φαντασία in Aristotle, *De anima* 3.3," *CQ* 32 (1982): 100–113.

31. *De Anima* 2.5.416b33–35, 417b20–27.

32. *De Anima* 2.6.418a14–16, 2.7.418a26f, etc.

33. *De Memoria* 1.449b10–15.

34. *De Sensu* 7.447a12ff.

35. The fact that φαντασία has many features in common with both sensation

and thought leads Aristotle occasionally to identify it with the latter (cf. the passages cited by Freudenthal, *Ueber den Begriff,* p. 53 n. 4), but more often he correlates it with the former (*Ueber den Begriff,* p. 53 n. 5). Freudenthal is surely not far off the mark when he writes, "Vor Allem aber ist ihre Identität mit der Wahrnehmung festzuhalten" (*Ueber den Begriff,* p. 53).

36. Plato, *Sophist* 264B, *Philebus* 38C-D.

37. *Eth. Nic.* 7.3.1147b3–5, *De Anima* 3.3.432a10–12.

38. *De Anima* 3.3.427b17–20.

39. In fact, on several occasions Aristotle seems to violate this corollary, but the violations are not grave and can be explained away: see Ross, *Aristotle,* 142–43, and Schofield, "Aristotle on the Imagination," 115–18.

40. *De Anima* 3.7.431a14–17, 3.8.432a8–14; *De Memoria* 450a23–25, 451a14–16; *De Insomniis* 1.459a14–22, 459b7–23.

41. For example, Rees, "Aristotle's Treatment of φαντασία," 496, and Aristotle, *De Anima,* ed. David Ross (Oxford: Clarendon Press, 1961), 38.

42. For the importance Aristotle attributes to metaphor, see e.g., *Rhet.* 3.2.1405a8–10, *Poet.* 22.1459a5–8. For later correlations of imagination and poetry or the other arts, cf. [Longinus], *On the Sublime* 15; Philostratus, *Life of Apollonius of Tyana* 6.19; Plotinus, *Enneads* 5.8.1.

43. This essay is an expanded version of a lecture presented at the Colloquium on Classical and Medieval Semiotics, Third International Summer Institute for Semiotic and Structural Studies, Victoria College, University of Toronto (June 1982).

# History, Technical Style, and Chaucer's *Treatise on the Astrolabe*

## GEORGE OVITT, JR.

*Drexel University*

Chaucer's *Treatise on the Astrolabe* is the oldest work in the English language whose concern is the description of a scientific instrument and a technological process.[1] Apart from this, the *Treatise* is significant for the student of the history of astronomy for the insights it provides into the development of observation, measurement, and record-keeping techniques that would come to make a rigorous and scientific astronomy possible. At the same time, because it provides the longest example of Chaucer's prose that is not a translation, the *Treatise* is important for students of the history of English literature in that it allows them to analyze Chaucer's abilities as a writer of prose, especially technical prose.[2] Also of interest is the history of the relations between the humanities and the sciences, for in the *Treatise on the Astrolabe* is clear evidence of the kind of technical expertise that a nonspecialist of the fourteenth century might have mastered. For the student of the troubled relations of the "two cultures," such evidence is invaluable.[3]

Yet, in spite of these obvious attractions, the *Treatise on the Astrolabe* has been virtually ignored by all of those constituencies that might be expected to take an interest in it.[4] Since it is impossible for a single essay to consider fully the literary, scientific, and historical significance of Chaucer's text, I intend in this preliminary investigation to suggest, first, the place of the *Treatise* and the scientific instrument it describes within the tradition of medieval astronomy. Second, I shall consider some of the issues raised by the way in which a fourteenth-century poet created a technical style capable of rendering the astrolabe and its functions into a form comprehensible to a "popular" audience. Finally, I shall make some general observations on the mode of scientific thought engendered by the use of a precision instrument—at once a technological artifact and a work of art—like the astrolabe.

Astronomy was accorded a unique status among the scientific disciplines of the Middle Ages. As early as the fifth century, long before the first wave of Arabic and Greek astronomical knowledge began to flow into the West, there was a sense of the sublimity of the study of the heavens. Isidore of Seville (c. 560–636), whose own contribution to the evolving science of astronomy was limited to the perpetuation of a cosmology lacking any reliance on systematic observation, nonetheless had a strong sense of the significance of the discipline: "[The] succession of the seven secular disciplines was terminated in astronomy by the philosophers so that it might free souls seduced by secular learning from worldly things and set them to contemplating higher things" ( . . . *scilicet ut animos saeculari sapientia implicatos a terrenis rebus abducerent, et in superna contemplatione conlocarent*).[5] The subordination of analysis and explanation of celestial phenomena to the contemplation of their metaphysical and moral efficacy engendered an attitude toward the heavens that would impede the development of a scientific astronomy until such time as philosophers were willing to see an inherent value in such worldly things as planetary motion.

Theological or metaphysical evaluations of the importance of astronomy similar to Isidore's can be found in the writings of other early encyclopedists like Macrobius (fl. c. 400), Martianus Capella (fl. 410–29), and Cassiodorus (c. 490–583). Macrobius, for example, describes the material universe as a hierarchical structure that has the central earthly sphere for both its physical and metaphysical nadir; the earth is created *ex defaecatis abrasum elementis*. The soul of man, containing as it does a spark of the primal being, spends its prison term on earth yearning for the stars. Macrobius's insistence on this dichotomy—built on platonic dualism and a gnostic mistrust of the material world—makes the stars spiritual emblems, invitations back to the primordial One, and also undercuts any merely physical interest in celestial phenomena.

Another and more interesting case of the subordination of astronomical knowledge to metaphysical ends can be found in

Martianus Capella's *De nuptiis Philologiae et Mercurii*. Martianus's rich allegory of the seven liberal arts is especially notable for its eighth book on astronomy; the roots of this abbreviated discussion of the highest quadrivial art are in Varro's *De astrologia*, a book which in turn goes back to Posidonius and to the astronomical handbooks of Geminus, Theon, and Cleomedes. One can trace echoes of Martianus's discussion in Bernard Silvestris, Thierry of Chartres, Adelard of Bath, and John of Salisbury.[6] Indeed, Martianus is even referred to as an honorable predecessor in Book I of Copernicus's *De revolutionibus*. What accounts for the long-term influence of Martianus's rather bombastic account of astronomical knowledge? Copernicus, for one, was impressed by Martianus's geoheliocentric system—an ingenious view that held that Mercury and Venus do not circle the Earth as the other planets do but circle the sun instead—but this view had no influence on the dominant two-sphere cosmology of the Middle Ages. No, what caused *De nuptiis* to have so great an influence was the success with which Martianus elicited a suitable theological meaning from the scientific material he treated; his allegory of planetary motions is another in a series of metaphysical descriptions of the longing for the heavens, not for the understanding of the mechanisms of their operation.

Among those influenced by Martianus was Johannes Scotus Eriugena (c. 810–77), whose rudimentary knowledge of Greek gave him access to works of celestial metaphysics but apparently not to works of celestial mechanics. His *De divisione natura* uses the pseudo-Dionysian *Celestial Hierarchy* to propound a theory of primordial causes that relates the "universe of creatures" to a generative Word.[7] Eriugena's theological cosmology influenced writers in the twelfth and thirteenth centuries—including Bernard of Chartres and Hugh of Saint Victor[8]—and helped to sustain a persistent metaphysical counterpoint to the physical and mathematical study of the heavens that began in earnest during the eleventh century. Indeed, one might detect in the "metaphysical astronomy" of the neoplatonic tradition—a tradition reaching from the *Timaeus*, through Chalcidius, to the school of Chartres[9]—an aspect of a larger issue, namely the struggle of the sciences to obtain a viable position in the organization of *scientia*.[10] The dominant position of theology and the subordination of the *artes liberales* and *artes mechanicae* to sacred doctrine might be seen to have slowed the development of astronomy by causing observation to be undervalued; the orderly appearances of the heavens were saved through reference to traditional texts in much the same way as the orderly interpretation of scripture was saved through the employment of traditional authorities and proved modes of analysis.[11] Isidore of Seville, for example, while describing the annual motion of the sun, observes that "it is plain that [the sun] has a motion of its own and does not move with the universe" because days and nights are not of equal length and because one may observe that it rises and sets in a different position each day. However, the notion of an independently moving sun created obvious problems for Isidore: How does one account for variations in the length of days or seasons if the sun's motion, which is *a priori* circular and uniform, carries it across a uniform distance? Isidore, unprepared to analyze the ecliptic (the sun's annual path across the heavens) and the effect that an observer's latitude has on the apparent motion of the sun, offered this answer instead: "[the sun] makes its annual orbits by unequal distances because of the changes of seasons" (*Etymol.*, 3.50). Here, the motion of the sun is seen as purposeful, and the phenomenon of seasonal change is itself the cause of the variation in distances that comprise the sun's annual course: "For going to the north, the sun restores the summer so that fruits may grow and what is green in the wet weather may ripen in the heat" (*Etymol.*, 3.50). Nature operates according to laws that account for the appearances of things; thus the sun also "bathes itself in the ocean" and later "passes by unknown ways beneath the earth to return again to the east" (*Etymol.*, 3.52). Such fanciful explanations of astronomical phenomena fill the *Etymologiae*: "The hinges [*cardines*] of the heavens are the ends of the axis and are called hinges because the heavens turn on them or because they turn like the heart [*vel quia sicut car volvuntur*]" (*Etymol.*, 3.38). The "hinges of the heart," while admittedly a pleasing image, suggest very little about the nature of the heavenly rotation that Isidore wished to explain. In reading Isidore, one comes to see that observation of astronomical phenomena is not the point; the *Etymologiae* records traditional texts, preserves the derivations of scientific and pseudoscientific terminologies, and aligns natural philosophy with the higher purposes of God's world. Like most other early medieval discussions of astronomy, the *Etymologiae* functioned primarily as a guide to reading the language of the heavens, not its laws. The true domain of such a text was not science but hermeneutics.[12]

The history of astronomy from Isidore of Seville and the other encyclopedists until the translations of the astronomical tables of al-Khwarizimi (1126), the *De compositione et utilitate astrolabii* of pseudo-Masha'allah[13] (c. 1133), and, most important of all, Ptolemy's *Almagest* (c. 1175), offers few works whose concern is the precise observation of planetary and stellar movements.[14] The Venerable Bede (673–735) did compose a work, *De temporum ratione,* that provided a detailed description of the problems of calendar construction, particularly the computation of the correct date for the celebration of Easter. While of considerable mathematical interest, this text, and the science of *compotus* that grew out of it, contributed little to development of observational astronomy.[15] Another important figure, Gerbert of Aurillac (c. 945–1003), was among the first to bring texts describing Arabic astronomical theories and instruments from northern Spain to Europe.[16] Gerbert also translated a number of scientific works, including works of astrology. Still, whatever intrinsic interest the careers and works of Bede and Gerbert have, they remain exceptional individuals during a time when astronomical knowledge went undeveloped. It took the translations and assimilation of Greek and Arabic texts during the twelfth century to provide the methods and tools necessary for the development of an astronomy based on observation and measurement.[17] Gerbert was in an intellectual avant-garde, with individuals like Daniel of Morley and Adelard of Bath, whose members would bring to the neoplatonic tradition in astronomy and cosmology the mathematical model and mathematical tools of Ptolemy.[18] This model, when used in conjunction with Aristotle's cosmological system as developed in *De caelo* and *Physica,* came to dominate the study of the heavens until the sixteenth century. However, the way first had to be prepared for the acceptance and assimilation of this Ptolemaic-Aristotelian system. Because Ptolemy's mathematics were often too difficult for young scholars, adaptations and nontechnical accounts of the new astronomy preceded this assimilation.

A century after the introduction of the *Almagest* and the diffusion of astronomical tables and astrolabes, a *corpus astronomicum* had developed within the universities of Paris and Oxford that gave the study of planetary motion a solid grounding in mathematics and measurement.[19] The most popular university textbook, John of Sacrobosco's (d. c. 1244–56) *De sphaera*, provided a much-simplified account of the heavens reminiscent of Isidore of Seville ("the sensible world is made in the likeness of the archetype . . .") but which also reveals the influence of Aristotle's *De caelo*, the *Almagest*, and al-Farghani's *Differentie scientie astrorum*.[20] Sacrobosco is of particular interest for this discussion because he provides a description of how the astrolabe could be used in the determination of the earth's circumference and because he is one of the writers to whom Chaucer makes specific reference in the *Treatise on the Astrolabe*.[21]

In addition to Sacrobosco, the medieval curriculum in astronomy made extensive use of Campanus of Novara's (d. 1296) *Theorica planetarum*, a simplified version of the *Almagest* that treated in detail the nature of planetary motion—a subject barely touched on by Sacrobosco.[22] Campanus, like Sacrobosco, apparently understood the principles of an astronomical instrument, in his case the equatorium. One fourteenth-century instrument-maker, Johannes de Lineriis, explicitly credits Campanus with having constructed this essentially three-dimensional astrolabe in order to create a model of the Ptolemaic system.[23] The equatorium provides a link with the larger subject of this essay, namely Chaucer and his *Treatise on the Astrolabe*, in that a work describing the equatorium has been attributed to Chaucer.[24]

From this brief sketch of the history of the traditions of medieval astronomy, we can make a useful distinction for the history of science between revolutionary discoveries and the gradual changes in modes of thought that make these discoveries possible. Furthermore, prerevolutionary changes in the theoretical structure of scientific thinking often depend upon the discovery and deployment of technological artifacts, with their potential for enhancing either preliminary observation or "postpartum" verification.[25] Thus, for example, interpretations of Galileo that neglect his debt to the impetus-theorists of the thirteenth and fourteenth centuries tend to present too "revolutionary" a view of scientific creativity, while interpretations that neglect the importance of Galileo's various experiments and observations tend to overemphasize the purely mathematical or rational aspects of his discoveries.[26] More recently, a complete description of the development of quantum mechanics requires that we consider the theoretical development of mathematical matrices, the practical development of cloud chambers and accelerators, the revolutionary insights of Pauli and the evolutionary context of twentieth-century physics within which these insights occurred.[27] In the case of medieval astronomy, while the introduction of the astrolabe into the West provided a sophisticated technological tool for the initiation of careful observation, significant astronomical discoveries did not occur until the sixteenth century because there existed neither the empirical methodology nor the critical habit of mind sufficient to create a break with the dominant Aristotelian-Ptolemaic cosmology.[28] A scientific insurrection of sorts followed the translation of Ptolemy into Latin, but the larger commitment to the defense of the theological status quo placed severe restrictions on how far a scientific theory could go; certainly theorizing did not keep pace with the accelerating technological change that was transforming the material life of Europe.[29] Even with the rise of the universities of northern Europe and the appearance of sophisticated scholar-scientists like Robert Grosseteste, Roger Bacon, and John Buridan, the theological orientation of natural philosophy was not displaced by a scientific methodology.[30] An instrument like the astrolabe promised the possibility of putting observation, precise measurement, and careful record-keeping in the service of astronomical theory—essential steps on the long road to the theoretical revolution of the sixteenth and seventeenth centuries.

Chaucer wrote the *Treatise on the Astrolabe* in 1391 to "Lyte Lowys," presumably his son.[31] His purpose in writing on such a difficult and, one might think, alien subject was ostensibly to satisfy the boy's desire "to lerne sciences touching nombres and proporciouns" (Intro.).[32] This characterization of Chaucer's intention supports evidence adduced by Poulle and others that astrolabe use served the needs of teaching geometry as often as it served the needs of observational astronomy.[33] In any case, Chaucer did intend to give the mysterious Lowys practical experience with the astrolabe as indicated by his statement that he has "yven [Lowys] a suffisant Astrolabie as for our orizonte, compowned after the latitude of Oxenforde" (Intro.) and by the fact that he has included a section of "conclusions" or problems designed to help his pupil translate theory into practice.

Yet, despite his opening remarks, Chaucer clearly wrote for a wider audience as well. The evidence for this contention is derived from the fact that a significant portion of the introduction to the *Treatise* is taken up with an apology for the use of "naked wordes in Englissh." It is true that Chaucer has used the vernacular for Lowys's sake—"for Latyn ne canst thou yit but small"—but the length and complexity of his apology would seem to indicate that he had other readers in mind:

> But natheless suffise to the these trewe conclusions in Englissh as wel as sufficith to these noble clerkes Grekes these same conclusions in Grek; and to Arabiens in Arabik, and to Jewes in Ebrew, and to the Latyn folk in Latyn; whiche Latyn folk had hem first out of othere dyverse langages, and writen hem in her owne tunge, that is to seyn, in Latyn. And God woot that in alle these langages and in many moo han these conclusions ben suffisantly lerned and taught, and yit by diverse reules; right as diverse pathes leden diverse folk the righte way to Rome. (Intro.)

This apology has both formal and material significance. Its formal significance derives from the evidence it presents concerning Chaucer's technical style. One notes particularly the care he took to be clear—the multiplication of examples to replace a simple summarizing statement; the redundant "that is to seyn, in Latyn," that nonetheless guarantees clarity; the selection of a perfectly apt, and perfectly expressive, metaphor with which to end the explanation of the babel of scientific "tunges." Provocative here is the phrase "and yit by diverse reules." Is Chaucer referring to the rules of different languages, or to the pedagogical possibility that modes of instruction will vary from language to language, or finally, to the possibility that the rules of astrolabe use will themselves alter? Most likely, Chaucer is acknowledging here the heterogeneity of modes of scientific discourse, while at the same time recognizing the unitary nature of the object of that discourse—in this case, the astrolabe. This point suggests the other, materially significant, aspect of the passage. When Chaucer uses the vernacular and writes that "I shewe the in my light Englissh as trew conclusions touching this mater, and not oonly as trewe but as many and as subtile conclusiouns, as been shewid in Latyn in eny commune tretys of the Astrelabie," he is taking a position regarding the expressive powers of the vernacular that was not altogether accepted in the fourteenth century.[34] Later in the "Introduction," Chaucer seems to return to this point with a further acknowledgement of the distinction between Latin and "lewd" languages: "I n'am but a lewd compilator of the labour of olde astrologiens, and have it translated in myn Englissh oonly for thy doctrine" (Intro.). In other words, Chaucer refuses to claim too much for his *Treatise*. He asserts that he creates nothing, nor does he claim originality for his text; he merely translates for Lowys what has been written in the "lerned tunges." This modest dismissal must be seen as both a rhetorical convention (what Curtius calls "affected modesty"[35]) and a sincere attempt to deflect criticism. Chaucer does do more, a great deal more, than merely translate from "Masha'allah's" *De compositione*, but it is also true that by writing "subtile conclusiouns" in the vernacular Chaucer was violating a learned convention. It may seem strange to us, living as we do in an age when the liberal arts are everywhere being displaced by the practical arts, to consider that Chaucer felt diffident about his undertaking precisely because it was a practical infringement on a primarily theoretical astronomical tradition based on a traditional university curriculum. Like Robert Sampson, whose courses in business writing attracted would-be court scribes to Oxford at around the time that the *Treatise* was being written, Chaucer was intruding in the domain of a conservative intellectual tradition by writing as an amateur and by popularizing his subject.[36]

The astrolabe that Lowys presumably held consisted of a circular disk, called the mother *(mater)*, into one side of which was inserted an alidade or pivotal sight. Chaucer describes the "moder" accurately as the "thikkest plate, perced with a large hool," but he does not, at this point, mention the alidade; instead, he describes a line that extends from the thumb-ring (by which the user holds his astrolabe) to the "netherist bordure" of the mother's "wombe" (I, 3–4). On the other side of the astrolabe were two thinner plates "compowned for diverse clymates [latitudes]," the rete and the tympan (usually called the *aranea* and *tubula regionum* in Latin). On most astrolabes, the tympan was inscribed with a stereographic project of the heavens—that is, a two-dimensional geometric representation of the spheres in the heavens—while the rete, described by Chaucer as "shapen in manere of a nett or of a webb of a loppe [spider]"

(I, 3), indicated the locations on the tympan of the brighter fixed stars.[37]

An examination of the first sections of "Masha'allah's" *De compositione* confirms Michael Masi's conclusion that Chaucer did not use this source in composing his own description of the astrolabe. Masi notes that while both Chaucer's *Treatise* and the *De compositione* are divided into two parts, one dealing with the construction of an astrolabe and the other with its use, Chaucer's description in Part I summarizes the parts of an already constructed instrument while "Masha'allah" gives detailed instructions that would allow a reader to build an astrolabe.[38] Nonetheless, as Masi notes, Chaucer's first section "appears written by a person well acquainted with the instrument's use" and confirms the fact that Chaucer did not merely copy out sources but knew enough about the astrolabe to provide a clear description of its construction and use. A comparison of certain sections from Part I of the *Treatise on the Astrolabe* with sections from *De compositione* dealing with the same material confirms Chaucer's originality and also reveals something of the characteristics of his technical style:

> This moder is dividid on the bakhalf with a lyne that cometh descending fro the ring doun to the netherist bordure. The whiche lyne, fro the forseide ring unto the centre of the large hool amidde, is clepid the south lyne, or ellis the lyne meridional. And the remenaunt of this lyne doun to the bordure is clepid the north lyne, or ellis the lyne of midnyght.
>
> Overthwart this forseide longe lyne ther crossith him another lyne of the same lengthe from eest to west. Of the which lyne, from a litel cros (+) in the bordure unto the centre of the large hool, is clepid the est lyne, or ellis the lyne orientale. And the remenaunt of this lyne, fro the forseide centre unto the bordure, is clepid the west lyne, or ellis the lyne occidentale. Now has thou here the foure quarters of thin Astrolabie divided after the foure principales plages or quarters of the firmament. (I,4–5)

Apart from one or two substantive questions raised by this passage—Chaucer could have been clearer in describing the *linea medii coeli* or "line of midnight," for example—this text is especially interesting for the insight it gives into Chaucer's

style. First, Chaucer attempts to standardize the technical terminology of the instrument he describes. This is an important
first step in all technical and scientific writing and one not
taken often enough in medieval Latin treatises on the astrolabe—not taken, for example, in "Masha'allah's" *De compositione*. Thus, for instance, Chaucer repeats certain key words
("bordure," "lyne," "large hool") and uses carefully constructed
parallel phrasing ("or ellis the line meridional . . . or ellis the
lyne of midnyght") in order to give the reader a quick grasp of
the operational terminology of the astrolabe within a context of
simple description. In this passage Chaucer also piles up prepositional phrases ("of the which lyne," "from a litel cros") in
order to clarify the precise nature of the relationships between
the parts of the instrument.

Yet at the same time there is a sparseness and economy in
this description that justifies Chaucer's rather conservative
style. For example, the point-by-point spatial organization of
the passage allows Chaucer to compress his description because such an organization gives him a momentary reprieve
from the necessity of describing the temporal processes for
which the astrolabe is used. Thus the sequence of prepositional
phrases serves to locate and fix the positions of the astrolabe's
parts relative to one another and to prepare "lyte Lowys" to
manipulate an instrument that can easily be visualized as a
taxonomy of spatially, if not functionally, related names. Chaucer duplicates the balance and symmetry of the astrolabe in the
structure of his prose, and he also fulfills his promise to "writen
unto a child twyes a god sentence" in order to make the "art of
memory" less difficult. Thus the *Treatise* here succeeds in being
clear partially because it follows the advice on the presentation
of spatial objects that was a part of the traditions of the art of
memory from the time of the pseudo-Ciceronian *Ad Heren-
nium*.[39]

Compared with Chaucer's *Treatise*, the description of the
quadrants offered in the *De compositione* is far briefer and less
schematic:

> Dividesque ipsum spacium quod fuerit inter ipsos circulos
> per 360 divisiones equales, et incipies scribere ab initio quarte
> occidentalis et meridiane ex puncto *a*, eundo ad punctum *c*
> continuatim usque in 360 gradus. Et elucidabis [tabulam] et
> equabis eam prout melius poteris. Deinde extrahes dyametra

illius que quadrant eam abscindens unum eorum per alterum super *c* punctum cuspidis, ita ut quadrantes sint equales: et facies in alia parte similiter.

[Then divide the space, which will be between the circles, into 360 equal divisions, and then begin to inscribe the gradations from the beginning of the SE quadrant, through 360 degrees, from point *A* to point *C*. And make the plate *(tabulam)* as clear and even as you can. Next, draw the diameters and divide the circle into quadrants so that one quadrant cuts the other at the center *C* and so that the quadrants are equal. Do the same thing on the other side.][40]

Here, and throughout the *De compositione,* "Masha'allah" displays a greater concern for the mathematics of astrolabe construction and astrolabe use than Chaucer, and he is not as interested in the language of description nor in the topics suggested by this language as Chaucer.

In describing the same "spacium quod fuerit inter ipsos circulos"—the second concentric circle inscribed on the *mater* and the one containing the "circle of the equinoxes" or equator—Chaucer demonstrates how different are his concerns and method of description from those of "Masha'allah":

The myddel cercle in wydnesse, of these 3, is clepid the cercle equinoxiall, upon which turnith evermo the hevedes of Aries and Libra. And understond wel that evermo thys cercle equinoxiall turnith justly from verrey est to verrey west as I have shewed the in the speer solide.[41] This same cercle is clepid also Equator, that is the weyer of the day; for whan the sonne is in the hevedes of Aries and Libra, than ben the dayes and nightes ylike of lengthe in all the world. (I,17)

Chaucer has certainly taken this definition of the equinoctial or celestial equator from Sacrobosco's *De sphaera.*[42] Note that unlike "Masha'allah," Chaucer chooses to describe the division of the concentric circles on the "wombe syde" of Lowys's astrolabe as a totality (I,15–16) and then to describe further the individual circles purely in terms of extended definitions. Chaucer also gives his somewhat ambiguous definition of the equinox in the context of this description of the "myddel cercle." Since the sun is in Aries and Libra for more than one day and night, Chaucer implies that there are more than two days a year when days and nights are "ylike of length." Still, in defining the operational terminology of the astrolabe and in adding to this terminology the basic conceptions of observational astronomy, Chaucer is clear enough and very careful to include every definition useful for understanding the ways in which the astrolabe provides a model of planetary relationships. Furthermore, Chaucer arranges his definitions according to the "order of space" so that the user can easily apply the text to the instrument he is handling. For example, after providing the basic definition of the "myddel cercle" of the equator quoted above, Chaucer moves to a brief discussion of the function of the "equinoxiall" in computing latitudes and in telling time. He then returns to another definition of the "equinoxiall," one that is fuller in its relationship to the principles of astronomy:

> This equinoxiall is clepid the gurdel of the first moeving, or ellis of the first moevable. And note that the first moevyng is clepid moevyng of the first moevable of the 8 speer, which moeving is from est into west, and eft ageyn into est. Also it is clepid girdel of the first moeving for it departith the first moevable, that is to seyn the spere, in two like partyes evene distanz fro the poles of this world. (I,17)

This elaborate expansion of Sacrobosco's discussion of the "girdle of the first movement" shows Chaucer at his meticulous and pedantic best. Yet one wonders what a child of ten tender years would have made of this circular and exhausting series of definitions of the equinoctial. There is nothing to match these passages in the *De compositione*, nor is there anything like Chaucer's care and verbosity in any other Latin astrolabe treatise known to me. Chaucer is operating here with a method that should be quite familiar to readers of his poems: he is taking the form of his narrative from one source and then packing into that form all of the erudition he can manage, delighting all the while in the naming of objects, the organizing of information, and the compounding of related and unrelated detail. Of course, Chaucer's encyclopedic method works quite well in the *Knight's Tale* or in the *Parliament of Fowls*, but can it work in a scientific treatise without creating problems for an audience that needs to know how a complex technological artifact actually works?

One type of problem created by the technical style of the

*Treatise* can be illustrated by a passage from Part I dealing with the circle of months:

> Next the cercle of the daies folewith the cercle of the names of the monthes, that is to say, Januarius, Februarius . . . December. The names of these monthes were clepid thus, somme for her propirtees and somme by statutes of lordes Arabiens, somme by othre lordes of Rome. Eke of these monthes, as liked to Julius Cesar and to Cesar Augustus, somme were compouned of diverse nombres of daies, as Julie and August . . . yit truste wel that the sonne dwellith therfore nevere the more ne lasse in oon signe than in another. (I,10)

Throughout this section of the *Treatise*, Chaucer lists parts, without attempting to clarify the nature of the relations of these parts or their functions ("Next this folewith the cercle of the daies . . ."; "Than folewen the names of the holy daies . . ."; "Next the forseide cercle of the A B C . . ."). This paratactic construction, while useful enough for enumeration, makes it difficult to evaluate the information that is presented—what does one need to remember in order to use the astrolabe? Parataxis, though it balances the successive concentric circles that Chaucer describes, also removes the possibility of selection and judgment:

> Than hast thou a brod reule, that hath on either ende a square plate perced with certein holes, somme more and somme lasse, to resceyve the stremes of the sonne by day, and eke by mediacioun of thin eye to knowe the altitude of sterres by night.(I,13)

This broad rule is the alidade, and its inclusion among the list of circles makes sense if one sees the astrolabe primarily as an object in space. But if one sees the astrolabe as a series of processes in time, then the inclusion of this description here makes less sense. In evaluating Chaucer's technical style, one must observe that a separation has been made between the configuration of the astrolabe's parts and the functional logic of the astrolabe as a whole. Chaucer has relegated most functional questions to Part II—to the series of "conclusiouns" that he has taken right out of the *De compositione*. In reading through Part I, it is clear enough what parts constitute the instrument Lowys holds, but missing from this description is a satisfactory picture of the astrolabe as an integrated and functional device. The "brod reule" described here "receives the rays of the sun" during the day but assists ("by mediacioun of thin eye") the user in knowing the altitudes of the stars at night. "Receiving" and "knowing" are very different functional words, and the effect of their parallel use is to unbalance the description of the astrolabe's use.

Chaucer seems throughout Part I of the *Treatise* to focus on names rather than on processes, and he sometimes digresses in order to develop the cercle of associations evoked by a particular name. For example, he writes of the zodiac that

> . . . in the zodiak ben the 12 signes that han names of bestes, or ellis for whan the sonne entrith into eny of tho signes he takith the propirte of suche bestes, or ellis that for the sterres that ben ther fixed ben disposid in signes of bestes or shape like bestes, or elles whan the planetes ben under thilke signes thei causen us by her influence operaciouns and effectes like to the operaciouns of bestes. (I,21)

The thoroughness of so many successive clauses offering alternative explanations of the astrological meaning of "zodia" ("in langage of Grek sowneth 'bestes' in Latyn tunge") is a reminder of the Chaucerian style more familiar to readers of the poems. It is also a reminder of the problems Chaucer often had in coming to the point when describing the astrolabe. Moreover, there is, in the nagging repetition of "or ellis," a kind of implicit skepticism about the stellar influences being described: can one take seriously so many possibilities? Does not one feel drawn to exactitude and precise definition after struggling to unscramble the various possibilities Chaucer suggests? Surely, technical discourse in English needed to develop a more economical way of rendering objects and processes into clear and visually stimulating language.

For Chaucer, the temptation to move away from the astrolabe and toward digressive matter was simply too great, as one sees in a passage like this one:

> And everich of these 12 signes [of the zodiac] hath respect to a certeyn parcel of the body of a man, and hath it in govern-

aunce; as Aries hath thin heved, and Taurus thy nekke and thy throte, Gemini thin armholes and thin armes, and so furth, as shall be shewid more pleyn in the 5 partie of this tretis. (I,21)

This passage, and much else in the same section of Part I, is thematically linked to the description of the "compas which that contenith a large brede" that is the representation of the zodiac on the astrolabe. Chaucer moves in this section from the description of the material imprinting of the zodiac on the disc of the astrolabe, to the "ymagyned" twelve-degree band of the heavenly zodiac (actually closer to eight degrees on either side of the ecliptic), to the lengthy description of the lore of the zodiac partially quoted above. Perhaps the brief definition of the ecliptic "lyne" and the long description of the functionally irrelevant astrological material represents a pedagogical device. Could it be that Chaucer is passing over the details presented in a text like the *De compositione* in order to come more quickly to material that is likely to be of more interest to his pupil? Is Chaucer hinting here at the world of "these 12 signes" that the astrolabe will open up so that tender Lowys will feel impelled to go forward in his studies? After all, as a technical writer Chaucer needed to keep Lowys interested. He insists, from time to time, that the boy pay attention—"Forget not thys, litel Lowys," and "Now have I told the twyes" are two, more intrusive examples. So is it not likely that the astrological material, which is not to be found in other astrolabe treatises, also serves to capture his student's attention?[43]

In other words, the limitations of Chaucer's description of the astrolabe from a technical point of view—limitations clearly seen when comparing Chaucer's text to "Masha'allah's" description of the instrument—are not the product of either his limited knowledge of the astrolabe or his limited interest in its construction but rather the consequence of his stylistic and pedagogical decisions. Chaucer set out to provide a concise, lucid, and interesting description of the parts of the astrolabe so that his son would know just enough to be able to begin solving the problems translated from "Masha'allah" in the second part of the *Treatise*. In this, Chaucer has been successful.[44] If read as an early technical treatise, as the earliest technical treatise in English, Chaucer's text is distracting because it seems unconcerned with the functional relationships of the parts of the astrolabe. Chaucer is also willing to digress from the instrument to extraneous material that might better be placed in the section of practical exercises.

These criticisms are inevitable if the *Treatise* is read within a context created by the rigidly structured modern technical paper. But if the *Treatise* is read from within the historical context created by medieval astronomy as practiced over the previous six hundred years, then what appear to be weaknesses in Chaucer's description of the astrolabe may be seen differently. The astrolabe could be used to design astrological charts, to solve problems in planetary motion, to tell time, and to work out the spatial relations of terrestrial objects. Yet the astrolabe, which we moderns take to be a technological artifact and nothing more, was for Chaucer a symbolic artifact as well. Lowys could read angular distances from the flat disc he held on his thumb, but he could also certainly read other things just as clearly. The history of medieval astronomy makes it clear that even as the heavens were made subject to observation and formal mathematical analysis they did not lose their mysteriousness or their symbolic value. Neither Chaucer nor Lowys could think of the astrolabe as merely a tool for measuring; neither could they look at the engraved *mater* and not think of the "bestes" of the zodiac or the armholes of Gemini. What the modern reader might take to be distractions from the purpose of the *Treatise* are really the whole point of both the text and the instrument it describes. Until a different principle of planetary order could be discovered, until a decisive break could be made with the two-sphere universe of medieval astronomy, the astrolabe could only see what its user wanted to see. The astrolabe Lowys held, and the lucid handbook his father gave him to explain its use, would prove out problems that had often been proved before and would continue to confirm the underlying orderliness of the heavens. What Chaucer described in the *Treatise on the Astrolabe* was not only a technological artifact and scientific instrument but also a picture of this order cast into metal.[45]

In 1620, when Francis Bacon set out to displace the conservative tribes of Aristotelian science who even then dominated the universities of northern Europe, he assumed that any revision of the old Organum must begin with experiments and with instruments: "The unassisted hand, and the understanding left to itself, possess but little power. Effects are produced by means of instruments and helps, which the understanding requires no less than the hand."[46] Bacon's insistence on the importance of using observational devices in the construction of scientific theories stemmed from his analysis of the deficiencies of Aristotelian deductive methodology. One should not, Bacon wrote, be fooled by Aristotle's "frequent recourse to experiment in his books. . . ," for Aristotle "had already decided, without having properly consulted experience as the basis of his decisions and axioms," the outcome of his investigations in natural philosophy.[47] There is some justice in these charges. The scientific methodology of the *Posterior Analytics*, modeled on the formalism of Euclidian geometry, does not rely on experiment but, at most, on experience.

Yet there is another misconception, equally harmful to the understanding of science, that grows out of Baconian empiricism. The icon of this empirical faith has always been Galileo's telescope, and the sole article of required belief is that, as with Galileo and the acceptance of Copernicanism, scientific discovery depends primarily on the gathering and interpretation of observations that are themselves made possible only through the technology of precise instruments. Indeed, the devaluation of all science done before the seventeenth century grew out of the conviction that a culture without a developed technology is necessarily a culture without science—a conviction that is wrong on two counts.[48] Modern, post-Machian discussions of the philosophy of science have demonstrated the limitations of the Baconian view of scientific method. So have Duhem's revelations concerning exact science in the thirteenth and fourteenth centuries and the subsequent reconsideration of the nature of scientific "revolutions."[49] We now know, for example, that the history of inertial physics begins not in the seventeenth century with Galileo, but in the fourteenth century with John Buridan and Thomas Bradwardine.[50] Likewise, the revolution in astronomy—inseparable from the reconsideration of projectile motion—depended on a great deal more than the invention of the telescope; for one thing, it depended on the philosophical willingness to reconsider the meaning of man's place in the universe.[51] Indeed, the history of science shows us the extent to which various "revolutions"—from heliocentrism to quantum mechanics—grow out of a combination of factors:

the development of mathematical languages, the enhanced sophistication of instruments, the randomness of inspirations, the social organization of the scientific enterprise, and the development of a technical language and style capable of making public the results of scientific investigation.[52]

Still, whatever the shortcomings of the Baconian program, one cannot deny his contention that the development of instruments has an essential place in the growth of scientific knowledge.[53] But it is important to distinguish between the use of scientific instruments as a physical activity and the use of scientific instruments as a habit of mind or as an extension of a particular kind of thinking. Specifically, in the case of the astrolabe, the point is not that astrolabe use effected a revolution in astronomical thinking; it did not. Indeed, the two-dimensional celestial geometry of the mater and the tympan might even be seen as obstacles to the visualization of a dynamic, three-dimensional universe. Clearly Chaucer's *Treatise on the Astrolabe* evinces no revolutionary inclinations; one could very well read off an Aristotelian-Ptolemaic universe from the face of Lowys's instrument. However, what the astrolabe and its use did create as a by-product of studies "touching nombres and proporciouns" had a great deal to do with late medieval developments in the natural sciences. The astrolabe made precise measurement, careful observation, and accurate record-keeping not only possible but necessary. The creation of a new scientific theory may not require the strict application of the scientific method (data gathering, hypothesis formation, hypothesis testing, and so on), but such creation does depend on the construction of chains of arguments binding observation, prediction, and explanation together with the grammar and syntax of mathematical languages. Properly used, the astrolabe created a problem-solving context in which the demands of the long-dominant Aristotelian final cause did not intervene. An astronomical problem soluble by using the astrolabe had first to be clearly stated; then observations were made and interpreted, often using data on relative star positions contained in charts and catalogues; this data was then interpreted and, perhaps, communicated in a work like the *Treatise on the Astrolabe* or the *De compositione* or one of the many other astrolabe treatises.[54] Before the use of the astrolabe became widespread in the twelfth century, and until writers like "Masha'allah" and Chaucer set down the procedures for the construction and use of an astrolabe, there simply did not exist many contexts within which such a recognizably scientific exercise could be performed.

## NOTES

1. R. T. Gunther, *Chaucer and Messahalla on the Astrolabe*, vol. 5 of *Early Science in Oxford* (Oxford: Oxford University Press, 1929), v.

2. Two studies that note the style of the *Treatise* are Sister M. Madeleva, *A Lost Language and Other Essays on Chaucer* (New York: Russell and Russell, 1967), 87–100; and Margaret Schlauch, "Chaucer's Prose Rhythms," *PMLA* 65 (1950):568–89.

3. A useful starting point for the consideration of the relations between the "sciences" and the "humanities" during the later Middle Ages is John E. Murdoch, "From Social into Intellectual Factors: An Aspect of the Unitary Character of Late Medieval Learning," in *The Cultural Context of Medieval Learning*, ed. John E. Murdoch and Edith D. Sylla (Dordrecht and Boston: D. Reidel, 1975), 271–348; also valuable is *The Interaction Between Science and Philosophy*, ed. Y. Elkana (Atlantic Highlands, N.J.: Humanities Press, 1974), esp. 51–113.

4. In addition to the stylistic studies noted above, the following contain some material on the *Treatise*: Chauncy Wood, *Chaucer and the Country of the Stars* (Princeton: Princeton University Press, 1970), 12–20; Florence Marie Grimm, "Astronomical Lore in Chaucer," *University of Nebraska Studies in Language, Literature, and Criticism* 2 (1919):1–96; *The Equatorie of the Planets*, ed. Derek J. Price (Cambridge: At the University Press, 1955), 93–118.

5. Isidore of Seville, *Etymologiae sive origines*, ed. W. M. Lindsay (Oxford: Oxford University Press, 1911), 3.71.

6. See Macrobius, *On the Dream of Scipio*, trans. William H. Stahl (New York: Columbia University Press, 1952), 1.14. On the scientific writings of the early Middle Ages in general, see Stahl, *Roman Science* (Madison: University of Wisconsin Press, 1962); also H. M. Klinkenberg, "Der Verfall des Quadriviums im frühen Mittelalter," in *Artes Liberales, von der antiken Bildung zur Wissenschaft des Mittelalters*, ed. Josef Koch (Leiden: E. J. Brill, 1959), 1–32. On the influence of Martianus, see Stahl et al., *Martianus Capella and the Seven Liberal Arts* (New York: Columbia University Press, 1971), esp. 56–71. For the geoheliocentric system, see Pierre Duhem, *Le Système du monde*, 10 vols. (Paris: A. Hermann, 1913–59), 3:52.

7. The Floss edition (Johannes Scotus Eriugena, *De divisione natura*, in PL 122) is still reliable and the source of the remarks contained here; Books 1 and 2 are also available in *Periphyseon, Liber primus and Liber secundus*, ed. and trans. I. P. Sheldon-Williams (Dublin: Dublin Institute for Advanced Study, 1968, 1972).

8. For Eriugena's influence in the twelfth century, see Brian Stock, *Myth and Science in the Twelfth Century* (Princeton: Princeton University Press, 1972), 7–23; also Maieul Cappuyns, *Jean Scot Erigène: Sa vie, son oeuvre, sa pensée* (Louvain: Abbaye de Mont Cesare, 1933), 128–79; for essential differences between Hugh of Saint Victor and Eriugena, see *The Didascalicon of Hugh of Saint Victor*, ed. and trans. Jerome Taylor (New York: Columbia University Press, 1961), 165 n. 47.

9. See Raymond Klibansky, *The Continuity of the Platonic Tradition* (London: Warburg Institute, 1939), 21–29.

10. The problems of the organization of the sciences and of their relationship to existing knowledge is treated in James A. Weisheipl, "Classification of the Sciences in Medieval Thought," *Medieval Studies* 27 (1965):54–90.

11. On the dominance of theology, see Ernest A. Moody, "Empiricism and Metaphysics in Medieval Philosophy," *Philosophical Review* 67 (1958):145–63; also M.-D. Chenu, *La Théologie au douzième siècle* (Paris: J. Vrin, 1957), esp. chap. 4, "Grammaire et théologie," for a discussion of the use of other disciplines as tools for the study of theology; this same subject is treated by G. Evans, *Old Arts and New Theology* (Oxford: Oxford University Press, 1980). For the tension between theology and the new sciences inspired by Aristotle's works in particular, see Edward Grant, "The Condemnation of 1277, God's Absolute Power, and Physical Thought in the Late Middle Ages," *Viator* 11 (1980):211–44; for the problem of "saving the appearances" see Duhem, *To Save the Phenomena, An Essay on the Idea of Physical Theory from Plato to Galileo* (Chicago: University of Chicago Press, 1969); an example of astronomical theory operating within the Aristotelian tradition of an immobile earth and of appearance-saving can be found in John Buridan, *Johannis Buridani Quaestiones super Quattuor Libris De Caelo et Mundo*, ed. Ernest A. Moody (New York: Medieval Academy, 1942), 226–30.

12. Isidore of Seville's *De natura rerum*, which treats astronomical and cosmological matters in a more detailed and systematic way than the *Etymologiae*, nonetheless reinforces the sense that the study of the heavens is primarily a mechanism for understanding sacred doctrine. In his preface, Isidore discusses his purpose: "Quae omnia, secundum quod a ueteribus uiris ac maxime sicut in litteris catholicorum uirorum scripta sunt, proferentes breui tabella notamus. Neque enim earum rerum naturam noscere superstitiosae scientiae est, si tantum sana sobriaque doctrina considerentur" (*Isidore de Seville, Traité de la Nature*, ed. Jacques Fontaine [Bordeaux: Féret, 1960], 167). For a comprehensive discussion of the encyclopedic tradition and its relation to early medieval science, see Richard McKeon, "The Organization of Sciences and the Relations of Cultures in the Twelfth and Thirteenth Centuries," in *Cultural Context of Medieval Learning*, 151–92.

13. Paul Kunitzsch, "On the Authenticity of the Treatise on the Composition and Use of the Astrolabe Ascribed to Messahalla," *Archives Internationales d'Histoire des Sciences* 31 (1981):42–62, has cast serious doubt on Masha'allah's (variously spelled Messahalla, Messallah, etc.) authorship of *De compositione et utilitate astrolabii*. Masha'allah's name will still be used here, but in quotation marks. The only edition currently available of *De compositione* is Gunther's (n. 1, above); Michael Masi is currently preparing a new edition that may perhaps settle the question of authorship, but see Kunitzsch, 42 n. 7.

14. See Duhem, *Le Système du monde*, 2:393ff, and 4:1–90.

15. Bede's works on time-reckoning have been collected in *Bedae, Opera de temporibus*, ed. C. W. Jones (Cambridge, Mass.: Medieval Academy, 1943). A treatment of medieval *compotus* is W. E. van Wijk, *Origine et développement de la computistique médiévale*, Les Conférences du Palais de la Découverte, Ser. D: Histoire des sciences, no. 29 (Paris: Université de Paris, 1954).

16. For the career of Gerbert, see Uta Lindgren, *Gerbert von Aurillac und das Quadrivium: Untersuchungen zur Bildung im Zeitalter der Ottonen* (Wiesbaden: Steiner, 1976); also *Dictionary of Scientific Biography*, s.v. "Gerbert."

17. A good account of the process of translating scientific texts from Arabic and Greek into Latin can be found in David C. Lindberg, "The Transmission of Greek and Arabic Learning to the West," in *Science in the Middle Ages*, ed. David C. Lindberg (Chicago: University of Chicago Press, 1978), 52–90; also George F. Hourani, "The

Medieval Translations from Arabic to Latin Made in Spain," *The Muslim World* 62 (1972):97–114; still valuable is Charles Homer Haskins, *The Renaissance of the Twelfth Century* (Cambridge: Harvard University Press, 1927), chap. 9.

18. For an insight into the nature of the shift in thinking that occurred as familiarity with Greek and Arabic astronomy began, see Daniel of Morley, *Liber de naturis inferiorum et superiorum,* ed. Karl Sudhoff, Archiv für Geschichte der Mathematik, der Naturwissenschaften und der Technik, vol. 8, no. 2 (Leipzig: F. C. W. Vogel, 1917), 31–40; for Adelard of Bath's account of the marvels of Arabian learning, see his *Quaestiones naturales,* in *Die Quaestiones Naturales des Adelardus von Bath,* ed. Martin Müller, Beitrage zur Geschichte der Philosophie und Theologie des Mittelalters, vol. 31, no. 2 (Munster: Aschendorff, 1934). That Adelard's wonder was often untempered by skepticism or science is demonstrated by his discussion, for example, of the "food on which the stars live": "Ut igitur illa animalia loco, compositione, forma, ratione his inferioribus digniora sunt, ita esu quodam cibis nostris admodum puriore uti debent et possunt" (p. 69).

19. Olaf Pedersen, "Astronomy," in *Science in the Middle Ages,* ed. Lindberg, 314–20.

20. I refer to the edition of *De sphaera* in *The Sphere of Sacrobosco and its Commentators,* ed. and trans. Lynn Thorndike (Chicago: University of Chicago Press, 1949).

21. "For let one take an astrolabe on a clear starry night and, sighting the pole [star] through both apertures in the indicator, note the number of degrees where it is. Then let our measurer of the cosmos proceed directly north until on another clear night, observing the pole as before, the indicator stands a degree higher. After this let the extent of his travel be measured, and it will be found to be 700 stades. Then, allowing for this many stades for each of 360 degrees, the girth of the earth is found" (*De sphaera,* p. 85).

22. Text with extensive commentary available in *Campanus of Novara and Medieval Planetary Theory (Theorica planetarum),* ed. and trans. with commentary by Francis S. Benjamin, Jr., and G. J. Tommer (Madison: University of Wisconsin Press, 1971).

23. *Campanus of Novara,* 32. On the equatorium, see Emmanuel Poulle, "L'Equatorire de Guillaume Gilliszoon de Wisserkerke," *Physics* 3 (1961):223–51; also *The Equatorie of the Planets,* ed. Price, passim.

24. The text of the treatise, together with an analysis of the grounds for the attribution to Chaucer, is in *The Equatorie of the Planets,* ed. Price.

25. The philosophical problems centering on how science is actually done, understood, and communicated are vast. I have found the following works especially useful: Karl R. Popper, "Truth, Rationality, and the Growth of Scientific Knowledge," in *Philosophical Problems of Science and Technology,* ed. Alex C. Michalos (Boston: Allyn and Bacon, 1974), 76–117; Peter Weingart, "The Relations Between Science and Technology—A Sociological Explanation," in *The Dynamics of Science and Technology,* ed. Wolfgang Krohn et al. (Dordrecht and Boston: D. Reidel, 1978), 251–86; Thomas Kuhn, *The Structure of Scientific Revolutions,* rev. ed. (Chicago: University of Chicago Press, 1970), 35–42 and passim; Margaret Masterman, "The Nature of a Paradigm," in *Criticism and the Growth of Knowledge,* ed. Imre Lakatos and Alan Musgrave (Cambridge: At the University Press, 1970), 59–90; for the Middle Ages specifically, see Rupert Hall, "The Scholar and the Craftsman in the Scientific Revolution," in *Critical Problems in the History of Science,* ed. Marshall Clagett (Madison: University of Wisconsin Press, 1969), 3–23.

26. A useful collection of recent scholarship on Galileo's methods and specific contributions is *New Perspectives on Galileo,* ed. Robert E. Butts and Joseph C. Pitt (Dordrecht and Boston: D Reidel, 1978), esp. 1–58 and 209–57.

27. The story of the development of quantum mechanics has recently been told in readable fashion by Heinz Pagels, *The Cosmic Code: Quantum Physics as the Language of Nature* (New York: Simon and Schuster, 1982), esp. 63–84.

28. Thomas Kuhn, *The Copernican Revolution* (Cambridge: Harvard University Press, 1957), has discussed the revolution in sixteenth-century astronomy in terms of the break with the Ptolemaic-Aristotelian system; A. C. Crombie, *Robert Grosseteste and the Origins of Experimental Science* (Oxford: Oxford University Press, 1953), would push the origins of modern scientific method back to the thirteenth century, particularly to Oxford and the group of scientist-scholars associated with the great bishop of Lincoln. One might argue against Crombie's thesis that, first, Grosseteste was exceptional in his concern for a truly verifiable system of natural philosophy and, second, that the method of falsification devised by Grosseteste was not systematically applied to problems in either astronomy or physics. John Murdoch, "From Social Into Intellectual Factors," has demonstrated the development of new analytical languages in fourteenth-century philosophy, but he stops short of claiming that these languages are modern.

29. Ironically, at least some of the impetus for technological change came from the Church—the theology that often retarded the development of scientific theory implicitly encouraged invention. See Lynn White, Jr., "What Accelerated Technological Progress in the Western Middle Ages?" in *Scientific Change*, ed. A. C. Crombie (New York: Basic Books, 1963) esp. 284–88; also idem, "Cultural Climates and Technological Advance in the Middle Ages," *Viator* 2 (1971): 171–202; for the theological impetus given technology by the Church, see Ernst Benz, "Fondamenti cristiani della tecnica occidentale," in *Technica e casistica*, ed. Enrico Castelli (Rome: CEDAM, 1964), 241–63. (Benz is discussed by White in "Cultural Climates," 186–87).

30. See Edward Grant, *Physical Science in the Middle Ages* (Cambridge: At the University Press, 1977), 83–90; an argument for the revolutionary character of thirteenth-century Oxford science is to be found in Crombie, *Robert Grosseteste*; on the conservativism of late medieval science see Anneliese Maier, *Ausgehendes Mittelalter*, (Rome: Edizioni di Storia e Letteratura, 1964), 425–57. Maier's evaluation of the progress of scholastic natural philosophy includes a discussion of fundamental assumptions that dominated theorizing and could not be displaced by any single thinker. One of these, the Aristotelian dictum "omne quod movetur ab aliquo movetur" ("everything that is moved is moved by another"), simply precluded any understanding of inertia. Maier also notes that scholastic natural philosophers "never measured anything" (455).

31. Whether or not Lowys was Chaucer's son and whether or not Chaucer wrote in 1391 (or 1392) are still debated questions. Discussion of both may be found in Robinson's notes (see n. 32, below).

32. I refer to the text of the *Treatise on the Astrolabe* in F. N. Robinson, *The Works of Geoffrey Chaucer*, 2d ed. (Boston: Houghton Mifflin, 1957), 544–63 (notes, pp. 867–72). References to this edition are cited by part and section number.

33. On the theory of the astrolabe, see Willy Harter, "The Principle and Use of the Astrolabe," in *Oriens-Occidens* (Hildesheim: George Olms, 1968), 287–311; John D. North, "The Astrolabe," *Scientific American* 230 (1974): 96–106; Henri Michel, *Traité de l'astrolabe* (Paris: Gauthier-Villars, 1947). On the construction of the astrolabe and its pedagogical use, see Emmanuel Poulle, "La fabrication des astrolabes au moyen âge," *Techniques et Civilisations* 4 (1955): 117–28; also Poulle's monograph, *Un constructeur d'instruments astronomiques au XVᵉ siècle, Jean Fusoris* (Paris: H. Champion, 1962), esp. 109–24.

34. The question of the use of the vernacular is thoroughly discussed in M. T. Clanchy, *From Memory to Written Record* (Cambridge: Harvard University Press, 1979),

258–65 and passim. Even as late as 1527, the use of the vernacular for scholarly discourse was considered suspect. See Alan Debus, *Man and Nature in the Renaissance* (Cambridge: At the University Press, 1978), 7, for the experience of Paracelsus in Basel. I say "as late as 1527" because, with the advent of printing and the dissemination of printed books, the movement to reach a broader audience through translations into the vernacular tended to diffuse some of the insistence on a language-based distinction between the "learned" and the "lewd." See Elizabeth L. Eisenstein, *The Printing Press as an Agent of Change*, 2 vols. (Cambridge: At the University Press, 1979), esp. 2:250–66.

35. Ernst Robert Curtius, *European Literature and the Latin Middle Ages*, trans. Willard R. Trask (New York: Harper and Row, 1963), 83–85.

36. For Sampson's career, see H. G. Richardson, "Business Training in Medieval Oxford," *American Historical Review* 46 (1941): 259–80. For other aspects of the relationship between practical and liberal education in the medieval universities, see Lon R. Shelby, "The Education of Medieval Master Masons," *Speculum* 39 (1964): 388ff.

37. Michel, *Traité de l'astrolabe* has a clear explanation of the theory of stereographic projection (pp. 27ff). O. Neugebauer, "The Early History of the Astrolabe: Studies in Ancient Astronomy IX," in *A History of Ancient Mathematical Astronomy* (New York: Springer-Verlag, 1975), gives useful background on the mathematical aspects of astrolabe use.

38. Michael Masi, "Chaucer, Messahala and Bodleian Supra 78," *Manuscripta* 19 (1975): 41–42.

39. For the *ars memoriae*, and especially its relation to the development of science, see Frances Yates, *The Art of Memory* (Chicago: University of Chicago Press, 1966), 368–89.

40. Latin text from Gunther, *Chaucer and Messahalla*, 196.

41. This reference to the "speer solide" supports Price's claim that Chaucer wrote the *Equatorie of the Planets*. See also Derek Price, "Chaucer's Astronomy," *Nature* 170 (1952): 474–75.

42. S. W. Harvey, "Chaucer's Debt to Sacrobosco," *JEGP* 34 (1935): 34–38.

43. See, for example, the astrolabe treatise by Henry Bate (written in "1274, quinto idus octobris"), *Magistralis compositio astrolabii Hanrici Bate*, ed. R. T. Gunther, *Astrolabes of the World*, 2 vols. (Oxford: Oxford University Press, 1932), 1:368–76. Chaucer's *Treatise* is also very different in this respect from the *Opus astrolabii* of Andalo de nigro (c. 1270–1342) that I have examined at the Library of Congress in an edition printed in 1475.

44. The modern student of the astrolabe may test the value of Chaucer's *Treatise* as a teaching aid by designing a model instrument and then trying to solve some of the problems of Part II. With some supplemental design instructions taken from the *De compositione*, one can, in fact, construct a workable astrolabe.

45. For the pervasiveness of this orderly cosmology, see J. Bruce Brackenridge, "Kepler, Elliptical Orbits, and Celestial Circularity: A Study in the Persistence of Metaphysical Commitment—Part II," *Annals of Science* 39 (1982): 265–98.

46. Francis Bacon, *Novum Organum*, in *The Works of Francis Bacon*, ed. Basil Montagu, 3 vols. (Philadelphia: Parry and McMillan, 1855), 3:345.

47. Bacon, *Novum Organum*, 3:351; see also Edith D. Sylla, "The A Posteriori Foundations of Science," *Synthese* 40 (1979): 147–87, for an analysis of the medieval use of Aristotelian assumptions and methods.

48. William Whewell, in his classic *History of the Inductive Sciences*, 3 vols. (London: Parker, 1837), declared that the technology of the Middle Ages contributed nothing to the development of science because science is purely theoretical (1:353–54).

That medieval technology had a great deal to do with the development of medieval and modern science has been shown by Lynn White, Jr. In "The Medieval Roots of Modern Technology and Science," in *Medieval Religion and Technology* (Berkeley and Los Angeles: University of California Press, 1978), 75–92, White points out that the exchange between science and technology was indeed a one-way process, but not, as Whewell suspected, a matter of science creating technology but of technology helping to create science.

49. See Duhem, *Le Système du monde*, 4:313–16. Dudley Shapere, *Galileo: A Philosophical Study* (Chicago: University of Chicago Press, 1974), 126–45, discusses the empirical and rational-deductive methods within the specific context created by the science of motion.

50. See Marshall Clagett, *The Science of Mechanics in the Middle Ages* (Madison: University of Wisconsin Press, 1961).

51. Kuhn, *The Copernican Revolution*, 100–133; also Tullio Gregory, "La nouvelle idée de nature et de savoir scientifique au XIIᵉ siècle," in *Cultural Context of Medieval Learning*, 193–210.

52. The complexity of scientific discovery is well represented by Thomas Kuhn in *The Structure of Scientific Revolutions;* on sociological issues in the history of science, see Robert K. Merton, "Social and Cultural Context of Science," in Merton's collected essays, *The Sociology of Science*, ed. Norman W. Storer (Chicago: University of Chicago Press, 1973), 173–90; also Karin D. Knorr et al., *The Social Process of Scientific Investigation* (Dordrecht and Boston: D. Reidel, 1981). An essential source is Einstein's own account of his work in *Albert Einstein: Philosopher-Scientist*, ed. Paul Arthur Schlipp, 2 vols. (Evanston, Ill.: Library of Living Philosophers, 1949), 1:2–95. For the randomness of inspiration, nothing is more eloquent than Einstein's discussion of the "free play of concepts" (7).

53. An interesting contemporary testimony to the importance of technology in advancing scientific knowledge is recorded by June Goodfield in *An Imagined World* (New York: Harper and Row, 1981), 44. Goodfield's story of scientific discovery, traced through the work of one scientist, presents a vivid and lucid insight into the complexities, and artistry, of scientific research.

54. Paul Kunitzsch, "Observations on the Arabic Reception of the Astrolabe," *Archives Internationales d'histoire des sciences* 31 (1981): 249–52, presents a comprehensive bibliography of astrolabe treatises.

# Creation and Responsibility in Science: Some Lessons from the Modern Prometheus

LEONARD ISAACS

*Michigan State University*

> Learn from me, if not by my precepts, at least by my example, how dangerous is the acquirement of knowledge, and how much happier that man is who believes his native town to be the world, than he who aspires to be greater than his nature will allow.
> —Victor Frankenstein, in *Frankenstein; or, The Modern Prometheus* by Mary Shelley

A cliché may be a truth not deeply enough pursued. There can be little doubt that the crudely sutured features of Victor Frankenstein's creation are a twentieth-century commonplace. Since 1931, more than twenty different Frankenstein monsters have emerged from the film studios' conception of a scientific laboratory, and the face is familiar in cartoons, T-shirts, and novelty-store windows. The evocative surname—somewhat indiscriminately applied to both the scientist and his creation—has conspicuously graced the news media in the last few years as critics have sought the most effective symbol to persuade the public of the potential hazards of certain kinds of molecular biological research. Mayor Alfred Vellucci could have been auditioning for the role of burgomaster in the classic films as he warned the citizenry of Cambridge, Massachusetts, that "something could crawl out of the laboratory, such as a Frankenstein"[1] or that "'those people in white coats' could build a Frankenstein."[2] The *Washington Star* caught the spirit with the headline "Is Harvard the Proper Place for Frankenstein Tinkering?"[3] An eminent defender of molecular biological research attempted to co-opt this rhetorical banner by referring to ill-conceived efforts at control as "our regulatory Frankenstein,"[4] while observers of the recombinant DNA debate have termed it "the Frankenstein Syndrome"[5] or "the Frankenstein Factor."[6]

The familiar face and the easy, almost reflexive references to the name should not be dismissed as just another pop culture stereotype; their widespread currency is only the most visible manifestation of a deeper and more significant cultural phenomenon. The story of Victor Frankenstein and his fearful creation should be viewed, I believe, as the twentieth century's living myth. The Frankenstein theme embodies and dramatizes many of the most frightening dilemmas that have resulted from the advance of twentieth-century science; as a consequence, its status as popular myth is not only understandable, but appropriate and potentially valuable as well.

Myths are to a culture what dreams are to the individual. It matters little whether we interpret them in the Freudian sense as communal projections of unconscious fears and desires that are normally repressed, or in the Jungian sense of collective visions that put us back in touch with life-furthering psychic powers. Both interpretations see myth as a link between a culture's outward beliefs and activities and its unconscious or unacknowledged desires, fears, and motivations. Myths are a collective way of dealing with the unknown, the problematic, and the paradoxical aspects of human existence. For the culture with its myths, as for individuals with their dreams, recognition, understanding, and acceptance may lead to the fruitful integration of what could otherwise become destructive or life-eroding tensions and conflicts.

The relationship between private dream and public myth could not be more strikingly illustrated than by Mary Shelley's own case. *Frankenstein* owes its genesis to a fortuitous contest among Percy Shelley, Lord Byron, Dr. Polidori, and Mary Shelley to compose the best ghost story. Students of Mary Shelley's work have seen sources of the *Frankenstein* novel in the biographical and psychological details of her life, in the intellectual environment in which she was raised, and in the extensive discussions she was privy to between Percy Shelley and Byron on the implications of contemporary scientific developments.[7] The direct inspiration, according to Mary Shelley's own recollection, was a "waking dream" in which

> I did not sleep, nor could I be said to think. My imagination,
> unbidden, possessed and guided me, sifting the successive

images that arose in my mind with a vividness far beyond the
usual bounds of reverie. I saw—with shut eyes, but acute
mental vision—I saw the pale student of unhallowed arts
kneeling beside the thing he had put together. I saw the
hideous phantasm of a man stretched out, and then, on the
working of some powerful engine, show signs of life and stir
with an uneasy half vital motion.[8]

That hideous phantasm was conceived in the imagination of a
nineteen-year-old woman in 1816. It emerged into the world in
1818 with the first publication of the novel, but it would not
truly come of age for another century and a quarter.

The tale centers on a scientist who, seeing the decay of death
"succeed to the blooming cheek of life," and "how the worm
inhabited the wonders of the eye and brain,"[9] believes that if
he "could bestow animation upon lifeless matter," he might
"renew life where death had apparently devoted the body to
corruption" (4;48) Though his animation succeeds, Victor Frankenstein is horrified by the result—"the miserable monster
whom I had created" (5;52)—and he flees the creature's initial
attempts at contact. The monster, at first a Rousseauesque noble savage—an artificial natural man—is left to find his own
way in the world. He learns to speak and read; and his education comes through books and observations of human behavior.
Rejected by his creator and by society, his originally benevolent
disposition turns violent.

Confronting his maker at last, the monster eloquently indicts
Frankenstein for his failure of responsibility. The creature re-
counts the details of his unhappy experience in the world and
urges Frankenstein to ameliorate his existence by creating a
mate for him. Frankenstein agrees but then reneges; and the
creature wreaks vengeance upon those Frankenstein most
loves. The scientist pursues his creation to the Arctic ice fields;
near death, he is picked up by the captain of a polar expedition,
Robert Walton, to whom he tells his story. Walton's voyage
testifies to his own strivings for knowledge and glory and
serves as both frame and foil for Frankenstein's cautionary tale.
The novel actually begins with Walton's discovery of the dying
Frankenstein and concludes, after Frankenstein's history has
been told, with Walton's account of the monster's final mo-
ments.

That the "ghost story" revolves around a scientist and his
technological creation rather than the spiritual horrors released

by trafficking with the occult clearly differentiates this work from all its Gothic literary predecessors. It was written at a time when science and technology seemed to hold limitless promise for the intellectual and material advancement of mankind. Mary Shelley's circle provided her with firsthand experience of the exultations of Promethean men in the possibilities of a revolutionary industrial age. Byron incorporated the latest astronomical and geological conceptions into his poetry[10] and confidently predicted a future for man in which "steam-engines will conduct him to the moon."[11] Shelley carried on experiments in physics and chemistry and conceived in lyrical drama a world in which Prometheus stands unbound and "beneficent man rules the forces of nature; the lightning is his slave."[12] Conversant with many of the most exciting contemporary scientific developments—in particular the discovery of Galvanic electricity in animals, which gave promise of making the "spark of life" an object of scientific study—Mary Shelley could well ponder the results of unbounded Promethean effort.

Myths that have provided a shared perspective on the problems of human existence for past cultures can often be reinterpreted to provide an additional dimension through which to explore contemporary concerns. In attempting to do this for her own time with the Prometheus legend, Mary Shelley may in fact have created the first *future* myth—one whose structure was to correspond even more closely with the developments of a later century than with the author's own, and thus lay waiting for human activity to catch up with it. For, sympathetically translated into twentieth-century terms, *Frankenstein* addresses to an astonishing degree many of the most troublesome social and ethical dilemmas raised by the progress of recent science. The centrality of the Frankenstein myth to the twentieth century's experience with science and technology can be most fully appreciated by a consideration of two paradigmatic examples. The first, the development of atomic weapons, is a drama essentially completed; the second, the issue of recombinant DNA and genetic engineering, is still in an early phase. If my analysis is persuasive, an understanding of the historically completed case may help us with, or at least recognize more clearly, the conflicting emotions and opinions raised by the recombinant DNA debate.

I begin with a detailed comparison between Mary Shelley's account of Frankensteinian creation and the historical development of the atomic bomb. In particular, I will identify a number of critical elements that are present in both the Frankensteinian and the atomic creation. I consider these common elements to be essential components of what I term a "Frankenstein scenario"; and in the latter half of this essay I will attempt to interpret the recombinant DNA controversy, including several of its more unusual aspects, in terms of such a Frankenstein scenario.

For the decade following 1945, J. Robert Oppenheimer was probably the most renowned scientist in America. As director of the Los Alamos Laboratory, he had headed the research and development effort that produced the world's first atomic bombs. On 6 and 9 August 1945, two of these weapons were exploded over Japanese cities, bringing the Second World War to an apocalyptic conclusion. Oppenheimer was widely honored as the "Father of the atomic bomb" and came to represent in the public mind the very image of the scientific/technocratic creator. The careers of Victor Frankenstein and Robert Oppenheimer bear striking similarities. At times the parallels are so resonant that one almost forgets which is the real-world and which the fictional scientist; they seem cut from the same mythic fabric.[13]

An appropriate place to begin is with the attraction that scientific inquiry held for each of these men. Early in the novel, Frankenstein tells his listeners what drew him to the study of science:

> It was the secrets of heaven and earth that I desired to learn; and whether it was the outward substance of things, or the inner spirit of nature and the mysterious soul of man that occupied me, still my inquiries were directed to the metaphysical, or in its highest sense, the physical secrets of the world. (2;28)

Similarly, Oppenheimer seemed as engrossed in metaphysics as in physics itself. A less widely ranging professional colleague believed that

> Oppenheimer was overeducated in those fields which lie outside the scientific tradition, such as his interest in re-

ligion, in the Hindu religion in particular, which resulted in a feeling for the mystery of the universe that surrounded him almost like a fog.[14]

His formal scientific training took place in the strange new world of quantum mechanics, where physics and philosophy met: questions of causality, determinism, and the statistical nature of reality were as much a part of discourse as the more traditional physical language of "mass," "particle," and "velocity." In Göttingen, as a graduate student, Oppenheimer "was particularly deep in Dante's *Inferno* and . . . would discuss with colleagues the reason why Dante had located the eternal quest in hell instead of in paradise."[15] While in Berkeley, as an associate professor of physics, he was "reading the Bhagavad Gita [in the original with a professor of Sanskrit]. . . . It is very easy and quite marvellous [sic]."[16]

Both Frankenstein and Oppenheimer, it is clear, pursue science in its original sense of "natural philosophy." In addition to that intrinsic appeal, Frankenstein's researches are motivated by personal creative satisfaction, hopes of glory, and a desire to contribute to the world's welfare:

> Wealth was an inferior object; but what glory would attend the discovery, if I could banish disease from the human frame, and render man invulnerable to any but a violent death! (2;31)

The reasons for Oppenheimer's undertaking the work that led to the explosive release of atomic energy are complex but analogous: the excitement of an unexplored realm of physics, the desire for the highest level of accomplishment, and concern for the welfare of a world in which the Nazis threatened to become the first possessors of an awesome atomic power.[17]

The two creators share as well a spiritual passion and a disregard for the ordinary demands of the body. Frankenstein was "engaged, heart and soul" (4;43) and "animated by an almost supernatural enthusiasm" (4;44). He "had worked hard for nearly two years" on his creation, and "for this I had deprived myself of rest and health. . . . My cheek had grown pale with study, and my person had become emaciated with confinement" (5;51; 4;48). Similarly, Oppenheimer "spoke with a kind of mystical earnestness that captured our imagination,"[18] and "he seemed to be aflame with an inward spiritual passion."[19] Oppenheimer's own two years of hard work on the mesa at Los Alamos between 1943 and 1945 had also taken their toll; waiting in the desert for the test that would unleash his creation, he was "too emaciated to sweat, he had kept on his familiar sloppy tweed suit, which now fitted him like a tent."[20]

The first element, then, of a Frankenstein scenario is an area of scientific research that is immensely attractive intellectually and, at the same time, one that gives promise of contributing substantially to the public good; its successful pursuit would garner both professional and public respect. Something like this combination of factors is probably necessary to nurture both the interest and dedication of the brightest and most original minds, without which revolutionary scientific/technological breakthroughs are unlikely.

What is the nature of such a breakthrough? (An especially apposite word, *breakthrough* conveys the implication of penetrating some notable barrier between the understood and the unknown.) In both the novel and real life, the thing that has been created and released is of terrifying, overwhelming aspect; the onlookers find it difficult to capture in words the quality of the climactic event:

> How can I describe my emotions at this catastrophe, or how delineate the wretch whom with such infinite plans and care I had attempted to form? . . . I had desired it with an ardour that far exceeded moderation; but now that I had finished, the beauty of the dream vanished, and breathless horror and disgust filled my heart. (5;51)

The description of an eyewitness to the atomic creation rivals that romantic account:

> The whole country was lighted by a searing light with an intensity many times that of the midday sun. . . . Thirty seconds after the explosion came, first, the air blast pressing hard against the people and things, to be followed almost immediately by the strong, sustained, awesome roar which warned of doomsday and made us feel that we puny things were blasphemous to dare tamper with the forces heretofore reserved to The Almighty. Words are inadequate tools for the job of acquainting those not present with the physical, men-

tal and psychological effects. It had to be witnessed to be realized.[21]

What gives the Oppenheimer story its most compelling Frankensteinian quality is suggested in the preceding quotations: humanity has succeeded in a *transcendent* creation. It is not merely that it has produced something it does not know how to control; rather, it has created a thing that in its very nature embodies forces and potentialities that exceed by several orders of magnitude anything to which it could previously lay claim. In July 1945 human beings had not yet set foot beyond their home planet, but they had brought the million-degree temperatures of the sun to a piece of the New Mexican desert. Within a month, two more miniature suns were lighted over Hiroshima and Nagasaki. The human race is marvelously resilient; though virtually all of central Tokyo had been leveled and 80,000 people killed in a series of conventional bombing raids, the citizenry adapted. The destruction was calamitous, but it was a calamity that could be understood as the cumulative result of small, assimilable horrors. But not all the military experience of the deputy chief of the Japanese General Staff, Kawabe, could help him make sense of the report he received on 7 August 1945: "The whole city of Hiroshima was destroyed instantly by a single bomb."[22]

Mary Shelley, intuiting the dark side of technological accomplishment, believed herself to be recasting the Prometheus legend for a nineteenth-century audience. The classical Prometheus stole fire from the gods and, concealing it in a hollow tube, transmitted it to mortal men. Victor Frankenstein's creation represents Prometheus run riot. Following the monster's initial disappearance, Frankenstein catches sight of him in the midst of a stupendous lightning storm in the high Alps. In the first conversation between creator and creature, Frankenstein reluctantly seats himself "by the fire which my odious companion had lighted" (10;103) and hears the monster's account of his unorthodox education, in which the discovery of fire plays a prominent part. The monster runs "with the swiftness of lightning" (23;212) and images of fire and lightning fitfully illuminate the narrative. Such resonant details speak convincingly to an age in which the hollow tube filled with fire has been fitted with inertial guidance and can be brought to earth on a computer-calculated trajectory.

The transcendent power that the scientist has released, and with which he must deal, is the heart of the Frankenstein myth. This transcendent quality, with its intimations of the godlike or the supernatural, lies behind the mixture of admiration, awe, and fear that such creations inspire. It accounts for those time-honored clichés of virtually every Frankenstein horror film: "Doctor, don't you think you've gone too far?"; "Perhaps there are some things we are not meant to know." On a somewhat more elevated intellectual level, Mary Shelley accomplishes the same emotional effect through her extended use of Promethean allusions, with their inescapable suggestion of retribution for those who display the hubris of appropriating godlike powers, whether for their own aggrandizement or for humanity's putative benefit. As Robert Jungk points out, confrontation with the transcendent power released in the real world through knowledge of nuclear processes engendered musings of a similarly mythic or religious nature:

> It is a striking fact that none of those present [at the Alamogordo test] reacted to the phenomenon as professionally as he had supposed he would. They all, even those—who constituted the majority—ordinarily without religious faith or even any inclination thereto, recounted their experience in words derived from the linguistic fields of myth and theology.[23]

The most provocative expression of this feeling may have come from Oppenheimer himself. In the shocked silence immediately following the first atomic explosion, a line from the Bhagavad Gita floated through his mind, the words of Krishna, avatar of a Hindu god: "I am become death, the shatterer of worlds."[24]

But godlike powers entail godlike responsibilities. From the first chapter of Frankenstein's narrative, this moral pervades the novel. Frankenstein speaks approvingly of his parents' "deep consciousness of what they owed towards the being to which they had given life" (1;24). As the novel emphasizes, next to the presumptuous animation itself, Frankenstein's greatest transgression is his abdication of responsibility for his creation. He rushes out of the room at the monster's first signs of life and flees the house at the monster's first tentative approach to him. As Prometheus becomes the symbol of Frankenstein's hubris

throughout the novel, so *Paradise Lost* serves to indict Frankenstein for his failure of responsibility. The monster is most eloquent in his Miltonesque references to the duties owed him by
Frankenstein. In a particularly memorable passage, he re-
proaches his creator:

> I am thy creature, and I will be even mild and docile to my
> natural lord and king, if thou wilt also perform thy part, that
> which thou owest me. Oh, Frankenstein, be not equitable to
> every other, and trample upon me alone, to whom thy jus-
> tice, and even thy clemency and affection is most due. Re-
> member, that I am thy creature; I ought to be thy Adam; but I
> am rather the fallen angel, whom thou drivest from joy for no
> misdeed. (10;101)

Is it, in fact, legitimate to draw a parallel between Frankenstein's and Oppenheimer's duties of responsibility? Frankenstein assembled his creation alone with his own resources, in
an attic chamber. On the other hand, Oppenheimer was the
scientific director of a multi-million-dollar research and development effort involving several thousand technical workers.
Moreover, administrative authority was exercised by General
Leslie Groves, overall head of the Manhattan Project, and
through him, by the secretary of war and the president. But it
is, ironically, this very organizational diffusion of responsibility
that makes the Frankenstein theme so contemporary. The technological breakthroughs capable of producing Frankenstein
creations in the twentieth century cannot be one-person projects; scientific knowledge and economic resources must be
provided by a large network of collaborators, supporters, and,
on occasion, overseers. Watergate and Vietnam serve as recent
reminders of the ease with which personal responsibilities can
be sacrificed to the demands of the team or to institutional
priorities. Oppenheimer is, in this sense, as fitting a representative of the twentieth century's organizational scientist as
Frankenstein is of the nineteenth century's scientific individu-
alist.

Thus when confronted with a request to allow a petition
against the atom bombing of Japan to be distributed to Los
Alamos' scientists, Oppenheimer

> knew that the military authorities would take action if he did
> not, and besides he was dubious about how far scientists

ought to go in trying to influence political decisions. He said the petition could not be circulated.[25]

In a similar discussion, Edward Teller reported that Oppenheimer told him

> that he thought it improper for a scientist to use his prestige as a platform for political pronouncements. He conveyed to me in glowing terms the deep concern, thoroughness, and wisdom with which these questions were being handled in Washington.[26]

At about the same time, Oppenheimer was asked to give his advice to the interim committee that was to counsel Secretary of War Henry Stimson on atomic matters, including the use of bombs. As one of the committee related, Oppenheimer

> didn't say drop the bomb or don't drop it. He just tried to do his job, which was to give us technical background. I think he did it well. Certainly he didn't try to influence us in any way.[27]

The interpenetration of scientific and political decision-making in the modern world has been such as to allow Oppenheimer (or any other contemporary scientist) to make a *prima facie* case for an absence of, or at least a widely dispersed, responsibility. For most critics of the atomic denouement, this defense does not fully persuade, and for them the monster's accusation still goes to the heart of the moral issue.

Even in its own time, Mary Shelley's novel symbolized the large-scale societal ramifications of individual technological creations. Technology as a whole was, in many ways, the monster, clearly linked to the new technological, industrial, economic, and social order that issued from the nineteenth century's "dark Satanic mills."[28] If one translates this symbolic critique into the equivalent twentieth-century terms, it becomes more than a cautionary account of the dangers attendant on a particular scientific creation; it comes to serve as a warning about the political, economic, and social structure that may then pose a powerful threat to the life and welfare of the ordinary citizen.

Oppenheimer's monster is both the atomic bomb *and* the atomic establishment that grew up around it and ultimately took it over. This interpretation leads to another of the novel's implicit themes: once the transcendent technological creation has been produced, it becomes independent of the original motivations and subsequent wishes of its creator. The creation comes to have a life and a momentum of its own. Frankenstein's monster, once out of his maker's laboratory, responds with all his superhuman capacities to the currents of the world in which he finds himself and develops his own imperatives. He tells Frankenstein that a solitary monster results in a dangerously unstable situation that must be corrected:

> We may not part until you have promised to comply with my requisition. I am alone, and miserable; man will not associate with me; but one as deformed and horrible as myself would not deny herself to me. My companion must be of the same species, and have the same defects. This being you must create. (16;152)

So the scientist becomes the servant of his creation, subject to its blandishments and threats. The monster attempts to persuade Frankenstein, by the most forceful arguments, to embark upon the production of yet another—and potentially even more dangerous—monster. *Mutatis mutandis*, this was the agonizing situation in which Robert Oppenheimer found himself only a few years after his creation of a functional atomic bomb.

Oppenheimer left the Los Alamos Laboratory shortly after the conclusion of the war. A year later, President Truman appointed him, along with eight other scientists, to the general advisory committee set up to counsel the Atomic Energy Commission on questions of science and technology. His colleagues elected him chairman, and the general advisory committee—given the extensive experience in atomic affairs of its membership—rapidly became a major force in shaping atomic policy. In September 1949, barely four years after the successful production of American atomic weapons, the Soviet Union detonated an atomic bomb of its own. Initiated by the urgings of Edward Teller—a physicist with intensely anti-Communist sentiments who had played a major role in the formulation of theories regarding thermonuclear fusion—a powerful movement developed within the government to embark upon the production of a new kind of atomic weapon that would maintain U.S. technological superiority over the Soviets. Based on the fusion of hydrogen atoms, this thermonuclear conception (the earliest version of which was referred to as the "Super") promised explosive yields thousands of times greater than the earlier fission devices, if extremely difficult theoretical and technical problems could be solved. Undertaking such a project would require a vast array of resources and a number of far-reaching political, economic, and technical decisions. The question of whether to launch a Super project inevitably became a major issue for the deliberations of the general advisory committee.

Victor Frankenstein had acceded at first to his monster's demands. But the enormity of what he might be unleashing upon the world and the possibility of an unlimited proliferation of new monsters following upon his creation of a mate engendered second thoughts:

> As I sat, a train of reflection occurred to me, which led me to consider the effects of what I was now doing. Three years before I was engaged in the same manner, and had created a fiend whose unparalleled barbarity had desolated my heart, and filled it forever with the bitterest remorse. I was now about to form another being, of whose dispositions I was alike ignorant; she might become ten thousand times more malignant than her mate. (20;176)

As chairman of the general advisory committee, Oppenheimer was faced with framing recommendations regarding the development of a device whose destructive potential was to be measured in megatons of TNT rather than the mere kilotons of the Hiroshima and Nagasaki weapons. In short, Oppenheimer was crucially involved in decisions regarding a second creation of whose political and military disposition he was alike ignorant, and which might become literally ten thousand times more malignant than its predecessor.

Like most tragic protagonists Frankenstein has learned from his experience. With a painfully acquired sense of the wider consequences of his actions, he takes on the heavy responsibility of opposing the development of second-generation monsters. Frankenstein's response to the frightening dilemma in which he found himself was simple and direct: he "tore to pieces the thing on which I was engaged" (20;177). In answer to the monster's promptings to recommence the project, Frankenstein tells him not to "poison the air" with his sounds of malice (20;179); his unrestrainable creation replies with the chilling imprecation: "Remember, I shall be with you on your weddingnight" (20;179).

Oppenheimer's response to his own dilemma was less dramatic and more ambivalent than Frankenstein's, but the doubts and second thoughts are equally apparent. Oppenheimer no longer believed that his responsibilities ended with the provision of technical expertise. In a letter to another of the general advisory committee members, Oppenheimer describes the mounting pressure to produce a Super and suggests some of his qualms:

> What concerns me is really not the technical problem. . . . It seems likely to me even further to worsen the unbalance of our present war plans. What does worry me is that this thing appears to have caught the imagination, both of the congressional and military people, as the answer to the problems posed by the Russian advance. . . . But that we become committed to it as the way to save the country and the peace appears to me full of dangers.[29]

The general advisory committee deliberated the question of a crash program toward the Super and concluded: "We believe a Super bomb should never be produced."[30] Nuel Davis describes what followed upon that recommendation:

> To their mournful astonishment, after a few weeks Oppenheimer and his committee saw their conclusions rehashed in the newspapers. Before Hiroshima, no one had decided anything. The scientists had assumed the government would decide, the government had assumed the military would decide, and the military had assumed they were expected to fry Japanese. Against this natural falling motion no one had interposed himself wholly except [Under Secretary of the Navy] Bard, too minor a figure to stop it. Now the falling motion had begun again, but someone had looked into the thermonuclear grave, taken thought, and stopped the motion into it. Someone had decided—and must pay.[31]

For both Frankenstein and Oppenheimer, the payment was delayed but inevitable. First, Frankenstein's closest friend is destroyed, and then Frankenstein's bride. Oppenheimer's punishment began in 1953, with a change of presidential administration. Although Oppenheimer had resigned from the general advisory committee more than a year earlier, and although his direct involvement in government policy and research was now minimal, his security clearance was revoked pending further review. According to Davis,

On December 21, Strauss [the new chairman of the Atomic Energy Commission and a longtime adversary of Oppenheimer] summoned Oppenheimer and told him of the President's order. Oppenheimer had then only a token link with the Commission—a consultant's contract which would expire in July and of which the commission had made no use since September. This was not the link that Eisenhower meant to break with his order, but rather the link of respect and confidence that bound the scientific community to Oppenheimer. He was their rallying point against the government's sick, unreal reliance on a yet unbuilt H-bomb.[32]

To have acquiesced in the decision would be to participate in his own repudiation; it "would mean that I accept and concur in the view that I am not fit to serve this government that I have now served for some twelve years. This I cannot do. . . ."[33] Oppenheimer challenged the executive order and underwent a formal hearing by the personnel security board set up by the Atomic Energy Commission to conduct the investigation. For several weeks every aspect of Oppenheimer's professional and private life was open to scrutiny. And, indeed, the security arm of the atomic energy establishment that Oppenheimer helped create did not stop short of the bridal chamber. Both his wife's past Communist associations and his overnight stay at the home of a former fiancée ten years earlier were entered into the record of the case, which was subsequently published. The revocation order was upheld and Oppenheimer, symbolically destroyed, was removed from the world of public affairs.[34]

Thus, as a result of what may be considered their most noble action—the attempt finally to exercise responsibility by limiting the world-endangering proliferation of what they helped bring into being—both Frankenstein and Oppenheimer end as victims of their creations. That moral lesson provided the epigraph at the beginning of this essay (4;46); in the series of cinematic *Frankensteins* it has more usually provided the dramatic closing. It accorded well with the conventions of the erstwhile Hollywood film code, which did not allow transgressors to exit unpunished at a movie's conclusion. But the kind of cinematic homiletics that places the entire weight of responsibility and guilt upon one character in a murderous social drama, especially when followed by a collective sigh of relief on the part of the audience, should raise suspicions. As other familiar cinema archetypes—detective and psychiatrist—are wont to observe: the absence of something is often as revealing as its presence. With regard to *Frankenstein* in particular, two elements that are inescapable in Mary Shelley's novel are thrown into even bolder relief by their (almost) consistent absence in the film versions.

The monsters of most cinematic *Frankensteins* are mute. A few others manage an occasional semiarticulate grunt. Shelley's monster, on the contrary, has many of the most powerful speeches in the novel. Both Frankenstein and Walton, the novel's narrator, are moved to sympathy by the monster's words; and Walton "call[s] to mind what Frankenstein had said of his powers of eloquence and persuasion" (p. 239). Clearly, the filmmakers believed that their audience would be discomfited by the monster's frequently repeated assertions: "I was benevolent; my soul glowed with love and humanity. . . . I was benevolent and good; misery made me a fiend" (10;101). Indeed, the monster at first used his great strength for humanity's benefit, saving a drowning girl and anonymously performing laborious chores for the overburdened De Lacey family. By silencing the monster, the films have increased his separation from us, making him both more alienated and more alien. He becomes a figure to be pitied and feared, but not one needing to be dealt with wisely and humanely. The fact that the creation is, at least in part, successful—that an intelligent and malleable, though extremely powerful, being has been produced—is comfortably forgotten.

Most of the misery, in fact, of which the monster complains derives from the response of human society—the second, and related, element that the movie versions generally ignore or greatly play down. The monster's reward for the girl's rescue (translated into her *murder* in many of the movies) is a gunshot wound; for the unselfish labor, the blows of a stick when the monster finally shows himself. The monster's laudable intentions stand in sharp contrast to the iniquities of human society as revealed not only by his own experience, but also through his overhearing the account of injustices to befall the De Lacey family and by his foray into historical scholarship: "I read of men concerned in public affairs, governing or massacring their species" (15;135). The creature's virtues of intelligence, strength, and benevolence are unappreciated or rejected by human society on the basis of instinctive reactions to his outward appearance or mistaken analyses of his motives. As a consequence, the benevolence is perverted to malice, the intelligence to diabolic cunning, and the strength to unrestrained destructive power.

The novel, then, strongly suggests that the scientist's creation has unbounded potentiality for good *or* evil, and that it is society which turns that creation into something monstrous. Although twentieth-century audiences may repress this implication, it is clear that society shares both an ambivalence toward the creation and considerable responsibility for the direction it takes. The fear and condemnation directed against the act of unnatural biological creation are balanced by the enthusiastic interest and approbation generated by many successful biomedical interventions. We already draw upon the "vaults and charnel-houses" as we remove corneas, kidneys, lungs, and even hearts from the dead to extend the existence of the living.[35] And where biological materials are not suitable or available, we devise mechanical substitutes: artificial joints of metal and plastic, artificial blood vessels, artificial hearts, electric pacemakers—in this last instance literally instilling a "spark of life." Spare-part surgery might be appropriately described as Frankensteinian activity with a good press.

Similarly, one sympathizes with Victor Frankenstein's desire to "banish disease from the human frame and render man invulnerable to any but a violent death" (2;31). And the strength and power of the "monster" are attributes that speak to many unconscious desires. In this sense, Frankenstein's error is not so much a matter of flawed intentions as of faulty execution; in other words, his failure is as much technical and aesthetic as moral. As one critic has perceptively remarked,

> [the] disaster either wouldn't have happened, or would not
> have mattered anyway, if Frankenstein had been an es-
> thetically successful maker; a beautiful "monster," or even a
> passable one, would not have been a monster.[36]

If one wants to imagine an aesthetically successful
Frankensteinian creation—and appreciate the appeal that such
an achievement would have for our society—one need do no
more than recall "The Six Million Dollar Man" or his mate, "The
Bionic Woman."

The novel's imputation of responsibility to society for turning
the creation into a monster requires little real-world elaboration. Scientific research in most areas of contemporary interest
is expensive, and society provides the funding; the scientists'
discoveries have not been their own property for several decades. Again, no better illustration could be found of the novel's
argument that the scientific creation was a force for good or ill,
and that society directed it toward malignity, than the Oppenheimer case. The technological effort to produce an atomic
bomb was not a matter of open debate during World War II, but
there is little doubt the American public, caught up in total war,
would have wanted it produced; and once produced, employed. In General Groves' words:

> If the bomb hadn't been used, in the first year after the war
> was over, the first Congressional investigation would have
> screamed the government was responsible for the blood of
> our boys shed uselessly.[37]

Oppenheimer and his associates were popular heroes, and
doubts about the morality of the bomb's development and use
did not appear in any significant fashion in American public
discussion until several years after Hiroshima.

This comparison between the fictional account of a monster's
creation in the laboratory of Victor Frankenstein and the historical account of the creation of the atomic bomb in the laboratory
of Dr. Oppenheimer and his coworkers has attempted to identify the significant themes common to the two narratives. These
shared elements, I believe, characterize certain especially troubling dilemmas that have resulted from the impact of scientific
or technological activity upon society. Such Frankenstein scenarios contain most or all of the following themes: (1) Nature

contains secrets that can be uncovered by the exercise of creative scientific activity; (2) the research area in which this kind of revolutionary breakthrough will occur is of such intense fascination—for its intrinsic interest and its potential for application—that it attracts the best and brightest minds; (3) the breakthrough involves an aspect of truly transcendent power, in the sense that forces or potentialities that exceed by several orders of magnitude those to which mankind has been accustomed are suddenly made available for human manipulation; (4) the creator does not try, or is not able, to exercise effective responsibility regarding the further development of his creation or the uses to which it is put; (5) the creation develops a momentum and imperative of its own; (6) opposition to that imperative is personally hazardous; (7) the transcendent power of the creation is, in principle, a potential force for good or ill; (8) the complex network of political, economic, and social relationships ("society") into which the creation is introduced determines the end to which that creation is directed; that is, society may transform a relatively undifferentiated creation into a monster.

These elements, drawn from the histories of Victor Frankenstein and Robert Oppenheimer, form the basis for the widespread currency of the Frankenstein myth. In arguing for the authentic status of Frankenstein as contemporary myth, my sense of that term is in close agreement with the formulation of Joseph Campbell. Based on his extensive study of the world's myths, Campbell identified four functions generally characteristic of an operative, living mythology: to waken and maintain a sense of awe in relation to the mystery of the universe; to offer an image of the universe that will be in accord with the knowledge of the time; to reflect the norms of a society's moral order; and to serve as guide for the conduct of life.[38] I think the discussion of the two case histories shows how fully the Frankenstein-Oppenheimer theme serves these functions.

I would like now to explore somewhat more deeply the mythic nature of that theme. One must surely be led to wonder how it happens that the twentieth century's most awesome technological creation should mirror so strikingly the terrifying creation of a nineteenth-century novel. The answer may be that Mary Shelley's prescient intuition and Robert Oppenheimer's historic career are apprehensions or reflections of the same underlying structural relationship—one that interconnects scientist, society, and nature.[39]

The natural universe was man's original and inescapably immediate environment. No representative of a modern culture can ever fully imagine the direct, all-pervasive, awe-instilling experience of nature that must have conditioned the thoughts and beliefs of the earliest people. In fact, the history of mankind is an account of the development of societies—artificial environments that insulate people from nature and thus, in some fundamental sense, oppose it. The tension of that opposition may be found in every culture from the most primitive to the most technologically sophisticated; no society has (yet) been able to differentiate itself completely from the natural environment. The progress of that differentiation, the measure of the material and psychological support that the constructed environment of society provides, has most often been assessed in terms of the knowledge—and through knowledge, the control—that humans have acquired in respect to the natural world.

Ultimately, human existence rests upon paradox—or, at least, upon apparently unavoidable contradiction. Human physical subsistence depends upon the bounty of the natural world. When a number of critical parameters of that natural world fall within certain limits, human society can lead a more-or-less satisfactory existence; when one or more of these parameters falls outside the normal limits, greater or lesser disasters are the result. Among the most obvious such parameters are the absolute amount and distribution of sunlight, precipitation, temperature, wind, fish and game, insects, disease organisms, and tectonic activity. The natural world, in which human beings' physical existence is grounded, is simultaneously potential provider and potential destroyer, inescapably beneficent *and* baneful. Human mental and psychological existence, on the other hand, is equally dependent on the world inside the skull. That inner world functions in such a way that individuals and, perforce, society can operate on the outer world, can understand and control aspects of the external universe so as to increase the possibilities for survival within it, actively and effectively resisting death. At the same time, however, that unique human mind makes us, unlike any other animal, truly aware of death and of its ultimate irresistibility.

Paradoxes such as these lie at the root of functional mythologies. For primitive man, myth was a symbolic system for relating the beliefs and activities of his society to the awesome, contradictory, and potentially overwhelming realities of the natural world. A system of conceptualization and belief that organizes the unknown, representing its multivariant aspects through symbols and images the mind can grasp, gives form—and thus, meaning—to an otherwise chaotic and terrifying assemblage of events. Since these symbols can be manipulated by the individual and by society, they contribute to a comforting sense that the external reality that they reflect can also be controlled, or at least, influenced. Thus myth enables human societies to believe that they have achieved a measure of understanding and rapport with the natural world.

A new tension, however, is generated by this understanding. As a society gains an increased sense of security through its conceptual ordering of the natural world, and as the understanding embraces more phenomena and grows more detailed, a need develops for individuals who can interpret and apply this understanding for society's benefit. These mediators between society and the natural world are greatly respected, but never more so than when natural disaster (such as drought, famine, flood) threatens the society's existence and the most expert intervention available is sought. As both conceptual and social structures have evolved, the role of mediator has been filled by shamans, priests, and scientists.

It is almost inescapable that under these conditions the mediators will develop interests and goals that are not necessarily identical with those of the society at large that they serve. As the extent and complexity of knowledge about the workings of the natural world grow, the role of mediator becomes more specialized. Individuals must be found who possess the appropriate interests, temperaments, and talents for the work. It should not be at all surprising that in many cases interest in the enterprise of further understanding the natural world, of uncovering its secrets, takes precedence over, or even eclipses, the concern for judicious application of such knowledge for society's unmitigated benefit. It should also not be surprising that society comes to respond with some ambivalence towards those who mediate its interactions with the natural world—with gratitude for the essential services provided but with awe and fear of those who have special knowledge and contact with the mysterious workings of the universe.

The grander the achievements of these mediators, the greater will be the intensity of this mixture of gratitude, awe, and fear. Mythic thinking, through its symbolic conceptualizations, helped bring into existence these powerful figures who intervene in the natural world. In doing so it engendered another paradox of the very sort that myth is meant to express: society creates powerful figures who, in serving society, may not always serve society. In other words, myth itself has created a new element that must be incorporated in some fashion into mythic consciousness. In earlier times this process produced the accounts of Prometheus and Faust. As the revolutionary impact of scientific knowledge and technological innovation began to make itself felt in the nineteenth century, the figures of Frankenstein and his unrestrainable creation took mythic form. By the late twentieth century they have become virtually emblematic.

The dramatic and highly charged controversy that erupted over certain kinds of molecular biological research puzzled many observers. A number of the scientists engaged in recombinant DNA work have expressed surprise at the fact that this experimentation strongly aroused the public, while other areas of potentially hazardous biological investigation (such as infectious disease organisms, tumor viruses, or even the presently banned bacteriological warfare research) elicited much less concern. I believe that this troubling issue, along with the conflicting emotions and opinions that it engendered, can be more fully understood if it is considered in the light of a Frankenstein scenario. My analysis of the recombinant DNA controversy will not focus upon parallels between the careers of Victor Frankenstein and some premier molecular biologist, as was possible in the case of Robert Oppenheimer. Rather, I examine the activities and opinions of a diverse array of scientists in terms of the common elements that have already been derived from the Frankenstein-Oppenheimer comparison. I will analyze the recombinant DNA controversy by examining the extent to which these critical elements are present; that is, by assessing how closely this area of scientific research fits a Frankenstein scenario as previously defined.

The first of these elements—a belief that nature contains secrets of intense interest that can be revealed by the exercise of creative scientific activity—was fundamental to the development of the arcane new field of molecular biology. The individual who most influentially articulated this belief and who therefore comes closest to being the spiritual founder of molecular biology was Erwin Schrödinger—not a biologist at all, but a physicist at the forefront of quantum theory. In *What Is Life?* first published in 1944, Schrödinger asked: "How can the events *in space and time* which take place within the spatial boundary of a living organism be accounted for by physics and chemistry?"[40] His preliminary answer was that "the obvious inability of present-day physics and chemistry to account for such events is no reason at all for doubting that they can be accounted for by these sciences."[41] Schrödinger's ideas drew the attention of a number of young physical scientists to a relatively unexplored area of biology; his book, in the words of one such recruit, "became a kind of *Uncle Tom's Cabin* of the revolution in biology that, when the dust had cleared, left molecular genetics as its legacy."[42]

A common background in quantum physics is not the only similarity between Erwin Schrödinger and Robert Oppenheimer; there is also a shared appreciation of the metaphysical and aesthetic dimensions of scientific activity. Schrödinger's ability to combine romantic sensibility with scientific insight is suggested by his use of epigraphs from Goethe to introduce many sections of *What is Life?* One quotation immediately follows the heading "Mutations" and clearly implies that a firm physical explanation will be found for the "jump-like" changes in hereditary information that form "the working-ground for natural selection."

> Und was in schwankender Erscheinung schwebt,
> Befestiget mit dauernden Gedanken.[43]
> [And what in fluctuating appearance hovers,
> You will fix by lasting thoughts.]

The quotation comes from *Faust*, Goethe's romantic reworking of the medieval legend in which the elements of beneficent Promethean activity far outweigh the unsavory aspects of necromancy.

Schrödinger's adumbration of a physical basis for the transfer of genetic information caught the imagination of bright and often unorthodox scientists. Preeminent among these were Francis Crick and James Watson, who transformed this intuition into a revolutionary explanation of the mechanism of heredity—an explanation whose empirical solidity and theoretical elegance have given it the status of a central dogma of molecular biology. Crick and Watson made a complementary pair. Crick possessed an irrepressible intelligence and enthusiasm, while Watson had an uncanny instinct for the scientific longshot and a single-minded, if not opportunistic, drive to pursue the quest at whatever cost. Watson and Crick reinforced each other in the belief that the actual physical and chemical details of the structure of the DNA molecule would be the key to revealing how the genes really functioned.

Intellectual fascination and professional ambition combined to make the structure of DNA an irresistible challenge. In phrases reminiscent of Victor Frankenstein, Watson relates that "sometimes I daydreamed about discovering the secret of the gene"[44] or that an x-ray photograph of DNA, "a potential key to the secret of life was impossible to push out of my mind" (30). Crick's enthusiasm for the tentative solution to the structure of the molecule quickly took the form of a tendency "to tell everyone within hearing distance that we had found the secret of life" (126). Thoughts of professional success and acclaim, however, did not lag far behind the visionary musings. With the conclusion of the work in sight, Watson reflected that "it seemed almost unbelievable that the DNA structure was solved, that the answer was incredibly exciting, and that our names would be associated with the double helix as Pauling's was with the alpha helix" (127). Watson proceeded to tell his sister that "Francis and I had probably beaten Pauling to the gate and that the answer would revolutionize biology" (127); and he persuaded her to spend an afternoon typing up the final draft of the scientific report to *Nature* by telling her that "she was participating in perhaps the most famous event in biology since Darwin's book" (140).

That assessment has proved completely accurate. Watson and Crick's paper, published in 1953, contained an especially memorable (and deliberately understated) sentence: "It has not escaped our notice that the specific pairing we have postulated immediately suggests a possible copying mechanism for the genetic material" (139). With their model of DNA structure Watson and Crick had provided an extraordinarily persuasive explanation for one of the most fundamental processes in living organisms—the almost-perfect reproduction of the genetic information that will be passed on to future generations, along with the one-in-a-million chance for error that provides the new material for future evolution. The development of molecular biology as a major field of research derives directly from this conceptual breakthrough.

The thirty-year period following Watson and Crick's discovery became a golden age of biology. Between 1958 and 1975, in fact, fully half the forty-five Nobel prizes given in the fields of physiology or medicine were awarded for work in the highly specialized realm of molecular biology. During this time molecular biologists developed theories that outlined, at least in principle, how DNA was able to control the functioning of living cells, and by extension, the organization and development of living organisms. With astonishing rapidity, details of that outline began to be filled in: how the hereditary messages encoded in the genes—now understood simply as segments of the DNA molecule—were translated into enzymes that controlled all the cell's (and the organism's) biochemical activity; how alterations in the DNA segments produced alterations in enzymes, causing the known hereditary diseases; and even how the genes were "turned on" or "turned off."

The discovery of procedures that make it possible to join, at will, pieces of DNA of particular interest thus provides a dramatic culmination to three decades of research activity. The use of such recombinant DNA techniques makes it conceivable for the first time to investigate the precise chemical makeup of the individual genes of living organisms. In addition, it allows detailed study of those portions of the DNA that are involved in the turning on or turning off of genes in normal development or in disease. In essence, a method now exists that promises scientists a comprehensive understanding of the gene, both in its structure and in its expression. Once a sufficient body of knowledge and experience is gained in this area, the vistas become limitless. Genes governing the abilities to carry out certain functions might be transferable between species; synthetic genes for new traits might be insertable; genes with defective informational content might be repaired or improved upon; and the expression of the genes might be subject to deliberate regulation. With this heady potential for exciting scientific developments, recombinant DNA research can hardly

avoid being both a source of intellectual fascination for molecular biologists and a focus for their professional ambitions—
the second element of a Frankenstein scenario. It is most likely,
therefore, to attract many of the brightest and most highly
motivated investigators, as the opportunity of an earlier breakthrough attracted Crick and Watson.

Recombinant DNA technology has not suddenly introduced
the possibility of human intervention in the evolutionary process. Human beings have consciously or unconsciously affected
evolution on this planet since well before the beginnings of
recorded history, as, for example, in the domestication of plants
and animals, in the breeding of animals or vegetable hybrids
leading to new varieties, and in the probable extermination of
whole species of mammals by post-ice-age hunters. In historic
times humanity has spread viral and bacterial disease organisms to continents previously free of them, has attempted to
mitigate their effects through vaccines and antibiotics, and has
adopted increasingly sophisticated techniques of selective
breeding for both plants and animals. Manipulation of vege-
tative or animal nature has been among the most characteristic
of human behaviors.

Yet the unparalleled developments in molecular biology, cap-
ped by techniques for recombining DNA, have created a feeling
that we are approaching momentous new choices:

> The methods of DNA synthesis . . . have come to fruition
> just in time to reinforce, and be reinforced by, the ability to
> juggle DNA sequences around and generate them in un-
> limited amounts that recombinant DNA technology pro-
> vides. Together, the two techniques provide mankind for the
> first time with almost absolute control over the material of
> our genes.[45]

Robert Sinsheimer, then chairman of the biology division at Cal
Tech, may have summed up this sentiment most succinctly
when he observed, "For the first time in all time, a living
creature understands its origin and can undertake to design its
own future."[46]

Sinsheimer has identified the key factor that makes these
new possibilities for intervening in evolution so different from
the old: the element of conscious design through construction
rather than just selection. The potential now exists for altering

organisms in a highly sophisticated fashion—for its own sake, for useful application, or for the information it would reveal about gene structure—by introducing new genetic elements *ad libitum.* One can now combine, in the same organism, genes whose natural occurrence is separated by many hundred millions of years of evolutionary divergence and isolation.

The transcendent nature of such potentialities is fully comparable with the animation of Frankenstein's creation or the release of atomic energy. This critical element of a Frankenstein scenario has not been missed by many participants or observers of the recombinant DNA controversy. Not surprisingly, though, the transcendent aspect of recombinant DNA research has been more emphasized by its critics than its proponents. Robert Sinsheimer raised this aspect when he asked,

> Do we want to assume the basic responsibility for life on this planet—to develop new living forms for our own purpose? Shall we take into our own hands our own future evolution?[47]

In a widely quoted letter to *Science,* biochemist Erwin Chargaff posed similar questions:

> Is there anything more far-reaching than the creation of new forms of life? . . . Have we the right to counteract, irreversibly, the evolutionary wisdom of millions of years, in order to satisfy the ambition and the curiosity of a few scientists?[48]

The Frankenstein parallels are obvious. And just as Victor Frankenstein feared that "future ages might curse me as their pest" (20; 177), so Chargaff feels that his generation has engaged "in a destructive colonial warfare against nature" and that "the future will curse us for it."[49] Chargaff's letter, in fact, explicitly invokes the Frankenstein scenario:

> If Dr. Frankenstein must go on producing his little biological monsters—and I deny the urgency and even the compulsion—why pick *E.coli* as the womb? . . . The hybridization of Prometheus with Herostratus is bound to give evil results.[50]

The transcendent qualities of the research show up as well in the frequent suggestions of humanity's being able to engage in godlike acts of creation. An article entitled "The Future of Genetic Engineering" speaks of "the God-like power that such facilities endows [sic] on us,"[51] and two full-length books on the topic appropriate that intimation directly into their titles—*Playing God* by June Goodfield[52] and *Who Should Play God?* by Ted Howard and Jeremy Rifkin.[53]

In their first efforts at transcendant creation Victor Frankenstein and Robert Oppenheimer spent little time worrying about their responsibilities to control the products of their Promethean activity. In contrast to this indifference—and, perhaps, motivated by the lessons of atomic energy—a significant number of the most prominent DNA researchers were sensitive to the potential hazards of their work. Quite early they attempted to assess the possible dangers and to prevent their occurrence through communal action.

The problem of responsibility for outcomes of the new research received a formal airing among the leading molecular biologists at the Gordon Conference on Nucleic Acids in 1973. Maxine Singer, the conference's cochair, described the issue clearly:

> We all share the excitement and enthusiasm of yesterday morning's speaker, who pointed out that the scientific developments reported then would permit interesting experiments involving the linking together of a variety of DNA molecules. . . . Nevertheless, we are all aware that such experiments raise moral and ethical issues because of the potential hazards such molecules may engender. . . . Because we are doing these experiments, and because we recognize the potential difficulties, we have a responsibility to concern ourselves with the safety of our co-workers and laboratory personnel, as well as with the safety of the public. We are asked this morning to consider this responsibility.[54]

As a result of that discussion, an open letter was sent to the National Academy of Sciences and the Institute of Medicine suggesting that the potential hazards of gene splicing to laboratory workers and the public should be seriously considered and that the National Academy should appoint a committee for this purpose. The letter was also published in *Science*, which afforded it wide visibility among professional scientists.[55]

The academy formed a committee on recombinant nucleic acids that included many of the leading investigators. Their report called for an international conference to explore the issue further, since the potential hazards would not respect national boundaries. Most significantly, however, the committee recommended that until such a conference could be held, a moratorium be observed on two types of experiments that seemed to pose the greatest potential threat. Moreover, the group emphasized that other experiments be "carefully weighed" and "not be undertaken lightly."[56]

These steps led to the well-known Asilomar Conference, which concluded that certain experiments should not be performed under any circumstances and that others might be carried out under conditions of containment appropriate to the estimated risks. Responding to the Asilomar recommendations, the National Institutes of Health—working through committees composed largely (though not exclusively) of research scientists—drew up a comprehensive set of "Guidelines for Research Involving Recombinant DNA Molecules."[57] These regulations established procedures for physical and biological containment that are binding upon federally supported investigators.

The NIH guidelines were attacked by a number of individuals and by such groups as Science for the People, the People's Business Commission, and Friends of the Earth. In addition to their doubts about whether the guidelines assured public safety, these critics objected to the exclusive character of the discussions that led to the guidelines' formulation. Other observers responded more favorably to the scientists' role in regulation. Daniel Callahan, a philosopher and director of the Institute of Society, Ethics, and the Life Sciences, called the decision of scientists at the Gordon Conference to disseminate a letter recommending formal studies of the potential hazards "a striking act of moral initiative and courage" (*Forum*, 31). Daniel Singer, a lawyer and one of the nonscientific participants at Asilomar, said he "was uplifted by the way the community of scientists had organized for social responsibility."[58]

While disagreement exists about whether the molecular biologists exerted a disproportionate influence on the formulation of procedures for the regulation of their research, their very involvement indicates that they took their collective responsibility seriously. At the least, the time and effort spent by a significant number of leading investigators—in raising the question of public safety, in debating the technical issues, and in proposing detailed procedures for regulation—clearly contrast with the abdication of responsibility by Victor Frankenstein, as well as by Robert Oppenheimer and most of his coworkers.

The Frankensteinian element that has probably loomed largest in the public's perception of the controversy is the threat of the creation's developing a momentum, a "life" on its own. While this expression could easily be interpreted as a social and political metaphor in the case of atomic energy, the most immediate and dramatic concern raised by recombinant DNA research was that it might *literally* become true. Critics of the research argued that the insertion of genes from other species into the host bacterium *E. coli* might have unexpected and catastrophic consequences. Genes conferring resistance to a variety of antibiotics, the ability to synthesize new toxins, or the ability to induce carcinogenic development of human cells might be introduced, perhaps unknowingly, into laboratory strains of bacteria. If these strains were released from the research area through infection of laboratory workers or by accidental discharge, these bacteria might—in the worst case—be able to infect the general population, possibly causing epidemics of unimaginable severity because of the lack of any kind of natural resistance to the new causative agents. Similar scenarios could be imagined for other bacteria designed to consume oil spills or plants genetically engineered to fix nitrogen. The guidelines, of course, were constructed to address just such concerns; and most researchers in this area believe that the protocols for physical containment, the use of specially enfeebled strains of bacteria, and the prohibition of certain experiments constitute an extremely effective safety procedure.

The introduction of genetic sequences from one species into another, however, does result in unprecedentedly modified organisms. Only one or a very few genes can be inserted into recipient organisms by recombinant DNA techniques, so *E. coli* will remain *E. coli* and a wheat plant will not become a bean stalk. In the strict sense, no new forms of life are created by recombinant DNA research. Yet in another sense, the resultant modified organisms may display gene combinations that have not previously existed in nature, so that they are in some degree novel, and they are living, reproducing creatures.

The leading scientific critics of recombinant DNA research placed great emphasis upon this consideration. Erwin Chargaff pointed to

> the awesome irreversibility of what is being contemplated. You can stop splitting the atom; you can stop visiting the moon; you can stop using aerosols; you may even decide not to kill entire populations by the use of a few bombs. But you cannot recall a new form of life. Once you have constructed a viable *E. coli* cell carrying a plasmid DNA into which a piece of eukaryotic DNA has been spliced, it will survive you and your children and your children's children.[59]

Robert Sinsheimer underscores the same point in distinctly Frankensteinian language:

> We are becoming creators, makers of new forms of life, creations that we cannot undo, that will live on long after us, that will evolve according to their own destiny. What are the responsibilities of creators for our creations and for all the living world into which we bring our inventions? (*Forum*, 79)

Once again the parallel to Mary Shelley's fictional account of Promethean creation is striking. Pondering the potential results of continuing his work (and creating a mate for the monster), Victor Frankenstein is horrified by the thought of the monster's uncontrolled reproduction, fearing that "a race of devils would be propagated upon the earth who might make the very existence of the species of man a condition precarious and full of terror" (20;177). Mayor Vellucci was thus sensitive both to the fears of his constituency and to a prime element of the Frankenstein scenario when he chose to express his opposition to recombinant DNA in Cambridge in the evocative phrase, "something could crawl out of the laboratory, such as a Frankenstein [monster]."[60]

Apart from the literal sense in which recombinant DNA techniques may produce results with a life and momentum of their own, there is a sociological sense in which this Franken-steinian element is present as well. When a novel and powerful technology promises results faster and more easily than more conservative alternative approaches—and in the case of recom-binant DNA research, results that may be quite unattainable by other means—that technology often exerts a compelling influ-ence. A University of Michigan professor reflected this tend-ency when he testified at a public hearing:

> At the moment, the university has a favorable position with respect to research on recombinant DNA. It is perfectly clear that other universities will proceed with . . . research on this subject. Should Michigan choose not to, we will lose our position.[61]

Moreover, opposition to such imperatives may be costly:

> Suppose there are two contestants for a grant who wanted to perform a particular project. . . . It can be approached by DNA technology; it can be approached by more subtle, per-haps more difficult, more time-consuming methods of tradi-tional molecular biology. Which one of those approaches is going to get the grant? (*Forum*, 249)

And it may be not only costly, but personally hazardous as well. George Wald described such concerns among the less-estab-lished faculty at Harvard:

> There came a crucial time after many meetings of our Biology Department . . . when the junior faculty was really carrying the ball in opposition to the recombinant DNA . . . when finally it came to a meeting with the dean. And when the dean sat down at that meeting he looked around and said, "Where is the Biology Department?" And indeed, we had heard the last of any talk in this direction from our junior faculty. (*Forum*, 136)

Though much of the preceding discussion has focused on the highly dramatic potential hazards that might arise in the very near future as a consequence of experimentation with recombinant DNA, the implications of this research over the longer term are at least as significant a social concern; and they are tied just as directly to the basic Frankenstein scenario. Indeed, there are indications that some of the criticism that was leveled against recombinant DNA research on the issue of public health and safety may actually have gained much of its force from a less clearly articulated concern with the broader social aspects of the work.

An awesome potential for good or ill is represented by gene splicing and associated techniques for conscious manipulation of the genetic material. The theoretical knowledge gained from a comprehensive understanding of gene structure, organization, and regulation is fundamentally related not just to genetic disease, but also to cellular differentiation, embryonic development, and cancer. Theoretical understanding and practical control over such processes could well lead in the future to the ability to treat genetic disease at the cellular level, to the regeneration of limbs, to the *in vitro* culturing of whole organs for transplantation back into the donor without rejection, to the control of immunological response and autoimmune diseases, and to the ability to turn off the continuous proliferation of tumor cells. Thinking of the biomedical future in these utopian terms, an enthusiastic molecular biologist might well be forgiven for imagining, along with Victor Frankenstein, "What glory would attend the discovery, if I could banish disease from the human frame, and render man invulnerable to any but a violent death!" (21;31).

While these prospects might seem visionary, there are a host of potential benefits that leading researchers have suggested as being closer to practical accomplishment. David Baltimore, professor of microbiology at MIT and a Nobel laureate, notes:

There are still many people who do not believe that genetic engineering is feasible, so let me offer to you a possible scheme to indicate how close we could be to attempts at genetic engineering. There exist numerous inherited diseases that result in abnormal hemoglobin formation. . . . One could remove a sample of bone marrow . . . add to the cells the genes of normal globin synthesis, or even regulatory genes . . . attached to some appropriate vector that would help to insert the genes permanently into the cells. The bone marrow would now be easily taken back into the individual because there would be no immunological barrier. . . . I have little doubt that within five to ten years just such an experiment will be attempted. (*Forum*, 238)

Still nearer to achievement is the prospect of engineering *E. coli* to produce medically important substances by inserting the relevant gene sequences. Research has progressed with amazing rapidity in this area, much of it carried out in the laboratories of new companies founded or staffed by leading molecular biologists. It is highly probable that insulin, human growth hormones, and the antiviral agent interferon will be produced in quantity for clinical purposes by recombinant DNA techniques in the immediate future.[62]

Similarly, a number of human genetic deficiency diseases might be ameliorated by the provision of sizeable amounts of the missing proteins. Nor are potentially beneficent applications of recombinant DNA technology limited to the biomedical domain. Considerable thought has been given to its use in agriculture for more sophisticated plant breeding, for biological pest control, and for increasing the efficiency of photosynthesis, carbon dioxide fixation, and nitrogen fixation (*Forum*, 225–26).

For many of the critics of recombinant DNA research, however, the very prospects of potential benefit become the sources of concern about potential ills. When one is dealing with transcendent powers, one scientist's dream may be another's nightmare. Thus, hopes of *E. coli* producing insulin generated fears of such bacteria carrying on their newly programmed function as unwelcome colonizers of the human gut. Similarly, images of wheat fields producing their own nitrogen through gene-engineered nitrogen fixation—and in the process lifting the burden of expensive oil-based fertilizers from the economies of underdeveloped nations—come up against visions of farmland choked by self-nitrifying weeds.

Earlier in this essay I argued that the avoidance of a significant element (like the monster's ability to speak) by one of the parties involved in a Frankensteinian dilemma was often as revealing as its presence. Virtually all the scientists supporting recombinant DNA research have conscientiously refrained from expositions of the possible benefits derived from modifying the human gene pool or genetically engineering human behavior. Some DNA researchers see the use of genetic engineering as a plausible future therapy in treating diseases caused by defects in single genes. Such genetic manipulation would affect the individual, but not the gene pool of the species. Most researchers, however, dismiss any near-term prospect for the kind of genetic engineering that could specifically direct the development of human mental abilities—or of any other complex characteristic that depends on very large numbers of genes—and that could transfer any such changes to future generations.

This latter kind of genetic engineering is, of course, the most energizing symbol of Promethean creation in the public consciousness. Although the sorts of genetically remade men and women that have graced the pages of the science fiction pulps seem far beyond the capacity (and, to be fair, the interest) of present-day molecular biologists, the very discovery of the powerful, and previously unsuspected, techniques for recombining DNA contributes to a certain disquiet. The unprecedented series of breakthroughs so far achieved by the ingenuity of molecular biologists must make us pause before disclaiming the possibility of even more spectacular accomplishments. Part of the intrinsic fascination of DNA is that its structure and the way its information is coded are so similar in all living organisms. There is a very large difference between being able to engineer genetically an *E. coli* cell and a human zygote, but those two manipulations have more in common with each other than either has with the erstwhile breeding of prize Guernseys. Although there are at present no scientific claimants for the task, and although the prospect is indeed a distant one, it is hard to dismiss summarily a possible future in which some revenant Frankenstein imagines that "a new species would bless me as it creator and source," and that "many happy and excellent natures would owe their being to me" (4;47).

For many of the most articulate critics of recombinant DNA research, however, the malign potential of these techniques comes to a focus in just this prospect—that they will be used for deliberate engineering of the human gene pool. To Jeremy Rifkin of the People's Business Commission,

> the real issue here is the most important one that mankind has ever had to grapple with. . . . With the discovery of recombinant DNA scientists have unlocked the mystery of life itself. It is now only a matter of time . . . until the

biologists will be able, literally through recombinant DNA research, to create new plants, new strains of animals, and even genetically alter the human being on the earth. (*Forum*, 19)

Erwin Chargaff warns that the "genetic inheritance of mankind is its greatest and most indispensable treasure, which must be protected under all circumstances from defilement" (*Forum*, 48). Ethan Signer, professor of biology at MIT, cautions that

recombinant DNA research is going to bring us one more step closer to genetic engineering of people. That's when they figure out how to have us produce children with ideal characteristics. Last time the ideal children had blond hair, blue eyes, and Aryan genes. . . . We're going to tinker with the human gene pool. (*Forum*, 235)

As Signer's remarks suggest, a major element motivating opposition to recombinant DNA research is the belief that it will be put to fundamentally inhumane and antisocial uses. Jonathan Beckwith of the Harvard Medical School fears that "we may move from the present technological fix to the genetic fix, once recombinant DNA techniques have provided the tools" (*Forum*, 244). He anticipates misguided attempts to control aggression and social protest by the introduction of genes that would break down testosterone, as well as the genetic engineering of workers so that they could be employed in factories with high vinyl chloride levels (*Forum*, 244–45).

The response to such charges is itself instructive. Stanley Cohen, professor of medicine at Stanford University and one of the leading recombinant DNA researchers, believes that "knowledge itself is not immoral, but what society chooses to do with that knowledge may sometimes be immoral" (*Forum*, 249). Replying to the particular issues raised by Beckwith, Cohen provides a counterargument:

Clearly society currently has the knowledge to eliminate testosterone production in aggressive individuals without resorting to recombinant DNA techniques, but castration of such individuals is not a socially acceptable practice. Similarly, methods to accomplish the eugenic goals that Dr. Beckwith finds abhorrent and that I find equally abhorrent also exist at present, but society has not applied these methods because society finds them similarly abhorrent. . . . [T]he real issue . . . is what is done with knowledge by society, not the knowledge itself. (*Forum*, 249)

Bernard Davis argues similarly in response to the invocations of deliberate and repressive engineering of the human gene pool:

Even if we could use genetic technology in this way, I would question whether the technological imperative would necessarily (or even likely) lead us to do so. For the simple but effective techniques of selective breeding and artificial insemination are already available and yet they are not being used to influence the human gene pool. (*Forum*, 135)

Although these exchanges between supporters and opponents of the research reflect widely differing perspectives on many issues, they indicate clear agreement on the two final elements of a Frankenstein scenario: that the transcendent power made available by recombinant DNA technology is a potential force for good or ill (though they disagree, of course, as to which of these polar directions the research is leading); and that it is the political, economic, and moral arrangements of society that determine whether the long-term results of such two-edged scientific creativity will be monstrous.

The collective behavior of the molecular biologists in the exercise of responsibility regarding their creative activity appears as an important exception to the Frankenstein scenario. Victor Frankenstein and Robert Oppenheimer developed an expanded concept of scientific responsibility as a result of painful experience in dealing with the forces they had brought into being. The community of scientists has also undergone a raising of consciousness with respect to their responsibilities—first among physicists after Hiroshima, and now among molecular biologists. The heightened awareness among the latter may be traced directly back to the experience of that earlier group of scientists. The biologists could not escape the knowledge of what it means, politically, socially, and morally, to manipulate transcendent power; nor could they ignore the example of the atomic physicists in finally exercising communal professional responsibility by laboring, in the years following 1945, for effective civilian regulation of their creation.[63]

If the physicists, in Oppenheimer's plangent phrase, "have known sin," their fall from innocence has at least been a persuasive object lesson. While prominent scientists have taken opposite sides on most issues raised by the recombinant DNA controversy, there seems to be a consensus on one significant point: both scientists and the public must be involved in, and share responsibility for, the regulation of scientific research when the consequences of that research affect the public's fundamental interests. Within that consensus there are, unsurprisingly, strong differences of opinion as to the nature and degree of hazard and the proper balance between competing concerns (such as freedom of scientific inquiry vs. public safety, effective regulation vs. creativity, and professional vs. democratic decision making in science policy). It would, however, be difficult at present to find very many scientists who deny the principle of shared involvement. The idea of a value-free science, unfettered by social concerns and unconnected to social consequences, has as much plausibility—even among scientists—as the divine right of kings.

A case may still be made that the degree of responsibility exercised by the biologists is not adequate. John Lear, for example, in *Recombinant DNA: The Untold Story* charges the scientists with something like Frankensteinian hubris for their very effective attempts to dissuade Congress from passing regulatory legislation significantly more restrictive than the National Institutes of Health guidelines. He thinks that congressional leaders such as Edward Kennedy "grossly miscalculated the lengths to which the scientists would go to maintain their freedom to experiment as they saw fit without regard to the wishes of the people."[64] Lear also criticizes proposals for relaxing some of the original restrictions in the NIH guidelines.[65]

If one grants that the scientists have reasonably fulfilled their collective obligations, there remains the question of individual responsibility. Reports of less than complete compliance with the NIH guidelines in some laboratories suggested that the temptations and pressures of DNA research were capable of leading at least a small ministry of experimenters into disturbing, if low-level, Frankensteinian practices.[66] Nevertheless, I believe that the recognition and exercise of responsibility by a majority of the leading molecular biologists represents a nota-ble departure from the example set by Victor Frankenstein.

The exercise of responsibility is the only element of recombi-nant DNA research that does not closely match the Franken-stein scenario I have outlined; all the other elements of that scenario are clearly in evidence. The myth of Frankenstein is, therefore, a highly appropriate symbol of the dilemmas posed by this research frontier. The power of this contemporary myth helps explain why work on recombinant DNA elicited wide-spread anxiety while other areas of potentially hazardous in-vestigation did not. In responding to this anxiety at the Academy Forum on Research and Recombinant DNA, Stanley Cohen argued that "what can be said of recombinant DNA research can be said of virtually all knowledge." Cohen noted, however, that "some participants of this Forum seem to have a special fear of genetic knowledge" (*Forum*, 249). The reason for that special fear, I suggest—and for much of the passion engen-dered—is that it is not true that what can be said of recombinant DNA research can be said of virtually all knowledge, or even of all scientific knowledge. Recombinant DNA research fulfills almost all the requirements of a Frankenstein scenario and is—for precisely this reason—special. We can identify other areas of science—like research with more traditional infectious dis-ease organisms—that contain one or two elements of this sce-nario; very few areas of science, though, embody the constellation of elements that characterizes a full-fledged Frankenstein scenario. Thus, most scientific activity is not Fran-kensteinian, as I have employed the term; but the production of nuclear energy and the potential production of genetically engi-neered organisms have enough of transcendent creation about them to trouble the public deeply.

The quality of that public response was nicely captured in an observation by Kurt Mislow of Princeton University. He re-ferred to

the broad sense of opposition that one feels on the part of many people here for all kinds of different reasons. The opposition is, in fact, necessarily emotional, necessarily irra-tional because it is not by the rules of the game that these

objections are made. We are not providing a data base, drawing conclusions, and providing inferences and so forth. We
are operating from a gut feeling. . . . To ignore the reality of
that gut feeling, I think, is to be, in the last analysis, unscientific. It is there. . . . It goes back to the fairy tales that we
heard when we were little kids. It is something very fundamental and I think we are making a tremendous mistake if
we ignore it. (*Forum*, 278)

People were searching for a symbolic framework to make
sense of events that had overtaken them. The fairy tales of
childhood play a large role in shaping our interactions with the
world; and in western culture, at least, Frankenstein and his
monster are as visible as Snow White and her dwarfs. The
extraordinary developments spun out by twentieth-century science have caused us to seize upon what might otherwise have
remained a minor fantastic tale, transforming it into a myth of
wide currency and powerful effect.

Functioning myths help sustain human life and institutions
in the face of a world that people do not control and that
threatens to overwhelm them. These myths present—generally
in powerfully dramatic form—the facts of life to which humanity must adjust. These facts may be not only harsh, but also
paradoxical and contradictory, and cannot help but be the
source of profound psychic tensions. The notably imagistic
character of a society's myths—as of an individual's dreams—
may be the mode in which the human mind can most easily
deal with such paradox and contradiction. These primary process images and relationships, as opposed to the more single-
valued conceptualizations of the rational consciousness, are
amenable to multiple levels of interpretation. By virtue of this
characteristic they may enable human beings to take in and
assimilate the contradictory aspects of human existence, yet at
the same time not incapacitate human action by too direct a
confrontation with paradox. This is the sense in which I claim
the Frankenstein theme is—appropriately—the twentieth century's living myth. It is a response to the same kind of stimulus
that engendered the myths of earlier societies, and its sustain-
ing function is the same as well.

While many of the myths that embody fundamental conflicts
in human relationships still profoundly affect us, other myths
dealing with our interaction with the natural world have not

fared as well. Much of the *mysterium tremendum* of the universe, before which humanity was both ignorant and powerless, has become the province of grade-school teachers. The results of twentieth-century science are, in some instances, more worthy of wonder than the traditional sources of awe in earlier myths.

That, of course, is precisely the problem. The science that demystified the old terrors, that explained the awesome forces of nature and brought them under increasing human control, has resulted in the creation of new facts of life that, in our frame of reference, are just as harsh, overwhelming, and paradoxical as those that transfixed our predecessors. It is not comfortable to live in a world in which the power of the atom is as much a force to be propitiated as the spirits of sun, wind, and rain ever were,[67] and where the possible appearance of an inadvertently engineered biological scourge carries some of the flavor that must have infused populations speculating upon the next outbreak of plague. In this world four or five nations have stockpiles of thermonuclear weapons, and several more have, or could quickly have, atomic bombs. Given a particular sequence of social and political events, it is conceivable that several hundred million human beings could be destroyed in the space of two hours, with several hundred million more following over the course of a few days or weeks with no further action. In this world a balance of terror keeps the peace—as nasty a paradox as ever troubled earlier people. To this *angst* there has now been added the more conjectural, but no less terrifying, danger of uncontrollable outbreaks of disease threatening the lives of millions—a new Black Death, perhaps, set loose on the planet by the advanced science that has brought the smallpox virus to the edge of extinction. These are the kind of transcendent powers that many earlier societies did not even imagine their gods and demons to possess.

In the face of this paradox of scientific progress, the transformation into myth of a nineteenth-century romantic narrative becomes comprehensible. The problems of understanding and responding to the world of atomic energy and genetic manipulation are, however, multivalent; they include irreducible social, political, metaphysical, ethical, and psychological dimensions. Any particular analysis of an issue of such complexity can be little other than a single slice through a knot of Einsteinian space-time, reducing a multidimensional reality to a three-dimensional projection that, it is hoped, can be more

easily grasped by our conceptual faculties. The mythic interpretation presented here is only one such three-dimensional perspective. The complexity of the interaction between science and
society in the twentieth century invites, indeed demands, a
variety of explorations along different axes. Thus the social
transformation of knowledge, the public character both of that
knowledge and of its application, the industrialization of scientific practice, the internal and external influences upon the
production and diffusion of scientific knowledge, and the responsibility for the social, economic, political, and psychological results of technological progress constitute only a partial list
of necessary areas of study. No single approach will prove
satisfactory; only when a significant number of these complementary perspectives are provided will the complex reality of
the original problem be engaged.

What is common to many of these analytic perspectives,
though, is their focus upon rational or mechanistic modes of
social interaction. It is not at all clear that the dilemmas discussed in this essay—engendered by science, that most rational
of human activities—can be truly understood and dealt with on
the basis of purely rational analysis, even from a variety of
perspectives.[68] Emotional and nonrational reactions may be—in
addition to reason—fully appropriate responses to the intrusion of transcendent power into our daily existence.

Understood in this context, the Frankenstein myth provides,
or can be interpreted to provide, twentieth-century society
with two incontestable benefits: it offers, as do most living
myths, warning and catharsis. In terms of its cautionary function, the myth can serve in much the same way as contingency
planners are helped by presentation of worst-case scenarios. By
pursuing, in image and imagination, the most deeply troubling
elements of our present situation to the bottom of the night, we
may find a greater urgency and inspiration for enlightening the
days. The complementary function of the myth—complementary in as twentieth-century a sense as particle and wave—also
helps us endure in the face of a newly harsh and potentially
tragic reality by offering psychic release. The myth of Frankenstein provides a classic catharsis for its audience. We see in the
horrifying account of transcendent creation the analogy or imitation of our present and profoundly troubling situation. We
identify with the sufferer and feel pity; we apprehend the
causes and feel terror. For a while, at least, we are thus purged

of feelings of pity and terror through an appreciation of the protagonist's (Frankenstein's or Oppenheimer's) increased perception and sensitivity, gained through his tragic experience. We, as well, may learn from that tragic experience in a personal, emotional, nonrational way that complements the more abstract lessons we derive from our imagistic contingency planning.

Having, perhaps, learned from Frankenstein—as he so forcefully admonished us at the very beginning of this essay—we should surely grant him the final injunction:

Farewell, Walton! Seek happiness in tranquility and avoid ambition, even if it be only the apparently innocent one of distinguishing yourself in science and discoveries. Yet why do I say this? I have myself been blasted in these hopes, yet another may succeed (p. 236).[69]

## NOTES

1. As quoted in *Time*, 18 April 1977, 45.

2. As quoted in *Science* 193 (1976):300.

3. As quoted in Michael Rogers, *Biohazard* (New York: Knopf, 1977), 196.

4. James D. Watson, "In Defense of DNA," *New Republic*, 25 June 1977, 14.

5. Rogers, *Biohazard*, 191–205.

6. Willard Gaylin, "The Frankenstein Factor," *New England Journal of Medicine* 297 (1977):665–67.

7. See, for example, Eileen Bigland, *Mary Shelley* (London: Cassell, 1959), 84–88; Richard Church, *Mary Shelley* (New York: Viking, 1928), 83–106; Ellen Moers, *Literary Women* (Garden City, N.Y.: Doubleday, 1976), 90–99; Marc A. Rubenstein, "'My Accursed Origin': The Search for the Mother in *Frankenstein*," *Studies in Romanticism* 15 (1976):165–94; Christopher Small, *Ariel Like a Harpy: Shelley, Mary and Frankenstein* (London: Gollancz, 1972); William Walling, *Mary Shelley* (New York: Twayne, 1972), 23–50.

8. Mary Shelley, "Introduction," *Frankenstein*, ed. M. K. Joseph (London: Oxford University Press, 1969), 9.

9. Mary Shelley, *Frankenstein* (New York: Everyman-Dutton, 1963), chap. 4, p. 45. Subsequent references to *Frankenstein* included in this text will be to this edition, which reproduces Shelley's original 1818 version. Citations will be identified in parentheses by chapter, with page numbers from the Dutton edition.

10. Douglas Bush, *Science and English Poetry* (New York: Oxford University Press, 1950), 100.

11. *Don Juan*, canto 10, st. 2.

12. Bush, *Science and English Poetry*, 103–4.

13. I am not attempting here a deliberate inversion of the naturalist interpretation of literature as mirroring objective or scientific reality; I am not implying that Oppenheimer's life was shaped by the requirements of a narrative tradition. Nor am I quite making Ezra Pound's claim that the function of literature is that it incites humanity

to continue living. I am, rather, suggesting that both the real world and the fictional narratives exemplify in striking fashion a mythic structure that reflects a fundamental problem of human existence: the paradoxical nature of the relationship between knowledge and power, between creation and responsibility. Later in this essay, I pursue a more detailed investigation of how the narratives of Frankenstein and Oppenheimer are apprehensions of the same underlying structural relationship—one that connects scientist, society, and the natural universe. To rephrase Pound, it is the function of *myths* (such as Frankenstein) to incite humanity to continue living.

14. I. I. Rabi et al., *Oppenheimer* (New York: Charles Scribner's Sons, 1969), 7.

15. Robert Jungk, *Brighter than a Thousand Suns* (New York: Harcourt Brace, 1958), 21.

16. J. Robert Oppenheimer to Frank Oppenheimer, 7 October 1933, in *Robert Oppenheimer: Letters and Recollections,* ed. Alice Kimball Smith and Charles Weiner (Cambridge: Harvard University Press, 1980), 165.

17. See, for example, Oppenheimer to William A. Fowler, 28 January 1939, in *Robert Oppenheimer: Letters,* 207; Oppenheimer to I. I. Rabi, 26 February 1943, in ibid., 250.

18. Nuel Pharr Davis, *Lawrence and Oppenheimer* (New York: Simon and Schuster, 1968), 161.

19. Jungk, *Brighter than a Thousand Suns,* 132.

20. Davis, *Lawrence and Oppenheimer,* 233.

21. General Thomas F. Farrell, as quoted in General Leslie R. Groves, "Report on Alamogordo Atomic Bomb Test," 18 July 1945, reprinted as Appendix P in Martin J. Sherwin, *A World Destroyed* (New York: Knopf, 1975), 308–14.

22. Jungk, *Brighter than a Thousand Suns,* 211.

23. Ibid., 201.

24. Davis, *Lawrence and Oppenheimer,* 240.

25. Alice Kimball Smith, *A Peril and a Hope: The Scientists' Movement in America* (Chicago: University of Chicago Press, 1965), 55.

26. Ibid., 56.

27. Davis, *Lawrence and Oppenheimer,* 246.

28. Small, *Ariel Like a Harpy,* 245–54.

29. Davis, *Lawrence and Oppenheimer,* 307–8.

30. Ibid., 318.

31. Ibid., 322.

32. Ibid., 343.

33. Ibid.

34. In this discussion I imply that Oppenheimer's opposition to the crash development of the Super was the reason for his subsequent demise as a politically important figure. This account necessarily omits an extended treatment of many other significant factors such as very influential opponents who became personal enemies, Oppenheimer's recommendations against several pet Air Force projects, and his support of a balanced-force concept of air defense rather than a near-total reliance on an atomic bomb-carrying Strategic Air Command. Also much of Oppenheimer's opposition to the Super was based on his assessment that it would be a waste of money until certain crucial theoretical problems were solved first. When this conceptual breakthrough later occurred, he supported the pursuit of this new research direction, perhaps fearing that some other nation might also have the idea and develop it first. Nevertheless, the hesitation and caution that Oppenheimer urged with regard to the Super was a major element in his political humiliation. The personnel security board

that judged him "found that, following the President's decision, Dr. Oppenheimer did not show the *enthusiastic* support [italics added] for the Super program which might have been expected of the chief adviser to the Government under the circumstances; that, had he given his *enthusiastic* support to the program, a concerted effort would have been initiated at an earlier date, and that, whatever the motivation, the security interests of the United States were affected" (Davis, *Lawrence and Oppenheimer*, 305).

For a comprehensive treatment of Oppenheimer's career as an influential political adviser during the Cold War period, see Philip M. Stern, *The Oppenheimer Case: Security on Trial* (New York: Harper & Row, 1969), 111–213. I have more generally relied upon Davis's *Lawrence and Oppenheimer* as a source of quotations because of its stylistic consonance with the tone of this essay, but Davis's treatment is consistent with Stern's more detailed account.

35. Gaylin, "The Frankenstein Factor," 666.

36. Harold Bloom, "Frankenstein, or the New Prometheus," *Partisan Review* 32 (1965): 614.

37. Davis, *Lawrence and Oppenheimer*, 244.

38. Joseph Campbell, *Myths to Live By* (New York: Viking, 1972), 214–15.

39. I am indebted to Jeffrey Johnson, Department of Sociology, San Francisco State University, for valuable discussions on this theme.

40. Erwin Schrödinger, *What is Life?* (Garden City, N.Y.: Anchor-Doubleday, 1956), 2.

41. Ibid.

42. Gunther Stent, *The Coming of the Golden Age* (Garden City, N.Y.: Natural History Press, 1969), 21.

43. Schrödinger, *What Is Life?* 33.

44. James D. Watson, *The Double Helix* (New York: Mentor–New American Library, 1969), 27. Subsequent page references to this edition will be included in the text.

45. Graham Chedd, "The Making of a Gene," *New Scientist*, 30 September 1976, 682.

46. As quoted in *Time*, 19 April 1971, 33.

47. Robert Sinsheimer, "Troubled Dawn for Genetic Engineering," *New Scientist*, 16 October 1975, 150.

48. Erwin Chargaff, *Science* 192 (1976): 938–40.

49. Ibid.

50. Ibid.

51. *New Scientist*, 17 October 1974, 166.

52. June Goodfield, *Playing God* (New York: Random House, 1977).

53. Ted Howard and Jeremy Rifkin, *Who Should Play God?* (New York: Delacorte Press, 1977).

54. *Research with Recombinant DNA: An Academy Forum* (Washington, D.C.: National Academy of Sciences, 1977), 24. Hereafter cited as *Forum* with subsequent references included in the text.

55. Maxine Singer and Dieter Soll, *Science* 181 (1973): 1114.

56. Paul Berg et al., *Science* 185 (1974): 303.

57. U.S. National Institutes of Health, *Guidelines for Research Involving Recombinant DNA Molecules* (Washington, D.C.: GPO, 1976).

58. Rogers, *Biohazard*, 100.

59. Chargaff, in *Science*, 938–40.

60. As quoted in *Time*, 18 April 1977, 45.

61. As quoted in *Atlantic*, February 1977, 59.

62. See, for example, Matt Clark et al., "The Miracles of Spliced Genes," *Newsweek*, 17 March 1980, 62–71; Jeffrey L. Fox, "Genetic engineering industry emerges," *Chemical & Engineering News*, 17 March 1980, 15–23; Walter Gilbert and Lydia Villa-Komaroff, "Useful Proteins from Recombinant Bacteria," *Scientific American*, April 1980, 74–94.

63. See, for example, Smith, *A Peril and a Hope.*

64. John Lear, *Recombinant DNA: The Untold Story* (New York: Crown, 1978), 167.

65. Ibid., 207–8.

66. See Janet L. Hopson, "Recombinant Lab for DNA and My 95 Days in It," *Smithsonian*, June 1977, 55–62; and *Science* 200 (1978): 516–17.

67. Throughout this analysis, whenever I have discussed the release of atomic energy, I have used nuclear weaponry to provide examples of transcendent power applied to potentially destructive ends. For many years, most of the American public would have agreed that a potentially beneficial use of atomic energy was the generation of electricity by nuclear reactors. As the real-world events at Three Mile Island and the cinematic events of *The China Syndrome* graphically suggest, even the putative benefits of this technology possess a disquieting potential for getting out of control. There is now serious public questioning of whether this particular scientific creation *can*, in fact, be domesticated under any circumstances.

68. For an articulate presentation of the case for an exclusively rational analysis, see Carl Cohen, "On the Dangers of Inquiry and the Burden of Proof," in *The Recombinant DNA Debate*, ed. David A. Jackson and Stephen P. Stich (Englewood Cliffs, N.J.: Prentice-Hall, 1979), 303–34.

69. This essay was developed thanks to a post-doctoral fellowship at the Institute of Society, Ethics, and the Life Sciences in Hastings-on-Hudson, N.Y.

# History and Geology as Ways of Studying the Past

## STEPHEN BRUSH

*University of Maryland*

The recent demise of the American Association for the Advancement of the Humanities, formed in self-conscious imitation of scientific organizations founded in the nineteenth century, calls attention once again to the difficulty many scholars experience in defining their place in the modern world. The humanities have replaced the moral sciences, not wanting to be too closely identified with religion on the one hand, nor to be considered a "soft" form of science on the other. Just when the role of the humanist seemed to be winning respect from the scientists, the recrudescence of religious fundamentalism confused the public by vilifying "secular humanism." It is hard enough explaining and defending what it means to be a humanist without having to decide whether one is secular or nonsecular.

There is still much confusion and disagreement about the differences between the sciences and humanities as ways of knowing the world and about their similarities as creative activities. My original reason for tackling this subject is the fact that professionally I was once a scientist and am now a humanist. As an historian of science I still keep a foot in each world, with one office in a physical science institute, another in a history department, and a perpetual wrangle with the university bureaucracy about where I should park my car. I can report some striking differences in the behavior of physicists and historians; these turn out to be clues to more fundamental methodological differences. (For the purposes of this essay I accept the claim of my colleagues that historians are humanists, not social scientists.) For example:

—Historians rarely "talk shop" at lunch or other social occasions; physicists will take advantage of the slightest opportunity to give an enthusiastic discourse on their latest experiment or calculation.

—The physics department has a daily tea/coffee hour at which such opportunities are maximized; the historians all seem to be working by themselves in the library or study at this time.

—When a historian talks about his research at a department seminar or professional meeting, he usually reads a paper; a physicist shows slides or transparencies and talks informally about them.

—Physicists frequently collaborate in writing papers and monographs; historians rarely do. (This was made quite clear to me once when I submitted a paper jointly written with another physicist to a historical journal; the editor simply could not understand how it was possible for two people to write a paper together.)

—Physicists generally send out "preprints" of papers submitted for publication; historians almost never do. (When I continued this practice after making the transition from physicist to historian, a historian asked me if I was not worried that someone would steal my ideas before I got them into print.)

—Physicists try (not always successfully) to give credit in their papers to other physicists who have contributed to solving a problem or opened up a new line of research; historians often insist that they will rely only on primary sources, dismissing what other historians have written as unworthy even of refutation.

As a first step toward comparing the sciences and the humanities, let us eliminate as many as possible of the nonessential differences. There is a tendency to take physics as the model for all science, yet many of the differences between physics and other sciences (primacy of general laws, mathematical deduction, laboratory experimentation, and so on) are similar to the alleged differences between the sciences and the humanities. Thus, rather than compare history with physics, one should compare history with geology, so at least we can say that both disciplines have a similar purpose—to reconstruct and interpret the past.[1] (I recognize that not all of geology has this purpose, but will limit myself to that part which does.) Let us compare historians and geologists who worked at about the same time and occupied roughly comparable positions of importance in their disciplines.

To begin, consider the German historian Leopold von Ranke (1795–1875) and the British geologist Charles Lyell (1797–1875). Ranke is generally called the founder of the modern school of critical historiography,[2] while Lyell is sometimes called the founder of modern geology.[3]

Both Ranke and Lyell are famous not so much for any single discovery about the past but rather for the establishment of a reliable *method* of making such discoveries; Ranke convinced historians to give priority to original sources, while Lyell persuaded geologists to favor explanations based on causes that can now be seen in operation. The earlier alternative in both cases was a literary-romantic tradition that relied on tremendous upheavals and invisible tendencies, possibly of supernatural origin.

Both have been criticized for their failure to discuss factors that are now considered essential: Ranke gave no serious attention to social, economic, and cultural history; Lyell excluded the origin of the earth from the domain of geology and denied that the earth's temperature and other physical conditions had been significantly different in the past.

A modern historian would immediately point out that Ranke represents a particular style of historical research and writing, and that other styles have at least equal claim to be regarded as "humanistic." A modern geologist would likewise object that Lyell's theoretical approach is not the only way to be scientific. And a skeptic could claim that any direct comparison of an historian and a geologist is meaningless since there is no single criterion by which both can be measured.

These objections can all be met by postulating that both humanists and scientists have a similar set of different styles or theoretical approaches. We need to find another historian (H) and another geologist (G) whose styles differ in the same way from those of Ranke and Lyell. Thus even if the relation "Ranke-Lyell" is neither true nor false but rather meaningless because historians and geologists are incommensurable, it may still be useful to consider the relation "H is to Ranke as G is to Lyell."[4]

In trying to identify Ranke's style one immediately encounters the frequent claim that it is "scientific." To admit this description as accurate would be to beg the question as to whether history differs from science. Moreover, it would smuggle into the discussion a pernicious misconception of what it means to be scientific. Consider instead whether terms such as *objective, empirical,* and *mechanistic* are appropriate.

Ranke's fame rests on his spectacular success in discovering and critically evaluating historical records, putting this information into a large number of comprehensive works, and inventing a method to train students to carry on this work. In the first instance the emphasis is on primary sources as the best evidence for the facts of history. If Ranke had done nothing more than collect such facts, it would be correct to call his style empirical, and I suspect this is what some commentators mean when they call him scientific. But it is now generally recognized that scientists themselves do much more than collect facts; they develop theories that may be supported by facts and may predict new facts, but are not completely governed by them.[5]

When Ranke went to Vienna and Venice in 1827–28, he found a rich collection of reports written by ambassadors to other European countries in the sixteenth and seventeenth centuries, and subsequently he found similar reports in other archives in Italy, Spain, and Holland. As a result he was able to write *A History of England, Principally in the Seventeenth Century,* based on sources that had never been fully exploited by English historians themselves.[6] This accomplishment may be seen as the discovery of new empirical facts, and Ranke's lust for such information seems to be in no way different from that of a scientist doing an experiment, collecting specimens, or finding the solution to an equation.[7] But there is also the judgment that some sources are more trustworthy than others—in particular that the Venetian ambassadors, representing a country geographically distant from England, would be more disinterested spectators than the French.[8] In any case it is desirable to have several independent eyewitness accounts of an event. Similarly, Ranke suggests that as a foreigner he can be more impartial in writing the history of a country than a native historian, or at least can bring a different perspective[9]—just as he claimed that, as a German Protestant, he could write a more balanced *History of the Popes* than Catholics had done.[10] In each case Ranke promises to go beyond empiricism to achieve *objectivity.*

Suppose, for the sake of argument, that the past has a real existence independent of ourselves.[11] Then objectivity means the closest possible approach to "how it actually happened"— the usual translation of Ranke's phrase *wie es eigentlich gewesen*. As Krieger notes,[12] Ranke intended to include knowledge of historical processes, not merely discrete facts; and as Iggers and Moltke point out, *eigentlich* does not mean "actually" in a restrictive sense but "essentially."[13] In addition Ranke definitely includes the explanation of causes in his conception of the historian's task. These causes are to be located in the nature of human beings: one can understand why this man acted in that way under those circumstances because we have other information from which we can infer his character and mental state.

In science this mode of explanation by causes acting in individual cases would be called mechanistic. This is not the same thing as deterministic, since it does not claim that there is only one possible outcome given those causes, although the lack of determinism may be attributed only to a lack of complete knowledge rather than to inherent randomness.

In history it would seem appropriate to call Ranke's causal explanations humanistic, at least insofar as they do not involve Divine Providence.[14] Thus he rejects Hegel's view that history is the unfolding of the World-Spirit's consciousness, since this denies any significance to individual human consciousness.[15] Things happen, Ranke argues, because of human actions, not because God or a World-Spirit wills them to happen. In this sense the phrase *secular humanism* is an accurate description of the attitude of most historians since Ranke.

At this point one can make a direct comparison with our geologist. Lyell argued that phenomena must be explained by causes we can now see in operation, not by postulating past catastrophes greater than any we have experienced in recorded history. For example, a detailed study of earthquake records shows that they produce rather frequent elevations and lowerings of the land in some areas. On the reasonable assumption that such seismic activity has been equally widespread in the past he infers that it could have changed the configuration of land and water, and that this in turn would have affected climates.[16]

Although modern geologists do not necessarily accept Lyell's extreme uniformitarian postulate that the magnitude of causes has never been much greater in the past, they agree with him in rejecting as unscientific the arbitrary invocation of major catastrophes completely unlike those in recorded history. In particular, the rapid deposition of all the geological strata following a global flood, a tenet of religio-scientific belief before Lyell, has been completely rejected. On the other hand, Lyell himself was willing to accept the Ice Age theory when he could see scientific evidence for it, and scientists in the 1980s are willing to consider the possibility that the extinction of dinosaurs was the result of the impact of an asteroid. Catastrophes may be invoked in science, provided that there is a convincing body of evidence that cannot be explained otherwise and that the same catastrophe explains more than one type of observation.

While no one would now deny that Lyell's method is scientific, some philosophers have promulgated doctrines that would exclude the entire enterprise of historical geology from the house of science. This is not because of any explicit hostility to the study of the earth, but results rather from the unthinking presumption that all sciences must be like physics. In particular Karl Popper once argued that a scientific hypothesis must entail predictions that can be tested by new observations, and that Darwinian evolutionary theory failed to satisfy this criterion because it only explained facts already known about past events.[17] Interpreted in such a strict sense, Popper's "falsifiability" criterion would eliminate *any* theory about the past or about large-scale phenomena (such as those in astronomy) that cannot be brought into the laboratory for controlled experiments. A similar line of reasoning underlies Popper's well-known denunciation of historicism.[18]

Although Popper recanted his statement that evolution is not a scientific theory, modern creationists have used it to claim equal time in the public school science classroom for their alternative theory of origins.[19] Ironically, their own creationist model includes the same arbitrary catastrophic postulates that had already failed to pass the much less stringent criteria introduced by Lyell. Ranke, on the other hand, is a scholar whose religious convictions impel him to seek the truth about history rather than distort it to fit a preconceived doctrine.[20]

Both Ranke and Lyell, in order to justify their explanations by means of causes acting on individuals, must deny any significant role to long-term trends. Ranke says it is not true that "the life of mankind reaches a higher potential in each epoch" in the sense that each generation surpasses the previous one—"this would be an injustice on the part of the deity."[21] All generations are different but equal in the eyes of God. It is not necessarily true that each generation is more moral than the previous one.[22] Lyell rejects the progressionist doctrine of his contemporaries, based on the assumption that the earth is gradually cooling off since its creation as a hot gaseous cloud. Since earthquakes are powered by internal heat, they would have been more frequent and violent if the earth had been hotter in the past; but then Lyell could no longer use the uniformitarian principle that geological phenomena are to be explained by causes of the same magnitude as we now observe them to be.[23]

A century earlier, Giambattista Vico had argued that knowledge of society and its history is more reliable than knowledge of nature because any creation is best understood by its creator.[24] People have made society, but God has made nature. Thus the humanist has an advantage over the scientist. Vico did not anticipate that the scientists' understanding of physics and chemistry would improve more rapidly than the humanists' understanding of psychology and sociology. Yet, before 1900 the historians were probably ahead of the geologists in understanding their respective subject matter, although it would be difficult to prove this statement.

This impression is supported by the respect Lyell pays to history at the beginning of his *Principles of Geology.* By the study of geology

> we acquire a more perfect knowledge of [the earth's] *present* condition, and more comprehensive views concerning the laws *now* governing its animate and inanimate productions. When we study history, we obtain a more profound insight into human nature, by instituting a comparison between the present and former states of society. We trace the long series of events which have gradually led to the actual posture of affairs; and by connecting effects with their causes, we are enabled to classify and retain in the memory a multitude of complicated relations—the various peculiarities of national character—the different degrees of moral and intellectual refinement, and numerous other circumstances, which, without historical associations would be uninteresting or imperfectly understood. As the present condition of nations is the result of many antecedent changes . . . so the natural world is the result of a long succession of events.[25]

Citing Niebuhr's *History of Rome*, Lyell writes:

> as we explore this magnificent field of inquiry, the sentiment
> of a great historian of our times may continually be present to
> our minds, that "he who calls what has vanished back again
> into being, enjoys a bliss like that of creating."[26]

Before Lyell, geology and history were part of the same
subject, since in the *Genesis* account the earth scarcely existed
before man, and the evidence for alleged events such as the
Flood was similar in character to that for human experiences.[27]
The geologist Abraham Werner, following the philosophy of
Christian Wolff, integrated human and geological history.[28]
The influence of historical writing on geological terminology
persisted into the nineteenth century in the use of words like
*monument, revolution,* and *accidents.*[29] Even at the end of the
nineteenth century, although Archibald Geikie regarded
Werner's mingling of the two disciplines as no more than a
rhetorical device to attract students to a fallacious doctrine,[30]
the respected geologist Eduard Suess combined evidence from
geology and history when he discussed the role of floods in
shaping the earth's surface.[31]

Ranke in turn uses a geological metaphor in explaining why
he had chosen to write about seventeenth-century England:

> When we contemplate the framework of the earth, those
> heights which testify to the inherent energy of the original
> and active elements attract our special notice; we admire the
> massive mountains which overhang and dominate the
> lowlands covered with the settlements of man. So also in the
> domain of history we are attracted by epochs at which the
> elemental forces, whose joint action or tempered antagonism
> has produced states and kingdoms, rise in sudden war
> against each other, and amidst the surging sea of troubles
> upheave into the light new formations, which give to subse-
> quent ages their special character.[32]

Both of the above quotations suggest that singular events
have long-term consequences but leave somewhat vague the
causes of the events themselves. Ironically, mountain-building
was the weakest part of Lyell's theory[33] so Ranke could not

have gained much by studying Lyell. Ranke does not, in fact, make frequent use of such metaphors from science, and one reviewer commented that "he keeps the golden mean between Carlyle and Buckle; treating history neither as a sort of Homeric battle, nor as an advanced geological era."[34] But he was, according to Thompson and Holm, "the first historical scholar who took cognizance of the history of science" and urged its serious study.[35]

George Macaulay Trevelyan (1876–1962) seems to be a good candidate for "H," the historian whose style is radically different from Ranke's.[36] Trevelyan was a defender of the literary tradition and an opponent of the scientific movement that dominated historical writing at the end of the nineteenth century. He chided the Rankean scholars for their "materialistic" lust for "crude documents"[37] and reminded them that the alleged "science of cause and effect in human affairs . . . does not exist and cannot ever exist in any degree of accuracy remotely deserving to be described by the word 'science.' " Whereas physical science can claim direct utility and/or discovery of causal laws, history can do neither. The only role of science in historical studies is to collect and weigh evidence as to facts, but not to guess at cause and effect.[38]

Trevelyan rejected the role of academic scholar and became a writer; he chose to educate and inspire the public through works that would be accepted as literature. That did not imply any less regard for accuracy; he asserted that, in any historical writing, "he will give the best interpretation who, having discovered and weighed all the important evidence available, has the largest grasp of intellect, the warmest human sympathy, the higher imaginative powers." History should help us to understand ourselves and to appreciate literature, tasks that he thought the scientific historians had neglected.[39]

Although to the historian and his reader "the deeds themselves are far more interesting than their causes and effects,"[40] concern for the individual events does not imply that they have no broader significance. The literary-romantic style balances concrete detail against grand visions of unity and progress. Trevelyan saw history as a process leading to and throwing light on the present; the historian need not refrain from any moral judgment but may properly point out where the tendency toward religious toleration and democracy has been accelerated or obstructed.[41]

The acceptance of a long-term trend in earth history, as well as an insistence on the educational and literary aspects of geology, characterized Archibald Geikie (1835–1924), the "G" whom I contrast with Lyell. Geikie accepted the progressive or directionist assumption of most nineteenth-century geologists, that the gradual cooling and contraction of the earth governed the nature of changes on its surface. Whereas Lyell aimed his writings at other geologists and delayed the preparation of a short textbook called *Elements of Geology* when he realized that it might interfere with sales of his multivolume treatise,[42] Geikie devoted much of his time to education and popularization. A recent article by David Oldroyd characterizes him as a romantic Whig historian (of geology), in terms almost identical to those frequently applied to Trevelyan.[43] While Geikie enthusiastically violated Lyell's dictum that cosmogony is not part of geology and saw earth history as inseparably connected with the grand story of cosmic evolution,[44] he also glorified the human importance of individual geological formations in his lectures on the influence of scenery on literature.[45]

In order to carry out a more detailed comparison, I have selected one historical topic on which both Ranke and Trevelyan published major works—the English revolution of the seventeenth century—and one geological topic discussed in some detail by both Lyell and Geikie—the source of volcanic energy.

One might suppose that the first problem for the historian of a civil war or revolution is to identify the two sides in the conflict. It is not enough to say that the English Civil War was a battle between the Roundheads or Puritans, who controlled Parliament, and the Cavaliers or Royalists who supported King Charles. We need to know who the Puritans and Royalists were; in other words, what information must we have about people in order to predict with some assurance that they would choose to support the king or the Parliament? Was this a struggle between different religious groups or different economic classes? The answer would presumably help explain the causes of the revolution; we can then look for particular events likely to aggravate the animosities between the parties and provoke hostile acts or outbreaks of violence.

Ranke, while perhaps not ascribing to that question the importance that later historians were to do, sees the division between parties as a combination of nationality, religion, and politics.[46] The "old Celtic stock" was dominated by but not integrated with the "Germanic race"; the former tended to be Catholic, the latter was mostly Protestant. The Germanic race was, however, split into two kingdoms (English and Scottish), each of which tried to preserve its independence; they differed on "ecclesiastical forms" (Episcopal, Presbyterian, and so on) both in the predominant tendency of the kingdoms as a whole and within each kingdom (especially the English). The desire of the Stuarts to unite the two kingdoms under a common strong government, and perhaps even a common church, aroused opposition between Protestant groups, partly on political grounds. By themselves the Catholics would never have been able to mount a serious challenge to the Protestant majority, but the threat that they might gain influence through the monarchy—because of the foreign policy and marriage of Charles I—was a source of instability.[47] Yet while Ranke suggests that popular fears that Charles I would bring England back to Catholicism aggravated opposition to his rule, Ranke declares "with absolute certainty" that Charles did not intend to do this.[48]

Thus for Ranke the composition of the two sides was not completely determined by ethnic or religious allegiances; each person had to weigh his loyalty to the king and to the Parliament, as affected by their behavior, against those allegiances. This is my interpretation of Ranke's very brief statements; the only other generalization I can find is that Cromwell's army regarded Charles I as the successor of William the Conqueror and themselves as the "successors of the Anglo-Saxon population, again after long oppression regaining the upper hand."[49]

Trevelyan begins his *England under the Stuarts* with a description of the upper, middle, and lower classes.[50] While fascinating to read, this account disclaims at the outset any attempt to explain the midcentury conflict in terms of previous divisions along economic lines, thus implicitly denying the validity of the causes of the revolution proposed recently by historians.[51] Trevelyan agrees with much of Ranke's analysis of the religious-political basis for the conflict, but he provides a much more detailed and subtle description of the theological differences of the English protagonists, while presenting a more simplistic view of the international situation. That is what one might expect of an Englishman writing about English history, as compared to a German on the same subject. If a literary approach to history is to have any value other than as literature, it must depend on the writer's ability to draw on his own experience and intuitive understanding of a familiar subject matter.

But Trevelyan's imaginative sympathy for seventeenth-century Englishmen is frequently dominated by his enthusiasm for the cause of Parliamentary democracy, his abhorrence of Stuart despotism, and his dislike of Catholicism. His work is a paradigm of the "Whig interpretation of history" criticized by Herbert Butterfield; every actor and every action is judged as a positive or negative contribution to the progress of freedom or liberalism.[52] This approach is sometimes defended as "humanistic" in the sense that it recognizes the importance of human values in the interpretation of history and uses the past for the moral inspiration and improvement of the present. From this perspective the alternative "value-free" approach may be criticized as an irresponsible attempt to evade the ethical dimension of human behavior. An extreme example of such criticism is the attempt made in England after World War II to blame Ranke for complicity in the rise of Naziism in Germany.[53]

Ranke himself summarized the two approaches in his famous dictum:

> To history has been given the function of judging the past, of instructing men for the profit of future years. The present attempt does not aspire to such a lofty undertaking. It merely wants to show how, essentially, things happened.[54]

Ranke does not mean that he intends to limit himself to establishing the empirical facts of history; to show how things happened entails finding causes for them. It is not good enough to locate these causes in the character of the participants in the events, even if one can claim personal knowledge of these men; thus he criticizes Lord Clarendon's contemporary history of the revolution for deducing all the calamities from the ministry of Buckingham: "One has here no professional historian, who searches diligently for remote causes, and perhaps (as has been our intention) endeavours to point out the opposing elements in the history of the world developed in the course of the strife. . . ."[55]

Ranke, no less than Trevelyan, needs to invoke putative laws of human nature in order to explain behavior.[56] Thus, "in politics personal gratitude is only a feeble motive" (the members of Parliament were not grateful to James I for allowing them to be elected)[57] and "In parliamentary assemblies the most influential speeches will be, not those which approach most nearly to the ideal of classical eloquence, but those which best correspond to the education and mental tendencies prevalent at the time" (on John Pym's effectiveness).[58] A comparable generalization from Trevelyan is that people do not generally defend freedom of speech except where the speech agrees with a popular view.[59]

But since both Ranke and Trevelyan assert that the behavior of Charles I was of crucial importance in provoking the revolution, we expect them to give a plausible explanation of this behavior based on all the available information. It is interesting to note that in one case both historians depart from their own principles in coping with this challenge—Ranke by issuing a moralistic judgment, Trevelyan by dismissing it with a pair of apodictic but uninformative phrases.

Consider the king's decision to assent to Strafford's execution under the bill of attainder passed by Parliament in May 1641. Ranke raves: "Verily it was a great moment for the King: what glory would attend his memory had he lived up to his convictions [that Strafford was not guilty of treason] and opposed to the pressure put upon him an immovable moral strength. To this end was he king, and possessed the right of sanctioning or of rejecting the resolution of Parliament: that was the theory of the constitution. . . ."[60] Trevelyan says, "The King's assent, as all men knew, could only be extorted by force," describes the shouts of the mob surrounding Whitehall, and concludes merely that "he gave way. Noise had conquered, as when the Bastille fell."[61]

Elsewhere Ranke discusses in detail the decisions, or failures to decide, of Charles I at critical junctures such as the movement of the Dutch against a Spanish fleet in English waters.[62] Trevelyan passes over these events rather quickly and saves his hermeneutic skills for the task of analyzing the decision to execute Charles. Now at last we learn that the king did not deserve to die and that his death actually obstructed the progress of democracy; yet sparing his life would not necessarily have rescued the country from chaos.[63]

One may agree with Trevelyan's opinion about the rights and wrongs of the English Revolution without admitting that historical writing should be slanted to reflect such an opinion. There are few royalists left to protest against that slant, but surely some readers would disagree with Trevelyan's justification for Strafford's treatment of the Irish: "A state of society so backward and so distracted could best be ruled as India was afterwards ruled by its English governors."[64] It is possible for historical writing to have literary quality without being prejudiced—as is indeed shown by large portions of Trevelyan's own work. Conversely, there is no reason why accuracy and fairness cannot be considered humanistic virtues.

Ranke's critics have accused him of bias in the other direction. It is claimed that his conservative political opinions, his approval of monarchy, led him to overlook the abuses of strong central governments and even to encourage the kind of thinking that allowed Hitler to come to power in Germany.[65] One could argue that objectivity in historical writing is impossible and that a writer like Trevelyan who flaunts his bias serves his readers better than one who conceals it. Nevertheless, Ranke impresses me as a scholar who is more concerned about accuracy than Trevelyan. Nor do I find him deficient in literary style; while not so emotional as Trevelyan, Ranke manages to tell an interesting story with some attention to the drama of exciting events.[66] Trevelyan calls Ranke's work "one of the great histories of our country, too much neglected," and I see no reason to dispute this statement.[67]

Perhaps my comparison of Ranke and Trevelyan is affected by the fact that Ranke himself established a new paradigm for historiography and thus determined the criteria by which historians, including himself, would be judged in the future. That would be in accordance with the view of Thomas S. Kuhn; but, rather than invoke the nebulous paradigm concept of his *Structure of Scientific Revolutions*, I prefer to use the distinction he later suggested between components of the "disciplinary matrix" shared by a scientific community.[68] Two of these are models and exemplars. A model may be simply a preferred analogy or a metaphysical commitment about the nature of reality. An exemplar is a concrete problem solution (reverting to an earlier sense of the term *paradigm*). One may prefer Ranke's or Tre-

velyan's model for the English Revolution, depending on one's
political orientation and one's judgment of the relative importance of different alleged causes of human action; this is still a
lively subject of debate among historians.[69] But one cannot, in
the twentieth century, be considered a professional historian
without giving allegiance to the methodology of critical use of
original documents, of which Ranke's work is almost univer-
sally regarded as the exemplar.


Both Charles Lyell and Archibald Geikie wrote extensively on
volcanoes, and indeed Geikie gained his reputation as a
geologist chiefly from his studies of vulcanism.[70] It might have
been interesting to compare their accounts of the great eruption
of Vesuvius in A.D. 79 with each other and with descriptions by
historians of its effects on Pompeii. But this event can hardly be
regarded as typical of the subjects treated by historians, nor can
we learn much about the modes of inquiry of geologists from
such a restricted topic. Rather than discuss accounts of a particular eruption or a particular volcano, I will consider the
views of Lyell and Geikie on the source of volcanic energy, the
relation of those views to more general theories about the forces
involved in geological change, and the issue of "progres-
sionism" in earth history.

In the first volume of his *Principles of Geology* (1820), Lyell
argued vigorously that geology should not include cosmogony.
He objected to the proliferation of highly speculative theories of
the earth's origin, insisting that geologists should not invoke in
their theories any causes that could not now be seen in operation. This prohibition of speculation about origins may have
served a useful function in avoiding the intrusion of theological
arguments about the origin of the earth.[71] But when Lyell
claimed that geological forces have always had roughly the
same magnitude and that there are no long-term directional
trends in the earth's history, he ran up against a very popular
theory; moreover, in justifying his uniformitarian doctrine he
made assumptions that appeared to violate fundamental results
of nineteenth-century physics.

The dominant theory before 1830 was that the earth had
originally condensed from a hot gaseous ball formed from a
rotating cloud as described in Laplace's nebular hypothesis. As
the ball cooled, it would form a solid crust but the inside would

remain fluid even now. This "central heat" concept had been suggested by Leibniz and worked out in detail by Buffon as the basis of his theory of the "epochs of nature." The evidence for this theory included: (1) indications that the surface temperature had previously been much higher than at present; for example, remains of tropical plants and animals found in arctic regions; (2) igneous rocks apparently formed at very high temperatures; (3) measurements of underground temperature showing a gradual increase with depth; and (4) lava in volcanic eruptions, ejected from some kind of hot underground reservoir.[72]

Just before he published his *Principles*, Lyell visited Paris and heard the French geologist Leonce Elie de Beaumont describe a new theory of the earth's surface features, based on the Leibniz-Buffon theory. According to Elie de Beaumont, the cooling fluid nucleus would contract more rapidly than the solid crust, so that the latter would repeatedly become unstable and collapse. Each of these "revolutions" would create a system of parallel mountain chains.[73]

Elie de Beaumont's theory avoided the arbitrary postulation of catastrophes to explain geological phenomena by providing an underlying uniform physical cause for the successive collapses of the crust. For that reason it was attractive to many geologists, although the regularity of mountain chains predicted by the theory was found to be greatly exaggerated.[74] But Lyell rejected the theory entirely. He was willing to admit that the earth has a store of internal heat that provides the energy for volcanic eruptions and earthquakes, but he denied that the store has diminished with time or that the earth had suffered any contraction. He attributed the change in surface temperature to rearrangements of the land and sea, these being due in turn to vertical motions of elevation and subsidence caused by earthquakes and volcanic eruptions. This subterranean activity is not sudden and global as in Elie de Beaumont's theory, but local and continual.[75]

Lyell's uniformitarian theory stood in a rather curious relationship to the mathematical theory of the earth's cooling developed by J. B. J. Fourier. Fourier's theory of heat conduction, together with his technique for analyzing functions or processes into components with different frequencies, was a major breakthrough in mathematical physics. It was the first physical theory to include in a quantitative way the principle of irreversibility, through the deceptively simple postulate that heat always flows from hot to cold, never from cold to hot.[76] This postulate establishes a direction in time: one goes from past to future, not from future to past. Applied to the earth's thermal history, Fourier's theory explains not only that the earth is cooling off but how rapidly it does so in terms of the heat capacity and thermal conductivity of its interior. Given the present temperature gradient at the surface (i.e., the rate of change of temperature with depth), one can estimate how long it has taken the earth to cool down from a specified high temperature.[77] All this is, of course, completely contrary to Lyell's assumption that the central heat remains constant—or is it?

When Fourier tried to estimate the time required for the earth to cool from a molten state, he found that it was so incredibly long that he did not even bother to write down the number. Had he done so, using the numerical values of the parameters that he considered appropriate, it would have been on the order of 200 million years. More significant at this point was his deduction that the effect of cooling on the earth's surface temperature at the present time is extremely small; in the past two thousand years it has been only $\frac{1}{288}$ degree.[78] The clear implication, at least for early-nineteenth-century geologists who were not accustomed to hundred-million-year time periods, was that the earth's cooling is irrelevant to the formation of its surface features.

Laplace pointed out that astronomical records can be used to check whether there has been any significant contraction of the earth by cooling; if the angular momentum of the earth is conserved, contraction would make it spin faster, thereby decreasing the length of the day. But there had not, in fact, been any noticeable change in the length of the day during the past two thousand years (such a change would have affected the timing of eclipses, for example). Lyell cited this result in support of his own assumption that the quantity of central heat has remained constant throughout geological history.[79] But he overlooked the fact that it is perfectly consistent with Fourier's model of slow cooling over a period of a hundred million years or so.

By the middle of the nineteenth century, geologists had come to accept the idea that the earth is much older than the biblical span of a few thousand years—partly because of Lyell's own emphasis on the immense quantity of time available for geological processes to produce their effects by gradual actions. Charles Darwin pushed Lyell's doctrine to its extreme when he suggested that the denudation of the Weald in England might have been going on for 300 million years.[80] But that rash statement, and other claims that geological time is unlimited, provoked a devastating attack by one of the most influential Victorian physicists, William Thomson (later to become Lord Kelvin). Thomson had taken up Fourier's heat conduction theory, at that time little known in Britain, and pointed out that the entire earth must have been molten something like a hundred million years ago. He asserted that uniformitarian geology represented a great mistake, being contrary to the laws of physics.[81] Lyell's assumption that the central heat is undiminished seemed to be supported by Fourier's calculations as long as time periods of only a few thousand years were under consideration in geology. But Lyell's success in persuading geologists to consider much longer periods ultimately undermined the credibility of his own theory, since the same type of calculation showed that the earth's temperature does change over periods of hundreds of millions of years.

There is a similar paradox in the fate of Lyell's views on organic evolution. The theory of central heat, as developed by Buffon and other naturalists, allowed the appearance of successively more complex forms of life as the earth's surface cooled down. Lyell's rejection of such "progression" in the organic world went along with his rejection of progression (due to cooling) in geological development.[82] But Darwin found the Lyellian earth, with its climate subject only to moderate fluctuations for indefinitely long periods, a very suitable environment for the gradual evolution of species by natural selection. Darwin's case was so convincing that Lyell himself had to accept it.[83]

But Lyell did not change his views on the invariability of central heat. In the third edition of his *Principles* (1834), he had argued that if the earth had in fact condensed from a hot fluid ball, convective cooling would have kept the temperature nearly uniform throughout until the crust began to form, and thus the nucleus could not now be much above its melting point, so the amount of residual heat was much less than his opponents supposed. He had also suggested that volcanic and tectonic activity in the crust was powered not only by heat flowing from the interior but by physical processes such as combustion and thermoelectric activity.[84] His ideas were quickly rejected by other geologists,[85] and a recent commentator has accused him of "attempting to contrive scientific arguments where none existed."[86]

But Lyell was able to find support for his doctrine in subsequent scientific developments. The fluidity of the earth's interior, which had been considered a consequence of the theory of central heat and had provided an explanation of the source of volcanic lava, was found to be inconsistent with well-established theories of phenomena such as ocean tides. Thomson himself insisted that the entire earth is a solid as rigid as steel.[87] The discovery of the convertibility of different forms of energy seemed to support Lyell's contention that vulcanism could be powered by chemical or electrical energy as well as by heat, and the detection of hydrogen in the 1834 eruption of Vesuvius appeared to confirm a prediction of the chemical theory. The reader of the eleventh edition of the *Principles* (1872) would quite likely be convinced that Lyell's theory had triumphantly withstood the test of time.[88]

But Lyell went astray in failing to recognize the implications of the great (C.P.) Snowy shibboleth of modern science, the Second Law of Thermodynamics.[89] It was William Thomson who first proclaimed in 1852 the Principle of the Dissipation of Energy, now known as the generalized Second Law of Thermodynamics: in all physical processes energy is conserved but tends to be transformed into less useful forms. The simplest example is the flow of heat from hot to cold: according to thermodynamic theory, heat cannot be converted into mechanical work unless a temperature difference is available and the flow of heat is controlled in a special way (as in a steam engine); once all the heat in a system has reached the same temperature, no further work can be extracted. This final state, which seemed to be an inevitable consequence of the natural tendency of heat to flow from hot to cold, was called the "heat death of the universe."[90] Thomson pointed out in his 1851 paper that the principle placed a limit on the time the earth is available for human habitation: at some time in the past it was too hot and at some time in the future it will be too cold.

Thomson argued that Lyell's uniformitarian geology must be abandoned because it violated the Principle of Energy Dissipation. Lyell might have replied that the principle itself was only a portentous way of stating what the progressionist geologists had already claimed about the directionality imposed on earth history by the outflow of central heat;[91] its generalization to other forms of energy was only postulated, not proved.

But Lyell was at a disadvantage here because physics was rapidly gaining prestige as a scientific discipline relative to geology in the late nineteenth century. Physics was becoming the most fundamental science, to which all others should ultimately be reduced. In any direct conflict between physics and geology, the physicists would refuse to give any ground while the geologists would be inclined to compromise. This change in the relations of physics and geology (which resulted in the current assumption, noted at the beginning of this paper, that all sciences are or should be like physics) is itself a result of the historical development that includes the conflict between Kelvin and Lyell.[92]

The first geologist to accept Thomson's restrictions on the age of the earth was Archibald Geikie. He suggested that denudation was not as slow as Darwin and others had supposed, hence would not have taken hundreds of millions of years to produce the observed effects. Referring to Thomson's denial of unlimited time, he said, "We have been drawing recklessly upon a bank in which it appears there are no further funds at our disposal. It is well, therefore, to find that our demands are really unnecessary."[93]

Thomson noted Geikie's "succession from the prevailing orthodoxy," but in the following years he and his colleagues reduced the age of the earth to only 10 to 20 million years, ignoring entirely the geological evidence for greater antiquity.[94] By 1889, even Geikie realized that the demands of the physicists were becoming unreasonable: "It is difficult satisfactorily to carry on a discussion in which your opponent entirely ignores your arguments, while you have given the fullest attention to his."[95]

While Geikie could point to some flaws in Thomson's deductions, he could not make a really fundamental criticism of it (such as T. C. Chamberlin was doing in America) because he accepted Thomson's basic assumption that the earth is cooling down from a molten state.[96] This assumption, shared by all major nineteenth-century geologists except Lyell, furnished the underlying cause of "progress" in the very definition of geology: "Its object is to trace the progress of our planet from the earliest beginnings of its separate existence . . . down to the present." It was still closely linked to evolution: "Geology shows that the present races of plants and animals are the descendants of other and very different races that once peopled the earth. It teaches that there has been a progress of the inhabitants, as well as one of the globe on which they have dwelt."[97] Since the earth was hotter in the past, we cannot assume "that the phase of nature's operations which we now witness has been the same in all past time," or that "at the present time all the great geological processes, which have produced changes in past ages of the earth's history, are still existent and active."[98]

To explain vulcanism, Geikie had to explain how liquid lava could erupt from an earth that Thomson had shown to be solid. His answer was that lava originated in subterranean magma, a substance so hot that, although ordinarily kept in a solid state by the pressure of the crust, it may be liquefied by any momentary decrease of pressure. Such a decrease may be caused by contraction (due to the slow cooling of the earth), which forces the crust to adjust itself to a shrinking nucleus by folding or rupture. The ridging-up of the crust relieves the pressure and liquefies the magma. Moreover, there are gases dissolved in the magma, which will escape violently when the pressure is released (like the carbon dioxide in an uncorked bottle of champagne). Geikie considered this combination of liquefaction of magma and explosive release of gases to be adequate to explain all the phenomena of vulcanism, and argued that the underlying contraction theory provided the only possible explanation of the formation of mountain chains and other geographical features.[99]

Yet Geikie had to admit that there was no good evidence that volcanic activity had been more intense in the past,[100] and he apparently found Thomson's solid earth hard to reconcile with his conceptions of magma. In any case he welcomed a new theory of vulcanism proposed by the Swedish scientist Svante Arrhenius in 1900. Arrhenius, following suggestions of several German geophysicists, suggested that the progressive increase of temperature with depth inside the earth causes not only liquefaction but vaporization.[101] It was known that at sufficiently high temperatures—above the "critical temperature"—a gas cannot be condensed no matter how high the pressure; more precisely, there is no longer a distinction between gas and liquid.[102] Arrhenius reasoned, on the basis of experiments with gases at lower pressures and temperatures, that the viscosity of this supercritical fluid would increase with temperature, so it would behave in some respects like a solid. For Geikie the main advantage of this theory was that it provided a continual source of high-temperature gas and fluid magma, whereas the solid earth of Thomson could offer only sporadic outbursts.[103]

For those readers unfamiliar with modern geology it may be helpful to point out that while Lyell's extreme uniform-itarianism has not survived into the twentieth century, the Arrhenius-Geikie explanation of vulcanism is even further re-moved from current ideas about the internal constitution of the earth.[104] The discovery of the existence of heat-generating ra-dioactive substances in the crust has made it unnecessary to attribute geothermal phenomena to a store of heat remaining from the earth's formation. In fact, it is considered quite possi-ble (as T. C. Chamberlin suggested as early as 1897) that the earth has not been cooling down at all but has been warming up.[105] Thus Geikie's insistence on explaining all volcanic and tectonic phenomena in terms of a diminishing store of central heat now seems no more justified than Lyell's insistence that the energy source for such phenomena has not changed with time.

Just as Trevelyan praised Ranke's work on English history while rejecting the premise that history should be a science based only on documents, Geikie's assessment of Lyell was ambivalent. In his book *Founders of Geology* Geikie made it clear that he did not accept Lyell's extreme version of uniform-itarianism but acknowledged the valuable contribution of his *Principles* to the development of the science:

> Lyell's function was mainly that of a critic and exponent of the researches of his contemporaries, and of a philosophical writer thereon, with a rare faculty of perceiving the connec-tion of scattered facts with each other, and with the general principles of science. . . . But Lyell, though he did not, like Sedgwick and Murchison, add new chapters to geological history, nevertheless left his mark upon the nomenclature and classification of the geological record.[106]

In the above discussion I have tried to emphasize the sim-ilarities between history and geology. I think there is a legiti-mate parallel between Trevelyan's Whig interpretation of the

English Revolution and Geikie's progressionist interpretation of vulcanism, just as there is between the philosophical grounds on which Ranke and Lyell denied the existence of any progressive tendency. The geologists do not depend on causes, general laws, and idealized mathematical models more heavily than the historians (contrary to Korner,[107] who claims this to be an essential difference between scientists and historians), but they articulate much more clearly the extent to which they do use them (as Hempel says).[108] Both Lyell and Geikie discuss the theory of central heat, whose mathematical aspects have been worked out by others (Fourier and Kelvin), but do not develop or test quantitative theories themselves.

The most striking difference between historians and geologists, at least in the examples I have considered, is that the latter are constantly interacting with each other whereas the former seem to work in isolation. Ranke never returned to the subject of the English Revolution, even to answer the reviewers of his book; he did not carry on a dialogue with other historians or take account of their findings in revising his own account. Trevelyan attacked the scientific historians in a general way but did not directly challenge their interpretation of specific historical events.

In the past few decades there has, in fact, been a rather heated controversy among historians about the causes of the English Revolution, which one might say is similar to the nineteenth-century debate among geologists about the causes of vulcanism. But as far as I can tell this is the exception that proves the rule; most historians consider the debate an embarrassing deviation from normal behavior rather than a welcome sign of liveliness in their profession.[109]

Scientific research is undoubtedly an intensely competitive activity, yet ever since the seventeenth century it has also been a cooperative activity in which researchers discuss, criticize, and modify their ideas at every stage. The person who has an important result is frequently torn between his desire to tell everyone about it at once and his fear that, following a premature leak, a rival will take advantage of the tip and beat him into print. On balance, the shift from the older practice of holding back one's discoveries until one can publish them in polished form in a major monograph to the newer practice of sharing information at an early stage through preprints and short articles seems to have accelerated progress in all fields of science. Perhaps history will always be a discipline in which the major achievements are book-length syntheses rather than brief papers. Yet it should be possible for historians to engage in vigorous debate with each other on specific questions of fact and interpretation and, more important, to change their conclusions as a result of such debate. It is no longer possible to argue that agreement can be expected only in those disciplines that deal with objective facts and mathematical theorems. We know that scientific revolutions may completely overturn theories that had been thought to have attained the status of eternal truth, yet our recognition of the provisional character of scientific knowledge does not prevent us from striving for a consensus on the basis of evidence available at a particular time.

# NOTES

1. Similar views were expressed by Edgar Zilsel, "Physics and the Problem of Historico-sociological Laws," *Philosophy of Science* 8 (1941): 567–79.

2. H. E. Barnes, *A History of Historical Writing*, 2d ed. (New York: Dover, 1961), 246; G. P. Gooch, *History and Historians in the Nineteenth Century* (1913; reprint, Boston: Beacon Press, 1959), 75. Among the encyclopedia articles on Ranke or on historical writing see *The New Encyclopedia Britannica, Macropedia*, 1981, s.v. "Ranke, Leopold von."

3. Among the encyclopedia articles on Lyell see *The World Book Encyclopedia*, 1975, s.v. "Lyell."

4. Lyell considered that geology should stand in the same relation to the physical sciences as history does to the moral sciences. See Mott Tuthill Greene, "Major Developments in Geotectonic Theory between 1800 and 1912" (Ph.D. diss., University of Washington, 1978), 86.

5. T. S. Kuhn, *The Structure of Scientific Revolutions* (Chicago: University of Chicago Press, 1970); S. G. Brush, "Can Science Come Out of the Laboratory Now?" *Bulletin of the Atomic Scientists* 32 (April 1976): 40–43.

6. Leopold von Ranke, *Englische Geschichte* (1859), English translation, *A History of England, Principally in the Seventeenth Century*, 6 vols. (Oxford: Clarendon Press, 1875). Cf. Leonard Krieger, *Ranke: The Meaning of History* (Chicago: University of Chicago Press, 1977). According to Lord Acton, Ranke was provoked to write this work by the "positive narrow standpoint of Macaulay's account"; see Herbert Butterfield, *Man on His Past: The Study of the History of Historical Scholarship* (London: Cambridge University Press, 1969), 88. Ranke influenced subsequent British historiography through S. R. Gardiner, who wrote an even more extensive treatise on the seventeenth-century English revolution.

7. On the sexual quality of Ranke's relation with his sources see Krieger, *Ranke*, 104–5. For a similar example from science see Bishop Sprat's *History of the Royal Society* (London, 1667), 344.

8. Ranke, *History of England*, 1:13. Lord Acton thought that this choice resulted from Ranke's bias in favor of the state: "the Venetians were on the governing side, and

viewed the state from the point of view of the trouble and difficulty of governing" (quoted in Butterfield, *Man on His Past,* 90). But another British historian admitted that, in contrast to Ranke, "none of our historians, except Hallam, has any pretensions to objectivity" (Henry Sidgwick, "Ranke's History of England," *Macmillan's Magazine* 4[1861]: 85–91, quoted from p. 86).

9. Ranke, *History of England,* 1:11.

10. From the preface to *History of the Popes* (1834), in Leopold von Ranke, *The Theory and Practice of History,* ed. Georg G. Iggers and Konrad von Moltke and trans. Wilma A. Iggers and Konrad von Moltke (Indianapolis: Bobbs-Merrill, 1973), 144–45.

11. "George Washington enjoys at present the epistemological status of an electron: each is an entity postulated for the purpose of giving coherence to our present experience, and each is unobservable by us" (Murray Murphey, *Our Knowledge of the Historical Past* [Indianapolis: Bobbs-Merrill, 1973], 16).

12. Krieger, *Ranke,* 142.

13. Iggers and Moltke, in Ranke, *Theory and Practice,* xix.

14. But see Peter Gay, *Style in History* (London: Jonathan Cape, 1975), 76–90.

15. Ranke, *Theory and Practice,* 49.

16. Charles Lyell, *Principles of Geology, being An Attempt to Explain the Former Changes of the Earth's Surface by Reference to Causes now in Operation* (1830–33; reprint, New York: Verlag von J. Cramer, 1970), vol. 1, chap. 23.

17. Karl Popper, *Unended Quest, An Intellectual Autobiography* (La Salle, Ill.: Open Court, 1976), pp. 167–180, and references cited therein.

18. Karl Popper, *The Poverty of Historicism,* 2d corrected ed. (London: Routledge & Kegan Paul, 1966).

19. Karl Popper, "Natural Selection and the Emergence of Mind," *Dialectica* 32 (1978): 339–55; "Evolution," *New Scientist* 87 (1980): 611. Cf. R. E. Kofahl and H. Zeisel, "Popper on Darwinism," *Science* 212 (1981): 873.

20. Gay, *Style,* 86–87.

21. From "Ueber die Epochen der neueren Geschichte" (1854), in Ranke, *Theory and Practice,* 53.

22. Ibid., 54, 56.

23. Lyell, *Principles,* 1:141–43 and other references given below (notes 73–83); Greene, "Major Developments in Geotectonic Theory."

24. *The New Science of Giambattista Vico* (3d ed., 1744), trans. Thomas Goddard Bergin and Max Harold Fisch (Ithaca, N.Y.: Cornell University Press, 1968), 96–97 (sect. 331).

25. Lyell, *Principles,* 1:1.

26. Lyell, *Principles,* 1:74; see also Leonard G.Wilson, *Charles Lyell, The Years to 1841: The Revolution in Geology* (New Haven, Conn.: Yale University Press, 1972), 215–16; D. R. Oldroyd, "Historicism and the Rise of Historical Geology," *History of Science* 17 (1979): 191–213, 227–57; M. J. S. Rudwick, "Historical Analogies in the Geological Work of Charles Lyell," *Janus* 64 (1977): 89–107.

27. Charles Coulston Gillispie, *Genesis and Geology: A Study in the Relations of Scientific Thought, Natural Theology, and Social Opinion in Great Britain, 1790–1850* (1951; reprint, New York: Harper & Bros., 1959); Stephen Toulmin and June Goodfield, *The Discovery of Time* (New York: Harper & Row, 1965).

28. Greene, "Major Developments in Geotectonic Theory," 54–58.

29. Rhoda Rappaport, "Borrowed Words: Problems of Vocabulary in Eighteenth-Century Geology," *British Journal for the History of Science* 15 (1982): 27–44.

30. Archibald Geikie, *The Founders of Geology,* 2d ed. (1905; reprint, New York:

Dover Publications, 1962), 208. Cf. Greene, "Major Developments in Geotectonic Theory," 58.

31. Greene, "Major Developments in Geotectonic Theory," 249–55.

32. Ranke, *History of England,* 1:9.

33. Greene, "Major Developments in Geotectonic Theory," 93 and elsewhere.

34. Sidgwick, "Ranke's History," 87.

35. James Westfall Thompson and Bernard J. Holm, *A History of Historical Writing,* 2 vols. (New York: Macmillan, 1942), 2:444.

36. This contrast may be found, for example, in Arthur Marwick, *The Nature of History* (London: Macmillan, 1970).

37. George Macaulay Trevelyan, *Clio, A Muse, and Other Essays Literary and Pedestrian* (London: Longman, Green, and Co., 1914), 4.

38. Ibid., 12, 30.

39. Ibid., 8, 24.

40. Ibid., 12.

41. Trevelyan, "Bias in History" (1947), reprinted in his *An Autobiography and Other Essays* (London: Longman, Green, and Co., 1949), 68–81.

42. Wilson, *Charles Lyell,* 503.

43. David R. Oldroyd, "Sir Archibald Geikie (1835–1924), Geologist, Romantic Aesthete, and Historian of Geology: The Problem of Whig Historiography of Science," *Annals of Science* 37 (1980): 441–62. On Trevelyan as a romantic Whig historian see also Marwick, *Nature of History,* 56–60, and the film "About Trevelyan" (Open University, Humanities Foundation Course A100/08).

44. Archibald Geikie, *Text-Book of Geology* (London: Macmillan & Co., 1882; 4th ed., 1903), Book 1.

45. Archibald Geikie, *Types of Scenery and Their Influence on Literature,* The Romanes Lecture, 1898 (1898; reprint, Port Washington, N.Y.: Kennikat Press, 1970); cf. other publications listed in Eric Cutter, "Sir Archibald Geikie: A Bibliography," *Journal of the Society for Bibliography of Natural History* 7 (1974): 1–18.

46. Ranke, *History of England,* 1:468.

47. Ibid., 2:39–40, 63.

48. Ibid., 2:45.

49. Ibid., 2:451–52.

50. George Macaulay Trevelyan, *England under the Stuarts* (1904 and rev. ed. 1925; reprint, London: Methuen, 1965), chaps. 1–2.

51. ". . . England, the revolutionary passions were stirred by no class in its own material interests" (Trevelyan, *England under the Stuarts,* 187). For a survey of recent interpretations see Christopher Hill, *Puritanism and Revolution, Studies in Interpretation of the English Revolution of the Seventeenth Century* (London: Secker & Warburg, 1958), chap. 1; *The English Revolution 1600–1660,* ed. E. W. Ives (London: Arnold, 1968); Jack Hexter, *Reappraisals in History* (Evanston, Ill.: Northwestern University Press, 1961), 117–62; Lawrence Stone, *The Causes of the English Revolution* (New York: Harper & Row, 1972).

52. Herbert Butterfield, *The Whig Interpretation of History* (London: Bell, 1931). J. H. Plumb, however, claims that Trevelyan's account is less biased than many of those published recently; see *G. M. Trevelyan* (London: Longman, Green and Co., 1951), 15.

53. Pieter Geyl, *From Ranke to Toynbee,* Smith College Studies in History, vol. 39 (Northampton, Mass.: Dept. of History, Smith College, 1952), chap. 1. (This is a discussion of the *Times Literary Supplement* 1950 article that made the charge.)

54. From *Geschichte der romanischen und germanischen Voelker von 1494–1514* (1824), in Ranke, *Theory and Practice of History,* 137.

55. Ranke, *History of England,* 6:9. Trevelyan calls Clarendon "the father of

English history" and says he "established the English tradition, which lasted for two hundred years: the tradition, namely, that history was a part of the national literature, and was meant for the education and delight of all who read books" (*Clio*, 35–36).

56. Krieger, *Ranke*, 4, who contradicts Iggers & Moltke in Ranke, *Theory and Practice of History*, lv.

57. Ranke, *History of England*, 1:398.

58. Ibid., 2:230.

59. Trevelyan, *England under the Stuarts*, 156–57.

60. Ranke, *History of England*, 2:269.

61. Trevelyan, *England under the Stuarts*, 202–3.

62. Ranke, *History of England*, 2:162.

63. Trevelyan, *England under the Stuarts*, 277–78.

64. Ibid., 180.

65. Geyl, *From Ranke to Toynbee*.

66. Gay, *Style*, 59–67. For a contemporary judgment see Sidgwick, "Ranke's History," 88: "The style of our author is careful, clear, and pleasing; not destitute of spirit or grace, though never rising to any great pitch of beauty or sublimity." Moreover, "We find in him hardly any traces of the phraseology stigmatized as German jargon" (87).

67. Trevelyan, *England under the Stuarts*, 514. H. E. Barnes said in 1937 that "Trevelyan's *England under the Stuarts* is the most brilliant piece of writing on this century since Macaulay's *History of England*" and did not even mention Ranke's work on English history (*History of Historical Writing*, 254–55).

68. T. S. Kuhn, "Second Thoughts on Paradigms," in *The Structure of Scientific Theories*, ed. Frederick Suppe, 2d ed. (Urbana: University of Illinois Press, 1977), 459–82.

69. See the works by Hill, Hexter, and Stone cited in n. 51.

70. Lyell, *Principles*, 1:312–98; Geikie, *Ancient Volcanoes of Great Britain* (London: Macmillan & Co., 1897). For historical background on this subject, see Karl Alfred von Zitell, *History of Geology and Palaeontology to the end of the Nineteenth Century* (London: Walter Scott, 1901), 254–80.

71. Rachel Laudan, "Redefinitions of a Discipline: Histories of Geology and Geological History" (Paper delivered at a conference, "Disciplinary Historiography and the Development of Disciplines," Bielefeld, W. Germany, September 1981).

72. S. G. Brush, *The Kind of Motion We Call Heat: A History of the Kinetic Theory of Gases in the Nineteenth Century* (Amsterdam: North-Holland, 1976), 551–55; Philip Lawrence, "Heaven and Earth: The Relation of the Nebular Hypothesis to Geology," in *Cosmology, History, and Theology*, ed. W. Yourgrau (New York: Plenum, 1977), 235–81.

73. Wilson, *Charles Lyell*, 259, 294–96; Philip Lawrence, "Charles Lyell versus the Theory of Central Heat: A Reappraisal of Lyell's Place in the History of Geology," *Journal of the History of Biology* 11 (1978): 101–28.

74. Lawrence, "Charles Lyell"; Greene, "Major Developments in Geotectonic Theory."

75. Lyell, *Principles*, 1:49–64, 112, 255; 3:240, 338f. Dov. Ospovat, "Lyell's Theory of Climate," *Journal of the History of Biology* 10 (1977): 317–29.

76. S. G. Brush, "Irreversibility and Indeterminism: Fourier to Heisenberg," *Journal of the History of Ideas* 37 (1976): 603–30; I. Grattan-Guinness, *Joseph Fourier 1768–1830* (Cambridge, Mass.: MIT Press, 1972); and "Joseph Fourier and the Revolution in Mathematical Physics," *Journal of the Institute of Mathematics and its Applications* 5 (1969): 230–53.

77. J. B. J. Fourier, "Mémoire sur les températures du Globe terrestre et des

132      Stephen Brush

espace planétaires," *Mémoires de l'Academie Royale des Sciences de l'Institut de France* 7 (1827): 570–604.

78. J. B. J. Fourier, "Mémoire sur le refroidissement seculaire du globe terrestre," *Annales de Chimie* 13 (1819): 418–37.

79. P. S. de Laplace, "Sur la diminution de la durée du jour par le refroidissement de la Terre," *Annales de Chimie et de Physique* 13 (1820): 410–17; Lyell, *Principles,* 1:141.

80. Charles Darwin, *On the Origin of Species by Means of Natural Selection, or the Preservation of Favoured Races in the Struggle for Life* (London: Murray, 1859), 282–87. For more conservative estimates from similar evidence, see John Phillips, *Life on Earth* (1860; reprint, New York: Arno Press, 1980), 130–36 and "On the Measure of Geological Time by Natural Chronometers," *Report of the 34th Meeting of the British Association for the Advancement of Science (1864),* 64–65.

81. William Thomson, Presidential Address to the Geological Society of Glasgow (1868); see Lord Kelvin's *Popular Lectures and Addresses* (London: Macmillan & Co., 1894), 2:44. A general account of this controversy is given by Joe D. Burchfield, *Lord Kelvin and the Age of the Earth* (New York: Science History Publishers, 1975), and more briefly in my *Temperature of History: Phases of Science and Culture in the Nineteenth Century* (New York: Burt Franklin & Co., 1978), chap. 3.

82. Martin J. S. Rudwick, "Uniformity and Progression: Reflections on the Structure of Geological Theory in the Age of Lyell," in *Perspectives in the History of Science and Technology,* ed D. H. D. Roller (Norman: University of Oklahoma Press, 1971), 209–27.

83. Lyell announced his conversion to Darwin's theory in 1864; see *Dictionary of Scientific Biography,* 1973, s.v. "Lyell, Charles."

84. Lawrence, "Charles Lyell," 125.

85. [George Poulett Scrope], Review of *Principles of Geology* by Charles Lyell, 3rd ed., *Quarterly Review* 53 (1835): 406–48.

86. Lawrence, "Charles Lyell," 125. Arguments did exist, but they were not to be discovered until later.

87. See Stephen G. Brush, "Nineteenth-Century Debates about the Inside of the Earth: Solid, Liquid, or Gas?" *Annals of Science* 36 (1979): 225–54.

88. See *Principles,* 2:32–33.

89. C. P. Snow, *The Two Cultures and a Second Look* (New York: Cambridge University Press, 1969), 15, 71–72.

90. Brush, *Kind of Motion,* 551–52, 555, 578, and 582 n. 52.

91. Ibid., 554–55, 559–60.

92. Ibid.

93. Geikie, "On Modern Denudation," *Transactions of the Geological Society of Glasgow* 3 (1871): 153–90 (quoted from 189). For the time-money analogy see Martin J. S. Rudwick, "Poulett Scrope on the Volcanoes of Auvergne: Lyellian Time and Political Economy," *British Journal for the History of Science* 7 (1974): 205–42.

94. Kelvin, *Popular Lectures,* 2:87; Burchfield, *Lord Kelvin.*

95. Geikie, Address of the President, Section C—Geology, *Report of the 69th Meeting of the British Association for the Advancement of Science, 1899,* 718–30 (quoted from 724). See also his 1892 address, reprinted in *Victorian Science,* ed. George Basalla et al. (Garden City, N.Y.: Doubleday, 1970), 373–96.

96. Geikie, *Text-Book,* 1:81–82; T. C. Chamberlin, "On Lord Kelvin's Address on the Age of the Earth as an Abode Fitted for Life," *Science,* n.s., 9(1899): 889–901; 10(1899): 11–18.

97. Geikie, *Text-Book,* 1:1.

98. Ibid., 1:3.

99. "Geographical Evolution" (1879) in Geikie, *Geological Sketches at Home and Abroad* (London: Macmillan & Co., 1882; New York: Fitzgerald, 1887), pt. 2, pp. 38–39; *Ancient Volcanoes*, 1:11–13. See also his *Text-Book;* but on p. 393 he has to invoke G. H. Darwin's theory to explain the configuration of continents.

100. *Ancient Volcanoes*, 1:13. But there have been variations and periods of maximum activity in the past (2:471).

101. S. Arrhenius, "Zur Physik des Volcanismus," *Geologiska Forenigens, Stockholm Forhandlingar* 22(1900): 325–420. For the earlier history of this idea see Brush, "Nineteenth-Century Debates."

102. Brush, *Kind of Motion*, 256–63.

103. Geikie, *Text-Book*, 1:355–56.

104. See Stephen G. Brush, "Discovery of the Earth's Core," *American Journal of Physics* 48(1980): 705–24.

105. T. C. Chamberlin, "A Group of Hypotheses Bearing on Climatic Change," *Journal of Geology* 5 (1897): 653–83.

106. Geikie, *Founders of Geology*, 404.

107. Stephan Korner, "On a Difference between the Natural Sciences and History," in *Biology, History, and Natural Philosophy*, ed. Allen D. Breck and Wolfgang Yourgrau (New York: Plenum, 1972), 243–50.

108. Carl G. Hempel, "The Function of General Laws in History" (1942), reprinted in *Aspects of Scientific Explanation and Other Essays in the Philosophy of Science* (New York: Free Press, 1965), 231–43.

109. Stone, *Causes of the English Revolution*, 30–32.

# Science's Fictions: The Problem of Language and Creativity

## STUART PETERFREUND

*Northeastern University*

Science is language-bound, as are the mathematical concepts and notational systems one uses to "do" science. Self-evident proofs like that of the squares of the sides of a right triangle $(c^2 = a^2 + b^2)$ depend on long chains of verbal axioms. Indeed, the very basis of number systems, as Gödel found out, is undecidable propositions—undecidable *because* the canons of provability cannot be extended to language.[1]

Language has an important role to play in the creative processes of science, as Max Black and Colin Murray Turbayne have noted in their discussions of metaphor-making in science. And Thomas S. Kuhn's notion of the *paradigm*, itself a language-related term, is similar to the notion of metaphor elaborated by Black and Turbayne. Jacob Bronowski, a literary scholar as well as a scientist and mathematician of some note, concludes that "all science is a search for unity in hidden likenesses."[2]

The language-bound status of science poses a number of problems that scientists and humanists of a positivist persuasion have sought to ignore. "The aim," as Gerald Holton has stated, "is to make one's work seem 'objective,' repeatable by anyone, or, as Louis Pasteur said, *inevitable*." Nevertheless, that very aim in science is a function of point of view, and point of view ramifies in the area of scientific content as well as that of scientific style: "Through the analyses of Robert K. Merton and others we know that disputes and priority fights exist as intense undercurrents. But their importance is generally disavowed by scientists, as are the deep thematic presuppositions underlying apparently 'neutral' presentations."[3]

Point of view and personal investment affect the neutrality

of language-bound science; moreover, the very status of language itself would seem to subvert the scientific enterprise. If, as Hans Eichner argues, science "studies nature, assumes determinacy, reasons ahistorically, and aims to establish timeless universal laws,"[4] it must do so with a language that has its own nature, is historically and culturally determined, and is subject to laws of its own. In fact, science's very origins dictate that it must be language-bound. As Husserl said, "natural philosophy," the original name of science, is descended from philosophy, with a language descended from philosophy's language of the "life-world."[5]

Despite the *prima facie* case for science's dependency on language, the official position on scientific activity and outcome is still a lot closer to the one identified by Pasteur and ratified by Eichner than it is to the position held by Black or Kuhn or Turbayne. Kuhn for his part questions science's power "to establish timeless universal laws," asking whether it helps "to imagine that there is some one full, objective, true account of nature and that the proper measure of scientific achievement is the extent to which it brings us closer to that ultimate goal."[6]

The reasons for the persistence of the official position are complex. However, one clear motive for holding that position emerges from Holton's comments. The reward for possessing scientific knowledge is power. The insight is hardly recent, being traceable at least back to Francis Bacon: "the true end of . . . Knowledge is a restitution and reinvesting (in great part) of man to the sovereignty and power . . . which he had in his first state of creation." Those best suited to reattain this power are the scientist, the mathematician, and the engineer. Those who are interested in "the creations of the mind and hand," the humanities and the fine arts, can continue to play quietly if they stay out of the way.[7]

Science's claim to power rests on more than its potential for wish-fulfillment. By focusing on the object half of the subject-object dualism, science provides the basis for establishing powerful technology. That technology in its turn provides a basis for arguing that science is capable of attaining even greater knowledge and greater power. The ready reliance of science on technology as its principal means of justification has been noted by Bronowski, who observes that science "admits no sharp boundary between knowledge and use."[8] Of course, other disciplines, such as the humanities, admit no such sharp boundaries either. But there is a significant difference between the sciences and the humanities in regard to the relative power of the technologies they can mobilize. Focused as they are on the subject half of the subject-object dualism, the humanities simply do not have much material power at their disposal. One can respond to a mugger scientifically by using a technology such as the martial arts, which makes use of leverage, acceleration of masses, angular momentum, and the like, or by using the technology of chemistry (a can of Mace); or one can respond to a mugger humanistically by means of eloquence or situational ethics to dissuade him from his actions. Western culture codifies the priorities and powers of the two technologies in the adage, "Shoot first and ask questions later." On a national and international scale, these priorities are at the basis of the current nuclear dilemma. The current administration's position is but a corollary of the adage quoted above: "Arm first and talk about disarmament later."

But power, as innumerable bloody revolutions have so eloquently shown, is something that one must constantly strive to justify. And science, as the vehicle of such powerful technology, must strive constantly to justify itself. On the most obvious level, science accomplishes this justification with extensive public relations campaigns that proclaim progress to be "our most important product" or pontificate that "without chemicals, life itself would be impossible." Other established institutions, most especially government, do much the same on this obvious level, but governments do something further that is interesting in this context: they ground their ultimate authority on some version of God's truth, which authorized the founding and continued existence of the state. As it turns out, science uses a similar logic of justification: its operations are predicated on the belief that it strives to reattain what Bacon calls "the sovereignty and power" of that "first state of creation." This reattainment depends entirely upon demonstrating the existence of a language, either in the scientific present or in that first state of creation, which is capable of describing Eichner's "timeless universal laws"—things as they ought to be, as ordained by God Almighty himself. Bacon's scientific program is also a program of language reform, aimed at reattaining the language of Adam. Nor is Bacon an exception in this regard.[9]

Science has an institutional commitment to perpetuating the

belief in a value-neutral, purely descriptive language medium, because such a belief, when held by the culture at large, ensures that science will maintain its power as an institution central to the culture. But at the same time it is necessary to make a start toward understanding the relationship between science's status as a language-bound human activity and its attainment of power.[10] Moreover, it is necessary to make a start toward understanding the role and influence of language in shaping the ever-shifting scientific accounts of how "things happen." The next three sections look at how science creates its myth of language, how the essentially mythic issues involved in that attempt at creation ramify as personal and cultural myths, and how an understanding of what is involved in the scientific language enterprise can be of use in reframing the study of the sciences to include the study of the humanities.

The myth of scientific language depends on the sort of dichotomizing that has traditionally attempted to separate ordinary language from poetic language, *Naturwissenschaft* (natural science) from *Geisteswissenchaft* (spiritual science, the humanities). In Eichner's rather glib formulation, "the former studies nature, assumes determinacy, reasons ahistorically, and aims to establish timeless universal laws. The latter studies human creations, assumes free will, takes a basically historicist approach, and focuses on the individual, unique, time-bound, and unrepeatable."

Such dichotomies function as operative truths, perhaps, but they are ultimately specious as dichotomies. If one looks closely at ordinary language, it turns out to be as self-referential and "foregrounded" as is poetic language. The linguists and stylisticians of the Prague Circle and those after them insist on the distinction because it is a precondition, an inaugural move essential to the operationalism of doing linguistics/stylistics. Moreover, it is an inaugural move containing a suppressed myth of language origins and development. Once upon a time, the world spoke "ordinary language." But then events gave rise to "deviance," and ultimately to "poetic language" as an entity distinct from its "ordinary" forebears.[11]

The dichotomy between scientific and humanistic discourse, which likewise originated as an operative truth, is also an ultimately specious dichotomy. If one looks closely at scientific discourse, as Holton has done, it turns out to be as partial, interested, and argumentative as humanistic discourse is.[12] But the distinction is necessary as an inaugural move to allow the operationalism of doing science to proceed. Moreover, the inaugural move is based on a myth, sometimes suppressed and sometimes not. Though it admits of some latitude in variation, the premises of the myth remain relatively constant. Once upon a time, there was a perfect language of words and objects, either without any syntax or without the annoying ambiguities of syntax. This language of words and objects named both the things of the universe and the principles underlying those things. Since that time, an intervening age has been responsible for debasing both the pristine language and its wisdom.

One important difference between the Prague linguists and stylisticians and those who propounded the myth of a scientific language concerns the avowed goals of the operations enabled by the inaugural move. Whatever suppressed ambitions they may harbor, the former overtly seek only to understand how ordinary language and poetic language differ. The latter stress that one of their principal goals is the apprehension, and perhaps the recovery, of that pristine language. Bacon's comments cited above make clear this goal, as well as that the object of the enterprise is power.

In all fairness to Bacon and the others having a part in creating the myth of scientific language, the battles they fought against Aristotle and scholasticism were begun long before the life of Aristotle himself. If it is true, as Alexandre Koyré asserts, that Galileo is essentially a Platonist in his thinking and that the Galilean legacy has a certain affinity with the Platonic legacy,[13] such is the case only because in Platonic dialogues may be found perhaps the earliest extant formulation of the myth of scientific language. Accordingly, this discussion of the myth should begin with a look at Plato.

The goal proposed by Socrates is not, properly speaking, scientific knowledge; rather, it is knowledge of the One, or the Good. Nevertheless, such knowledge is of "how things happen"—of process—and its reward is to be power. The education of Glaucon in the *Republic* aims to teach him how to use language to discover the truth, in order that he may be fit to lead; and the exile of the poets from the ideal *polis* that Glaucon is being trained to lead is justified on the grounds that their poems are second-order imitations of the essential truth—obfuscations of it rather than elaborations or elucidations.[14]

According to Socrates, to be a lawgiver speaking essential truth is to participate in a precedent as old as human language itself. In the *Cratylus*, both Socrates and the dialogue's namesake agree, despite their numerous disagreements, that the lawgivers are responsible for conferring names and that those names are the origins of language itself. The truth-status of these origins is a point of contention between Socrates and Cratylus and will be important in subsequent discussion of the myth. For now it is important to note that for Socrates these names are the vehicles of originary truth, as indeed all names properly given thereafter are the vehicles of essential truth. Socrates gets Hermogenes to agree "that there is but one principle of correctness in all names, the earliest as well as the latest," and that "the correctness of all names . . . was based on the intention of showing the nature of things named." The means of showing the nature of the object, according to Socrates, is sound-symbolism raised to the level of near-perfect mimesis.[15]

This notion of the nature and origin of language is used by Socrates as the pretext for doing dialectic. He gets Hermogenes to agree that lawgivers and judges are made, not born, and that the making entails learning how to ask questions and make replies in order to arrive at the vantage point that allows one a glimpse of originary truth. Then, facing Hermogenes, Socrates inquires, "And the man who knows how to ask and answer questions you call a dialectician?" "Yes, that is what I call him," Hermogenes replies (*Cr*, 31).

But the operations that proceed based on the myth of a scientific language never quite reconcile the outcome of those operations with the order described by the originary myth. Socrates can persuade Hermogenes that dialectic is the means to penetrate the ambiguities and uncertainties of everyday reality and that the goal of such activity is to arrive at the true and essential names (and principles) of things. But Socrates does not fare so well in his discussions with Cratylus, who is a sophist and a follower of Heraclitus.[16] To be both is to see language as an origin rather than as the access to originary truth and to believe that truth inheres in flux and process rather than in a stable order beyond flux and process. Cratylus is, furthermore, able to see the manner in which Socratic dialectic takes the polar oppositions in the very process of question-and-answer, coopting the subject who answers the question in the process of dissipating any potential for confusion about originary matters. That is, the strategy mobilized by Cratylus entails the refusal to allow one of the two options posed by the Socratic question to stand as the answer at once chosen by the subject and ratified by Socrates. For example, the principle of a perfect word-object language that may nevertheless be debased and abused depends on the Socratic assumption that one may speak either the truth or a lie, but not both at the same time. But Cratylus simply will not buy the inaugural assumption that it is a matter of either-or: "Why, Socrates, how could anyone who says that which he says, say that which is not? Is not falsehood saying that which is not?" (Cr, 155).

Socrates defers to the cleverness of Cratylus, as he is to do with increasing frequency throughout the remainder of the dialogue. What Cratylus has done is to hasten the unpacking of the Socratic position by positing an alternative notion of language origins, one that holds that language arises in the attempt to reconcile the antithetical elements and very nature of human experience itself, rather than in any attempt to rule out either pole of the antithesis. Socrates himself, even without the intervention of Cratylus, severely qualifies his own myth of language origins and at the same time reinstates the antithetical way of looking at the world with the shadows-on-the-cave-wall analogy of the Republic and the hermaphroditic origins myth of the Symposium, respectively. But at the end of the Cratylus, the sophist has shown the Socratic myth of language origins and his program of certain knowledge for what they are: an attempt to subvert antitheses rather than to mediate them, the attempt to subvert the world of process itself. While Socrates argues that if the Heraclitan notion of flux and antithesis is true, "no man of sense can put himself and his soul under the control of names and their makers to the point of affirming that he knows anything," he nevertheless reinstates the Heraclitan notion with a provisional affirmation that is itself an antithesis: "Perhaps, Cratylus, this theory is true, but perhaps it is not. Therefore you must consider courageously and thoroughly and not accept anything carelessly . . ." (Cr, 191).

In his closing remarks Socrates reveals the motives for his own language project when he consigns Cratylus to the countryside, while staying himself within the gates of the polis. The countryside is the place of natural origins—those of language as well as of the human species itself. The model Cratylus has advanced may hold true for the natural origins of language, but it is a model ill-suited to the large-scale managerial and problem-solving tasks one encounters in the highly structured, powerful systems of order like that of the city-state. That is, even if the Cratylan-Heraclitan model of language were naturally correct, it would be ill-suited for the tasks that are culturally mandated for the lawgiver of the *polis*. The same agenda of concerns operates in Bacon's myth of scientific language.

Bacon's myth of scientific language begins with the assumption that knowledge is power. The assumption is rather grittily stated as the third aphorism of *The New Organon*, although that is by no means Bacon's only articulation of the principle: "Human knowledge and human power meet in one; for where the cause is not known the effect cannot be produced. Nature to be commanded must be obeyed; and that which in contemplation is as the cause is in operation as the rule" (*NO*, 1.3).

For Bacon as for Socrates, perfect knowledge and power are pristine knowledge and power. In the case of Bacon, for whom Christianity is a force to be reckoned with, the pristine state has been specified as that occurring in the Garden of Eden, where the perfect word-object language spoken by Adam led to perfect human knowledge and power:

> the true end of . . . Knowledge is a restitution and reinvesting (in great part) of man to the sovereignty and power (for whensoever he shall be able to call the creatures by their true names he shall again command them) which he had in his first state of creation. And to speak plainly and clearly, it is a discovery of all operations and possibilities of operations from immortality (if that were possible) to the meanest mechanical practice.[17]

To make the myth of scientific language a reality, Bacon suggests a twofold program: first the corrupting influences must be recognized and extirpated; next, the corrupt language must be reformed in accord with the model posed by the perfect, pristine language. In an interesting move that has him playing Moses the lawgiver and scribe of the Edenic language, Bacon identifies for condemnation "idols" of four sorts. "To

these for distinction's sake I have assigned names, calling the
first class *Idols of the Tribe;* the second, *Idols of the Cave;* the third,
*Idols of the Market Place;* and fourth, *Idols of the Theatres" (NO,*
1.39). The way that these idols have been set up is through the
debasement of language. As an idol of the last sort, which is
identified interchangeably as an idol of theory, Aristotle occupies the same place of dishonor for Bacon as the sophists did
for Socrates. "Aristotle . . . corrupted natural philosophy [sci-
ence] by his logic: fashioning the world out of categories; as-
signing to the human soul, the noblest of substances, a genus
from worlds of the second intention" (*NO,* 1.63), and so on. The
remedy for these excesses, according to Bacon, is large doses of
that "science" of language, grammar. Only through using
grammar to work one's way back to the classical languages, and
thence to language before Babel, can the individual hope to
approach that lost power or language:

> Concerning speech and words, the consideration of them
> hath produced the science of grammar. For man still striveth
> to reintegrate himself in those benedictions, from which by
> his fault he hath been deprived; and as he has striven against
> the first general curse by the invention of the other arts, so
> hath he sought to come forth of the second general curse
> (which was the confusion of tongues) by the art of grammar;
> whereof the use in a mother tongue is small, in a foreign
> tongue more; but most in such foreign tongues as have
> ceased to be vulgar tongues, and are turned only to learned
> tongues.[18]

And yet, for all its positive outlook and energy, Bacon's
enterprise shows signs of the malaise that will ultimately doom
its posterity, the logical positivism of the early twentieth century. His own prose, which should be exemplary as the implementation of the language/science reform project, is often
vexed with apparent antitheses and self-contradictions of the
sort that began to worry Socrates toward the end of the *Cratylus.* Bacon's *Essays* are especially notorious in this regard. It
may be, as Stanley Fish has argued, that "the difficulty . . . lies
in the assumed equation of scientific and objective" and that in
Bacon's project "the mind has the role of villain," exhibiting a
tendency to hasty generalization, confusion of subject and object (or projection and reality), suppression of contradictory

and/or anomalous evidence, and ready seduction by the forms of language itself rather than by the phenomenal reality those forms allegedly report. It may be, in other words, that "these defects of knowledge are responsible for the confused state of knowledge at the present time"[19] in which Bacon writes. But the Baconian enterprise, notwithstanding the accolades of Cowley, Wilkins, and the Royal Society that claimed him as a spiritual progenitor, neither recovered the originary language it postulated nor attained the power and knowledge Bacon had set as *desiderata*. In fact, there is not a little irony in the fact that Bacon's life ended in disgrace owing to his own abuse of power while he was the solicitor of James I. One might also recall here that Socrates, for all his hopes of teaching the lawgivers to act justly and in accord with the knowledge made accessible through dialectic, was perceived by the rulers of Athens to be a corrupter of the city's youth and was given the choice of death or banishment.

This same myth of scientific language can also be seen in the work of Galileo and Newton. As Husserl points out, Galileo is responsible for the "surreptitious substitution of the mathematically substructed world of idealities for the only real world . . . our everyday life-world."[20] This activity had the force of substituting the *quadrivium* (arithmetic, music, geometry, astronomy) for the *trivium* (logic, rhetoric, grammar) as the fundamental notational and meaning base of the sciences. But as the *quadrivium* derives from the *trivium*—that is, cannot be spoken until the *trivium* is spoken—this substitution is yet another instance of attempting to posit the origins of scientific language as existing prior to the origins of ordinary language.[21] Galileo's motivations are quite visible in the introduction to the Third Day of *Dialogues Concerning the Two New Sciences*:

We bring forward [*promovemus*] a brand new science concerning a very old subject.

There is perhaps nothing in nature older than motion, about which volumes neither few nor small have been written by philosophers; yet I find many essentials [*symptomata*] of it that are worth knowing which have not ever been remarked, let alone demonstrated.[22]

Newton is an interesting amalgam of the tendencies found in Galileo and Bacon. The former English scientist subscribes to the notion of the *prisca sapientia,* or pristine wisdom of the sort allegedly engraved on the missing but presumably recoverable Smargadine tablets of Hermes Trismegistus. So on the one hand he apparently is anticlerical and antischolastic, as Galileo is. Yet Newton's principles of cause-and-effect, as they are set out at the beginning of Book 3 of *Principia Mathematica,* are covert references to the Genesis account that also provides a starting point for Bacon. And again like Galileo, Newton moves away from questions of origins with all deliberate and ob-fuscatory speed, mathematizing nature as quickly as he might.[23]

Lest the myth of scientific language appear to be an artifact that died out with the nineteenth or twentieth centuries, we might pause to consider the case of Einstein. The German-American physicist makes a distinction between the language of science and the language of art: "If what is seen and experienced is portrayed in the language of logic, we are engaged in science. If it is communicated through forms whose connections are not accessible to the conscious mind but are recognized intuitively as meaningful, then we are engaged in art. Common to both is the loving devotion to that which transcends personal concerns and volition." Thus far it seems as though the truths accessible to science and art (the humanities are interchangeable with the latter) are on the order of separate but equal. But then Einstein goes ahead and claims that this "language of logic" has access, however darkly, to the divinely ordained structure of the universe: "I do not believe in a personal God and I have never denied this but have expressed it clearly. If something in me which [*sic*] can be called religious then it is the unbounded admiration for the structure of the world so far as our science can reveal it." The being responsible for this structure, as Einstein says elsewhere, is God, immanent as "the intelligence manifested in nature."[24]

What accounts for this need to create a myth of scientific language? Of course, there is a need to justify the arrogation of power to oneself as a function of explaining how things happen in the universe. But this need has more to do with the logic of justification, in the Miltonic sense of explanation coupled with argument for the justice of providence, than it does with any objective notion of how things happen, if such a notion were, in fact, attainable. The need to create a myth, glimpsed in its largest sense, is the need to justify the use of language itself, as well as those activities made possible by language. In a certain sense, it is possible to see how the cases of *both* Socrates *and* Cratylus, *both* Bacon *and* the scholastics, have merit. Language has its beginning in antithesis, whether those origins are of the individual or his culture. The myth of the self, as Freud observes, descends from those "primal words" that we attach to our first experience of the world-as-process. Process brings change and change gives rise to antithesis—mother-present versus mother-absent, comfortable versus uncomfortable, and the like. Primal words accordingly mean in an antithetical mode, as both poles of process, until we have spoken ourselves along to greater coherence. "Peekaboo" denotes the process of absence to presence; "bye-bye," the same process played out in the opposite direction. The words, therefore, denote *both* absence *and* presence, not one or the other. Only when socialization and language acquisition have proceeded are the distinctions involved made sharper and more operative. Nevertheless, in the dream state one has access to these primal words and their originary contexts, which are both antithetical and the ground of all signification.[25]

Beyond the individual, the myths of a culture are likewise grounded in antithesis. Lévi-Strauss views myth as the attempt to mediate between antitheses and explain the culture into its present folkways by doing so. Is humanity descended from the gods or is it arisen from the primeval slime of the earth? Are we products of nature or products of culture? Myth says we are neither; myth says we are both; myth never says we are one or the other.[26] Even the myth of a scientific language is rooted in an earlier myth, itself an attempt to reconcile an earlier antithesis. The ground of all meaning, as Douglas R. Hofstadter has so eloquently argued, is antithetical regression. If there is an originary myth, it might as well be the paradox stated by the Cretan Epimenides, "All Cretans are liars." If Epimenides is right, then he is lying, so he cannot be right; but if he is lying, then he is telling the truth; but of course he cannot tell the truth by definition; and so on.[27]

In an apt anticipation of Hofstadter, the poet Shelley recognized that "every original language near to its source is in itself the chaos of a cyclic poem; the copiousness of lexicography and the distinctions of grammar are the works of a later age and are merely the catalogue and form of the creations of poetry."[28] True though this may be, Shelley's world, like Hofstadter's, is a world already spoken into existence. If language performance is still the prerogative of every native speaker, language competence is an assumed, innate capacity of all, unless otherwise demonstrated in the individual instance.[29] To say as much is to recognize the imperative felt by Socrates, Bacon, Galileo, Newton, Einstein, and uncountable others to get on with the work of doing the science or *technē* of one's choice rather than talking about it or about its impossibility. Vico makes the point quite well: primal poetry uttered by the giants who were the sires of the "greater gentes" was a means of reconciling their first profound awareness of absence and presence in the myth of Jove; but the "greater gentes" soon moved beyond that primal poem, at the same time using it as a basis for the elaboration of their wisdom, metaphysics, logic, morals, economy, politics, history, and the like. Once there was language, there were things to do with language.[30]

At the same time, because the justifications provided by language are tendered in the interest of maintaining the power of the speaking party, the myths of how things happen in the world are fraught with political significance. Galileo locked horns with a rather weak version of natural philosophy; but what nearly killed him was a potent regime of political tyranny in the form of the Inquisition, which viewed Galileo's thought as heretical, not the scholastic physicists who, if Simplicio is any epitome, were ready to cast off Aristotle anyway. Newton might well have lost his chair at Cambridge if he had expressed the covert Unitarian beliefs that caused him to assign as the source of universal gravity the absconded "Jeova sanctus unus," this notwithstanding the fact that pillars of orthodoxy like Boyle lauded his accomplishments in physics.[31] And Einstein's belief in the God of Spinoza did not help his reception in Germany before the rise of Hitler and mandated his emigration once that rise occurred. Despite causing him to deny irrationally the validity of Heisenberg's work, this belief seems, if anything, to have been an advantage in helping Einstein to arrive at the notion of nonrigid inertial systems, as well as that of a universe that is finite but unbounded.[32]

Nevertheless, the myth of scientific language has been a coercive force in its own right on more than one occasion. Placed in the hands of those in power, especially if those hands have control of language through the medium of written language, such a myth has the ability to foster schemes of order that deny the truth of individual experience. In one of his marvelous blanket indictments of the idea of order fostered by Enlightenment thought, including the thought of Newton and the *philosophes* intellectually responsible for the French Revolution, the poet William Blake professes to

> know too well that a great majority of Englishmen are fond of The Indefinite which they Measure by Newtons Doctrine of the Fluxions of the Atom. A Thing that does not Exist. These are Politicians & think that Republican Art is Inimical to their Atom. For a Line or Lineament is not formed by Chance. A Line is a Line in its Minutest Subdivision[s] Strait or Crooket. It is Itself & Not Intermeasurable with or by any Thing Else. Such is Job but since the French Revolution Englishmen are all Intermeasurable One by Another. Certainly a happy state of Agreement to which I for One do not Agree. God keep me from the Divinity of Yes & No too the Yea Nay Creeping Jesus from supposing Up & Down to be the same Thing as all Experimentalists must suppose.[33]

Nor is Blake's vendetta a relic of a bygone era. The positivists and their spokespersons are still among us, always and all too willing to propose their a priori categories, then carve up experience to fit—even willing to destroy science in the name of science. Eichner, for example, holds that "the Romantic 'research tradition' radically departed from the high road of modern science; that it attempted to undo . . . the methodological progress made since Galileo and Descartes; and that it proved unproductive in the sciences except where it compromised with the established methods it had set out to refute."[34] Eichner's argument is simply a recent revival of positivist nostalgia.

The methodology of Galileo, and Descartes as well, was none too clean, as Husserl, Koyré, and even Kuhn have shown. The alleged empiricism of Galileo often involved what Kuhn calls "analytical thought experimentation," which is done in one's head or one's cups, but not in one's laboratory. As a methodology it is quintessentially modern, but a good deal closer to the methods of Eichner's *Geisteswissenschaft* than to his *Naturwissenschaft*. Says Kuhn, "The analytical thought experimentation that bulks so large in the writings of Galileo, Einstein, Bohr, and others is perfectly calculated to expose the old paradigm to existing knowledge in ways that isolate the root of the crisis with a clarity unattainable in the laboratory."[35]

As to the productivity, or lack of productivity, of the romantic tradition, we should remember the centrality of the notion of metamorphosis, or becomingness, to romantic thought. While this notion may not have produced results in the thought and writings of the *Naturphilosophen*, the influence of the notion itself continued to be strong throughout the nineteenth century. Metamorphosis is a concept crucial to Lyell's geology and Haeckel's morphology alike. And even if one for some reason wishes to discredit these scientists individually, or to say that geology and biology are not "hard" sciences, or are "byways" departing from "the high road of modern science," Eichner's argument remains extremely questionable. The notion of eternal becomingness, as a restatement of the Heraclitan world view, influenced Pater and Nietzsche, to be sure, but it also influenced Hilbert and Einstein. The mathematical field equations of Hilbert, for example, bear witness to the importance of metamorphosis in his thought. As Leon Chai has recently argued, "content becomes less concrete, in a sense less 'absolute.' The affirmation of Heraclitus's concept of 'eternal flux' in Walter Pater and Nietzsche, and, in a very different realm, Hilbert's argument that the mathematical infinite can always be reduced to the finite, are reflections of this change."[36] This shift from Democritus (and Galileo and Newton) to Heraclitus (and Hilbert) is precisely isomorphic to the shift from mechanistic to organic metaphors that characterizes the romantic revolt. It is also the shift from stasis to becomingness that Carlyle envisions when he enjoins his reader to "close thy *Byron*; open thy *Goethe!*"[37] We may now understand how the dynamics of language acquisition itself may subsume and eclipse previous attempts to separate the objective and the subjective, the impartial and the interested.

One of the failures inherent in some, but by no means all, discussions of the methods and metaphysics of scientific inquiry has been to read the scientific text as though the stated intent of the author and the actual agenda of the text itself were one and the same. Many commentators, especially Karl Popper and his positivist supporters, have not sufficiently allowed for the nuances of point of view or the modalities of argument.[38] Students of literature, especially those trained during the halcyon days of the New Criticism, now old and defunct, would never dream of reading a text solely as the expression of authorial intent, lest they be charged with succumbing to the wiles of the "intentional fallacy." Every doctorate in literature knows that what Wordsworth says he does in the preface to *Lyrical Ballads* and what he actually does in the ballads themselves are not the same thing.[39] And yet the tendency has been to read scientific texts as though stated intention and accomplishment followed the identical agenda of concerns. Granted, as Holton has shown, science is in large measure responsible for perpetuating the myth of its value-neutrality and inevitability; but the time has come to see what happens when one shifts the emphasis from reading *science* to *reading* science.

Indeed, a scientific text, such as Newton's *Principia Mathematica* or Einstein's *Relativity: The Special and The General Theory*, invites, in fact begs, this shift of emphasis. Most exemplars of the genre begin with a mythic embryon, a small text about how the larger text came to pass. Thus most scientific texts (textbooks are not texts in this sense) can be viewed in a certain sense as expressionistic. They are, in other words, texts about their own making as texts. In that sense, the scientific text often contains a mythic element, cast in the form of a myth of self, that a careful reading can recover.

At this point, I should clarify the notion of a myth of self. Such a myth is intimately tied to the process of language acquisition itself—is, in fact, a means of mediating or attempting to resolve the antithesis that is the ground of linguistic meaning. That antithesis, it was stated above, has to do with the primal perception of process as a phenomenon comprising the movement from absence to presence or presence to absence, usually the former in the primal situation. Our sense of how things happen, to the extent that it is based on primal perception, is closely tied to our notion of how we "happen." During the course of acculturation, such primal perception merges with the culture's corpus of perceptions about how things happen. And in the case of myth in scientific language, the myth of self arising out of primal perception may influence the culture's corpus of perceptions about how things happen in the very process of merging with that corpus.

The dynamic in question can be approached from several different perspectives. Vico propounds the formula *verum et factum convertuntur*, which signifies "the idea that the concept of truth converts into the created or actually performed effect of some human action." As Howard N. Tuttle argues, "the *verum-factum* formula is true because knowing and being in the civil world—epistemology and ontology—are unified. The truth signifies the conversion of intelligible structures into human creations."[40] The process of conversion that Tuttle talks about has, for Vico, its origins in the language acquisition process. That process begins when thunder and lightning, the first radical demarcation of absence and presence in progress, occurs in the primal, prelinguistic world. The human inhabitants of that world

> were frightened and astonished by the great effect whose cause they did not know, and raised their eyes and became aware of the sky. And because in such a case the nature of the human mind leads it to attribute its own nature to the effect, and because in that state their nature was that of men all robust bodily strength, who expressed their very violent passions by shouting and grumbling, they pictured the sky to themselves as a great animated body, which in that aspect they called Jove . . . who meant to tell them something by the hiss of his bolts and the clap of his thunder (*NS*, 117–18, 119).

So, too, for Freud the origins of language are tied to the change from absence to presence and have the effect of projecting the ways of the individual "happens" onto the world of "things happening." That Freud chooses to ground language in sexual desire rather than religious awe is accidental rather than substantial, a function of cultural time and place and personal mythos rather than a deep-seated disagreement with what Vico has to say. As Lévi-Strauss has shown, the differing originary ground or premises of a given myth are less significant in their difference than is the dynamic of mediation significant in its similarity.[41] But to return to Freud: he summarizes with approval the work of the philologist Sperber, who argues that language has its origins in the process leading from sexual absence to sexual presence, and that, as it is subsequently used, language identifies the way things happen in undifferentiated process on the basis of that initially articulated sexual model:

> He [Sperber] says that the first sounds uttered were a means of communication, and of summoning the sexual partner, and that in later development the elements of speech were used as an accompaniment to the different kinds of work carried on by primitive man. This work was performed by associated efforts, to the sound of rhythmically repeated utterances, the effect of which was to transfer a sexual interest to the work. Primitive man made his work agreeable, so to speak, by treating it as the equivalent of and substitute for sexual activities. The word uttered during communal work had therefore two meanings, the one referring to the sexual act, the other to the labor which had come to be equivalent to it.[42]

Despite their superficial differences, Vico and Freud agree in one very important respect: the nexus of the myth of the self and the world of things happening is the act of metaphoric projection. The speaker understands how things happen in line with how he happens only after he has spoken the external world into coherence as the result of a "bodying forth" of sorts (*NS*, 129). At the primal level such bodying forth lends coherence to desire (Freud) or prohibition (Vico), or to a world compounded of desire and prohibition alike. But this union of ontology and epistemology still lacks an important element—a teleology. At a certain point, bodying forth ceases to be satisfactory by itself: stating *that* things happen or *how* things happen is not the same as understanding *why* things happen. One moves from silence to articulation, from antithesis to coherence, but for what purpose beyond the stasis of desire gratified or prohibition accepted?

The solution for the Judeo-Christian world in which most of the science and scientists under discussion have existed is apparently to adopt some form of theodicy. In its orthodox, religious context, such a theodicy posits a satisfying third term for the originary antithesis, which it interestingly enough reverses from absence-presence to presence-absence. There was a paradisiacal state, then there was a fall. This antithesis will be resolved by either a messianic era or a Messiah, who will return the righteous fallen to a state of paradisiacal innocence as good if not better than the original state. As the result of accepting this precept, the true believer suddenly has an answer for every why: Providence.

But a theodicy need not be orthodox to be operatively valid for an individual. Indeed, in the cases of Newton and Einstein, the lack of commitment to established Anglicanism and Judaism, respectively, does not prevent them from having very definite views on God's will, as it is established in their science. Speaking of the poet Wordsworth, but in terms that are suggestively applicable to this discussion, M. H. Abrams identifies what he calls "the theodicy of the private life . . . which translates the painful process of Christian conversion and redemption into a painful process of self-formation, crisis, and self-recognition, which culminates in a stage of self-coherence, self-awareness, and assured power that is its own reward."[43]

The original account of this process, according to Abrams, is Augustine's *Confessions*, which narrates the Bishop of Hippo's account of how he came to merge his myth of self with his culture's corpus of perceptions of how things happen, then found himself in a spiritual crisis arising from a desire to know why things happen. As a result of the crisis, Augustine undergoes conversion, the experience of which opens up teleology to him, making Augustine an expert on why all manner of things happen.

This synopsis of the *Confessions* is not without point: the work is a scientific as well as a religious text. Augustine is one of those Alexandrine polymaths whose desires include a "thirst to know the power and the nature of time, by which we measure the motions of bodies, and say, for example, this motion is twice as long as that." Augustine's desire is gratified only after his conversion, which makes accessible to him that perfect, mythic, prior language—one older than Greek or Latin and accessible to the inward perceptions of the saved only. This is the lawgiver's language sought by Socrates, the Adamic language sought by Bacon, the perfect calculus sought by Newton, the better mathematical language sought by all scientists who fail to realize that mathematical language, like Einstein's universe, is most assuredly finite if not in fact bounded. This perfect language makes itself known to what Augustine calls "memory":

The memory also contains the principles and unnumbered laws of numbers and dimensions. None of these has been impressed on the memory by a physical sense, because they have neither color nor sound, nor taste, nor sense of touch. I have heard the sound of the words by which these things are signified when discussed: but the sounds are one thing, the things another. For the sounds are one thing in Greek, another in Latin; but the things themselves are neither Greek nor Latin nor any other language.[44]

The net effect of a personal theodicy is to cause a perception of congruence, if not outright fusion, in the way the individual happens, the way things happen, and the articles of faith that constitute the individual notion of providence. Such a personal theodicy is the most articulate, but by no means the only, expression of the myth of self in scientific literature.[45]

In his psychobiography of Newton, Frank E. Manuel argues that Newton's circumstance of birth as a posthumous child led him to undertake a lifelong pursuit of the evidence that would confirm the existence of the absconded, unavailable father (Father?). Newton's belief that there is a connection between his lineage and divine providence is expressed more than once in Newton's notebooks by the anagram *"Isaacus Neuutonus—Jeova sanctus anus."*[46] The evidence that Newton finds for the existence of that absconded father-God is literally everywhere. The "General Scholium" at the end of Book 3 of the *Principia* argues down Descartes's idea of vortical planetary motion, in part by making the more regular circular or elliptical model of motion the result of the all-pervasive presence of the paternal *"Lord God* παντοκράτωρ, or *Universal Ruler.* . . . He endures forever, and is everywhere present; and, by existing always and everywhere, he constitutes duration and space" (*MP*, 543–47, esp. 544–45).[47]

Nor does Newton restrict his search for evidence of this father-son relationship to the laws and equations of mechanics, celestial or otherwise. He finds evidence for the veracity of his personal theodicy as the result of a close and curious reading of Biblical prophecy. The inertial system that is Newton's celestial universe seems to have been readily applicable as a model for the "motion" of those reconciled with their father-God after the Last Judgment: ". . . his survey of Old Testament prophecies and the Revelation of John led Newton to find proof that the earth will continue to be inhabited by mortals after the Day of Judgment, for ever and ever. On the day of his Coming, Christ will judge not only the dead but also the quick. . . ."[48] The "General Scholium" actually closes with a hint of the epiphanic and apocalyptic possibilities in store for the true believer able to open his heart and allow for the joining of the Spirit without and the spirit within:

> And now we might add something concerning a certain most subtle spirit which pervades and lies hid in all gross bodies. . . . But these are things that cannot be explained in few words, nor are we furnished with that sufficiency of experiments which is required to an accurate determination and demonstration of the laws by which this electric and elastic spirit operates (*MP*, 547).

Newton's textual hermeneutics in response to Biblical prophecy are certainly not without interest, but it is the physical realm of mechanics, whether terrestrial or celestial, that provides Newton most clearly with the middle term necessary for linking the personal and the providential. Newton's model for matter is a "bodied-forth" human projection that is acted on by "forces," all of which can in some way be traced to the father-God Newton seeks. If things happen as a result of divine forces, and if things happening are but a bodying forth of Newton himself, then the physical realities of the Newtonian universe may be said to reveal the design that adumbrates the metaphysical realities of Newton's relationship to his father-God.

This notion of bodying forth, mentioned above with Vico, is also a Newtonian concept. The "body" is the indivisible unit of Newtonian matter, whether that unit is posited as the basic constituent of mechanics, as in the *Principia*, or as the basic constituent of light, as in queries 30 and 31 of Book 3 of the *Optics*.[49] Moreover, the metaphor latent in the term *body* is exploited by Newton himself in his discussion of how one deduces the basic properties of the unit. There are five such properties—extension, hardness, impenetrability, mobility, and inertia—which in number correspond to the five senses. And one learns of these five properties by means of the senses. For example, "that all bodies are impenetrable, we gather not from reason, but from sensation" (*MP*, 399). That is, the "body" of Newtonian matter or the "corpuscle" (L. "little body") of Newtonian light, each with its five properties, is a projection of the human body, with its five senses. Newton creates matter in his image, as it were.

But there is an apparent contradiction between the five essential properties of matter and the five senses. The properties of matter seem all in all to betoken deadness, obduracy, transience, and insusceptibility to qualitative change, whereas the senses betoken life, flexibility, access to permanency, and the awareness of qualitative change. The apparent contradiction turns out to be evidence of the workings of Newton's personal theodicy. The argument in the conclusion of the *Optics* serves as a gloss on that theodicy, asserting as it does that the fall from pristine language and pristine wisdom after Babel "blinded" and "deadened" humanity in such a way that even the best and the brightest could only perceive the world as an aggregation of blind and dead bodies:

> And no doubt, if the Worship of false gods had not blinded the Heathen, their moral Philosophy would have gone further than to the four cardinal Virtues; and instead of teaching the transmigration of Souls, and to worship the Sun and Moon, the dead Heroes, they would have taught us to worship our true Author and Benefactor, as their Ancestors did under the Government of Noah and his Sons before they corrupted themselves (*O*, 405–6).[50]

Yet despite the apparent corruption of Newton's universe, that "true Author and Benefactor" still maintains a powerful efficacy as the First Cause of material phenomena and providence alike. Newton states in the concluding paragraph of the *Optics* that natural philosophy gives one access to knowledge of the First Cause and helps the individual frame a notion of duty in accord with providential elaborations of that first cause. In fact, one has access to such knowledge because Newton assumes at the outset that all material phenomena—the breath of life itself, motion, light—originate with the same God that has not been worshipped properly since Noah and his sons. The second of the "Rules of Reasoning in Philosophy" that preface Book 3 of the *Principia* states that the same natural effects originate in the same natural causes: "As to respiration in man and beast; the descent of stones in *Europe* and in *America;* the light of our culinary fire and of the sun; the reflection of light in the earth, and in the planets" (*MP,* 398). All of these natural causes may be traced back to that pre-Babel First Cause. Respiration in man, according to Genesis 2:7, is the result of *nephesh,* of God breathing the breath of life into the nostrils he has formed out of the dust of the earth itself. The descent of stones, the confounding of languages, and the imposition of gravitational limits to human aspiration are all the result of God's reaction to the building of the Tower on the plains of Shinar, as chronicled in Genesis 11:1–9. Creating the light of the sun is the act of God described in Genesis 1:16. Having created primal, undifferentiated light as his first act of creation, God then separates that light into sun, moon, and stars. Hence, this separation is also the cause of the first reflection, at least insofar as the moon and the planets, indistinguishable in primitive astronomy from the stars, reflect the light of the sun.

By elaborating the properties of the time- and space-bound universe of bodies, Newton hopes to establish the dependency of those bodies on the timeless, infinite presence of God as a First Cause. Insofar as the bodies are the surrogates or projections of Newton himself, he can establish his own relationship—indeed, kinship—to that first cause. Newtonian physics is the means for Newton to reaffiliate personally with God the Father, the father who is his God.

Though he sought no such personal reaffiliation, Einstein still conceived of a universe whose process and outcome are tied to the working out of a personal theodicy that links the world of the individual, the world of process, and a God responsible for the *telos* of the former and the workings of the latter.

The reason that Einstein does not seek personal reaffiliation is that his God is not the sort of anthropomorphic father-God of Newton. As Einstein says in a 1927 letter,

I cannot conceive of a personal God who would directly influence the actions of individuals, or would directly sit in judgment on creatures of his own creation. I cannot do this in spite of the fact that mechanistic causality has, to a certain extent, been placed in doubt by modern science. My religiosity consists in a humble admiration of the infinitely superior spirit that reveals itself in the little that we, with our weak and transitory understanding, can comprehend of reality. Morality is of the highest importance—but for us, not for God (*HS*, 66).

Some six years earlier, Einstein had specified his belief "in Spinoza's God, who reveals himself in the orderly harmony of what exists; not in a God who concerns himself with the fates and actions of human beings."[51]

Although Einstein's God does not appear to resemble Newton's to any great degree, his deity does reveal some traditional theistic trappings. First, its condition is that of absolute priority. Einstein had tried approaching physics without any *a priori* assumptions, such as the assumption of the existence of an order-giving spirit, but to no avail. At the beginning of *The Meaning of Relativity*, he complains "that the philosophers have had a harmful effect upon the progress of scientific thinking in removing certain fundamental concepts from the domain of empiricism, where they are under our control, to the intangible heights of the *a priori*." In order to rectify the situation, Einstein argues, it has been necessary for physics to appropriate the *a priori* categories of space and time from the realm of the numinous to the realm of the phenomenal. "This is particularly true of our concepts of time and space, which physicists have been obliged by the facts to bring down from the Olympus of *a priori* in order to adjust them and put them in a serviceable condition."[52]

Second, the appropriation that Einstein mentions so casually is actually the result of the experience of religious conversion, or something nearly akin to it. Beginning as Mach does, with no assumptions, failed to allow Einstein the latitude to conduct "analytical thought experimentation," the activity that Kuhn recognizes as one of Einstein's greatest scientific strengths. And yet there was something attractive in the iconoclasm of Mach's purely sensationalist epistemology. The crisis arising from the desire to see the world as it really is versus the desire to fathom its significance led Einstein to his conversion experience. "I began with a skeptical empiricism more or less like that of Mach. But the problem of gravitation converted me into a believing rationalist, that is, into someone who searches for the only reliable source of Truth in mathematical simplicity" (*HS*, 67).

Third, the conversion that takes place is to a belief in a living being, not a principle or formula. A 1942 letter to Lanczos expands on Einstein's initial response to Heisenberg's Uncertainty Principle ("God does not play dice with the Universe") to indicate his belief in a god that, while not anthropomorphic, at least has certain distinctly human order-seeking proclivities:

> You are the only person I know who has the same attitude towards physics as I have: a belief in the comprehension of reality through something basically simple and unified. . . . It seems hard to sneak a look at God's cards. But that he plays dice and uses "telepathic" methods (as the present quantum theory requires of him) is something that I cannot believe for a single moment (*HS*, 68).

The substitution of the card-playing metaphor for the dice-playing metaphor is interesting and significant. Cards, especially tarot cards, are the vehicle of fortune-telling, or theodicy, while dice are antitheodicy, as in the Roman soldiers' rolling dice for Jesus's clothes at the Crucifixion. On a more significant level, however, certain card games bind mathematical probability with laws or protocols of certainty in a way that dice cannot be bounded. Each time a die is rolled, assuming uniform distribution of weight over the mass and faces of the cube and a control over the uniformity of the rolling motion, the odds are one in six that a given face will turn up. The odds do not change with the number of throws, nor is it by any means certain that a given face will turn up at all in an infinite series of rolls. Card games such as casino or bridge, however, distribute all the cards evenly to all the players. In casino, if a given card—say, the good ten (of diamonds)—does not turn up on the first deal, the chances increase that it will turn up on the second deal. The odds against its appearance decrease from one in fifty–two to one in forty (the number of undealt cards remaining in the deck), and those odds continue to decrease until the end of the game or the appearance of the good ten, whichever occurs first. Once the card has appeared in a given deck of casino, there is zero probability that it will appear in that deck again. In bridge the entire deck is dealt, which means that all fifty-two cards are potentially in play. The odds of a given card appearing are further lowered by rules, such as following suit, declarer being able to play his and the dummy's hand at the same time, the lead being initially to the left of the declarer and thereafter in the hand of the person winning the trick, and so on. Such tactics as "finessing" for a potentially dangerous high card or "pulling trump" to improve one's own trick-taking ability with a cross-ruff are meant to reduce probability to certainty through the adoption of certain a priori assumptions and the implementation of a certain protocol in their behalf.

The net force of Einstein's card-playing metaphor is to confer all significance, whether of the individual or of the world of process, upon the systematic and comprehensive rather than the discrete and unique. This is the result of Einstein's belief in a God that creates systems of all sorts rather than monads of any kind. Just as no playing card has any numerical value independent of a system of values, no individual has any value independent of a system of individuals. The crisis of the post-World War II era, according to Einstein, "concerns the relationship of the individual to society," which is deteriorating on all fronts. According to Einstein, all human beings "feel insecure, lonely, and deprived of the native, simple, and unsophisticated enjoyment of life. Man can find meaning in life, short and perilous as it is, only through devoting himself to society."[53] And as for bodies in social systems, Einstein's included, so for bodies in inertial systems. "There is no absolute (independent of the space of reference) relation to space, and no absolute relation in time between two events, but there is an absolute (independent of the space of reference) relation in space and time . . . (*MR*, 30-31). Here Einstein begins to replace the Cartesian space-time coordinates with a space-time continuum, both space and time being, in Einstein's synthesis, cooriginal with light itself.

This replacement effectively unifies the world of the individual, the world of process, and the God responsible for both. An Old Testament God, although without the fatherly attributes of Newton's deity, the God in question is the one that by saying "Let there be light" brings the universe into existence. With the same sort of dissembling that leads Newton to say *"hypotheses non fingo,"* Einstein establishes his God as the primal source of all systems:

> The theory of relativity is often criticized for giving, without justification, a central theoretical role to the propagation of light. . . . In order to give physical significance to the con-

cept of time, processes of some kind are required which enable relations to be established between different places. It is immaterial what kind of processes one chooses for such a definition of time. It is advantageous, however, for the theory, to choose only those processes concerning which we know something certain. This holds for the propagation of light *in vacuo* in a higher degree than for any other process which could be considered. . . .

From all of these considerations, space and time data have a physically real, and not a mere fictitious significance. . . . (*MR*, 28–29).

Not only is the significance of the system of the universe and those who seek to understand it anchored in the propagation of light, but, according to Einstein, the very age of the universe itself may be determined on the basis of the deployment of the space-time continuum, which is to say the deployment of light, via the stars and star-systems that occupy space-time. The universe of Einstein is $10^9$ years old, and its origins coincide with the origins of a system of light: ". . . the 'beginning of the world' really constitutes a beginning, from the point of view of the development of the now existing stars and systems of stars, at which those stars and systems of stars did not yet exist as individual entities" (*MR*, 129).

If Einstein's God is the God of Light and Creator of the Universe known in the Old Testament and to the Israelites, then it is not too difficult to understand the nexus of theodicy and physics in Einstein's description. Rather than a personal messiah, Judaism awaits the advent of a messianic era in which people will unite to form a harmonious system, or community. Rather than a Last Judgment, Judaism believes in the revelation of the harmony and order of the universe that is God's creation, at which time error and unbelief will cease to exist. The physicist helps to promulgate system, or community, by understanding the principles on which physical systems are founded—principles that reveal an important analogue for social systems in revealing the harmony and order at the basis of the universe, while cleansing the world of error and unbelief. The religion of a physicist, according to Einstein, partakes of "the unbounded admiration for the structure of the world so far as our science can reveal it" (*HS*, 43). The moral imperative posed by this understanding is to make social order and natural order as nearly isomorphic as possible. Immortality, if it were possible, must be the immortality of structure. The physicist, whether proclaiming the Law of Conservation of Matter or pleading for the rapprochement of the individual and society, is the prophet of that structure.

In this brief summary I shall underscore some of the implications of the preceding two sections, as well as point the way for future study of some of the issues raised in those sections. Two of the implications seem especially germane. First, in a given period, it is highly likely that the myths and metaphors that privilege discourse will resemble each other across discipline lines much more closely than those myths and metaphors will resemble the figures within the same discipline at different times in its history. The second implication is logically and cognitively prior to the first, in a sense, but can only be recognized after the first: myth and metaphor are at the basis of the language that bounds all disciplines. Whatever may be the technological ramifications of a given interpretation of reality, one can only understand its psychological and affective ramifications by understanding the values and images latent in those myths and metaphors. A corollary to this second implication is that myth, metaphor, language itself—all are rooted in the body and its relationship to the otherness that surrounds it.

The first implication suggests that a unified study of discourse by period might approach its subject matter by fastening on a myth or metaphor characteristic of the period in question, as well as by understanding the transition from one period to another on the basis of the shift from one family of myths or metaphors to another. In the Europe of the Middle Ages and early Renaissance, for example, the metaphors and myths that privilege physics, statecraft, and poetry all set forth an explanatory model based on the immanence of force within bodies. Aristotelian physics describes objects as moving because they are endowed with the "potential" for doing so. The force or potential of movement exists immanently within the body in motion or capable of being in motion. The divine right of kingship is likewise a conception that makes force, in the form of God's will, immanent in the king who is God's vicegerent. Sir

162 STUART PETERFREUND

Philip Sidney's *Apology for Poetry* portrays the poet as a "maker,"
endowed with the same creative power within his universe of
words that God the Maker possesses in the universe.

Yet, by the end of the Renaissance and beginning of the
Enlightenment, force in the explanatory model has migrated to
a position outside the body. Immanence has been replaced by
obduracy, and the power of immanence has become abjectness
in its absence. As we have seen, the relationship of force and
body in Newtonian physics reverses the Aristotelian model.
The divine right of kingship has given way, at least in England
after the Civil War, to the conception of a large, potentially
destructive force existing in a "state of nature," which may
make the individual body's life "nasty, brutish, and short," to
use Hobbes's phrase, unless this force can be understood and
the individual's relationship to it stabilized. The protection of
life, liberty, and property that Locke sees as the main purpose
of civil government is accomplished by taking the potentially
destructive forces emanating from the state of nature and sta-
bilizing them. Lockeian civil government and the Newtonian
inertial system of the world have a good deal in common in
their description of the force-body relationship. John Dryden
feels cut off from the possibilities of immanence glimpsed by
Sidney. Dryden remarks that his is the age of "the second
temple"—the one built by the crabbed reason of uninspired
mediocrities rather than the divine inspiration of Solomon. The
poetry of the past is suddenly seen as a force that threatens the
individual poet, since he no longer possesses the immanent
force to recapitulate it.[54]

One possible reason for this reversal of polarities in the force-
body model common to all three discourses is that metaphors
themselves have a life-span. In Vico's model, they pass from
metaphor, to metonymy, to synecdoche, to irony, before the
occurrence of a *ricorso,* or renewal of this tropaic dialectic. If
irony gives the lie to the first figure, it stands to reason that the
figure emerging after the *ricorso* will oppose itself to the first
figure by somehow inverting or subverting it. But whether or
not one agrees with Vico, it is commonly understood that
metaphors undergo a process of decay, whereby they move
from a fresh and powerful explanatory status to the status of
metaphoricity to the status of dead metaphor to the status of
cliché. For example, after the rise of the city in the late Middle
Ages and early Renaissance, the metaphor "the body politic"

helped to explain the complex interactions of hierarchically ordered constituencies under the "headship" of a king inspired by immanent divine right. When Charles I lost his head in 1649, the metaphor's efficacy was correspondingly reduced. The literature of the period down through the Restoration abounds with images of physical disorganization, corruption, and decay—images in part arising from the fantasy projection of what it might be like to be a body ungoverned by a head. By the late eighteenth and early nineteenth centuries, the metaphor virtually ceases to exist. *Electorate* and *body politic* become nearly interchangeable terms. The phrase now sounds trite and tired, except, perhaps, when it is used for humor to describe a particular electorate (such as nudists) or a particular candidate (such as a strikingly attractive woman or a former athlete, male or female).

If myth and metaphor are at the basis of all disciplines, and if the relationship of the body to otherness is at the basis of all myth and metaphor, it is possible to understand the reversal of force-body models as the fluctuation between the complementary but paradoxical notions of priority. There is finally no definitive answer to whether the self comes before the other, or the other comes before the self, just as there is no originary truth but the truth of paradox itself to be derived from the statement "All Cretans are Liars." However, one makes the choice in the body-otherness paradox necessarily and arbitrarily, as a sort of inaugural *découpage*. If self precedes otherness, then the force-body model displays immanence. If otherness precedes self, then the force-body model displays forces acting on passive bodies.

Moreover, it is possible to see how this body-otherness paradox gives way to a preliminary taxonomy of discourses. It is no coincidence that physics focuses on the infinitesimal and the infinite (or nearly infinite), whereas literature, for example, focuses on individual human beings. The discourses of the *trivium*, from which the humanities are descended, are the discourses of the life-world. Their scale is apposite to their subject. The forces and bodies of the human life-world dictate that scale. The discourses of the *quadrivium*, from which the sciences are descended, are themselves descended from the *trivium*. Are these secondary discourses focused on a world that is larger or smaller than the life-world of the *trivium*? Are these secondary discourses focused on a world that is *both* larger *and* smaller than the life-world of the *trivium?* The paradoxical nature of the discourses that comprise the *trivium*—their very rootedness in paradoxicality itself—dictate that the universe addressed by the *quadrivium* be of both scales. Hence the microscope and the telescope, models of the atom and models of the universe. Between and at the origins of both the infinitesimal and the infinite stands the word-using human being, origin of metaphor, myth, and paradox alike, still occupying that medial position described by Pope in the *Essay on Man*, the one who is, for the sciences and the humanities alike, "The glory, jest, and riddle of the world."[55]

## NOTES

1. Jacob Bronowski, *Science and Human Values*, rev. ed. (1965; reprint, New York: Harper and Row, 1972), 38–40, makes the point in his discussion of Thomas Hobbes's discovery of Euclid. As Bronowski notes, "Even Euclid's geometry of the plane needs more than twenty axioms" (39–40). The theorem itself, of course, is the discovery of Pythagoras, and not Euclid. Gödel's discovery is recounted in *On Formally Undecidable Propositions* (1931; reprint, New York: Basic Books, 1962), which contains the paper on provability and some discussion of it. A helpful exposition of Gödel's discovery and its significance is found in Douglas R. Hofstadter, *Gödel, Escher, Bach: An Eternal Golden Braid* (1979; reprint, New York: Vintage Books, 1980), 17–19, 438–60, 696.

2. Bronowski, *Science and Human Values*, 12–13.

3. Gerald Holton, *The Scientific Imagination: Case Studies* (Cambridge: At the University Press, 1978), 237.

4. Hans Eichner, "The Rise of Modern Science and the Genesis of Romanticism," *PMLA* 97 (1982): 8–30 (esp. 25). For the "anarchist" and "cultural determinist" views of how language informs one's perception of the world, see, respectively, Paul K. Feyerabend, *Against Method: Outline of an Anarchistic Theory of Knowledge* (Atlantic Highlands, N.J.: Humanities Press, 1975); Benjamin Lee Whorf, *Language, Thought, and Reality: Selected Writings*, ed. John B. Carroll (Cambridge: M.I.T. Press, 1956).

5. See Edmund Husserl, *The Crisis of European Sciences and Transcendental Phenomenology*, trans. David Carr (1954; reprint, Evanston, Ill.: Northwestern University Press, 1970), 48–59.

6. See Thomas S. Kuhn, *The Structure of Scientific Revolutions*, rev. ed. (Chicago: University of Chicago Press, 1970), 171. See also Max Black, *Models and Metaphors: Studies in Language and Philosophy* (Ithaca, N.Y.: Cornell University Press, 1962) and Colin Murray Turbayne, *The Myth of Metaphor*, rev. ed. (Columbia: University of South Carolina Press, 1970).

7. See *The Philosophical Works of Francis Bacon*, ed. James Spedding, Robert Leslie Ellis, and Douglas Denon Heath, 12 vols. (Boston: Brown and Tagard, 1860–76), 3:222. See also *The New Organon, Or True Directions Concerning the Interpretation of Nature*, in *The New Organon and Related Writings*, ed. Fulton H. Anderson (New York: Liberal Arts Press 1960), 1:5–7. Subsequent references to *The New Organon* will appear in the body of the essay as *NO* plus the section and paragraph numbers.

8. Bronowski, *Science and Human Values*, 7.

9. For a survey of attempts to recover the Adamic language, see Stanley Fish, *Surprised by Sin* (New York: St. Martin's Press, 1967), 107–30. See also Russell A. Fraser, *The Language of Adam* (New York and London: Columbia University Press, 1977).

10. Actually, a very impressive start has been made toward understanding the relationship of language and power, principally by Michel Foucault. See *The Order of Things: An Archaeology of the Human Sciences* (New York: Random House, 1970). Foucault's treatment of the matter, however, is more synoptic and general than what is attempted here.

11. For the case as made by the Prague Circle theorists, see Bohuslav Havránek, "The Functional Differentiation of the Standard Language," and Jan Mukařovský, "Standard Language and Poetic Language," both in *A Prague School Reader on Esthetics, Literary Structure, and Style,* ed. and trans. Paul L. Garvin (Washington, D.C.: Georgetown University Press, 1967), 3–16, 17–30, respectively. For a telling rejoinder to the Prague Circle and their enormous linguistic progeny, see Stanley E. Fish's two essays: "How Ordinary is Ordinary Language?" *New Literary History* 5 (1973): 41–54; "Normal Circumstances, Literal Language, Direct Speech Acts, the Ordinary, the Everyday, the Obvious, What Goes without Saying, and Other Special Cases," *Critical Inquiry* 4 (1978): 625–44.

12. Holton postulates the existence of eight *themata* that influence scientific discourse. See his *Thematic Origins of Scientific Thought: Kepler to Einstein* (Cambridge: Harvard University Press, 1973), and *The Scientific Imagination,* 3–24.

13. Alexandre Koyré, *Metaphysics and Measurement: Essays in Scientific Revolution* (Cambridge: Harvard University Press, 1968), 16–43.

14. See John Sallis, *Being and Logos: The Way of Platonic Dialogue,* Philosophical Series, vol. 33 (Pittsburgh: Duquesne University Press, 1975), 401–48.

15. *Plato, with an English Translation,* trans. Harold N. Fowler, rev. ed., Loeb Classical Library, 12 vols. (1939; reprint, Cambridge: Harvard University Press, 1953), 6:131, 133. Subsequent references to this edition of the *Cratylus* will appear in the body of the essay as *Cr,* plus the page number.

16. Fowler states that Cratylus was a follower of Heraclitus on p. 5 of the "Introduction." Socrates himself implies it on p. 191.

17. *Philosophical Works of Francis Bacon,* ed. Spedding, Ellis, and Heath, 3:222.

18. *Bacon: The Advancement of Learning,* ed. William Aldis Wright, 5th ed. (1868; reprint, Oxford: Clarendon Press, 1926), 2.16.4.

19. Stanley E. Fish, *Self-Consuming Artifacts: The Experience of Seventeenth-Century Literature* (Berkeley, Los Angeles, and London: University of California Press, 1972), 78–85.

20. Husserl, *The Crisis of European Sciences,* 48.

21. For this gloss on Husserl, see James E. Swearingen, *Reflexivity in Tristram Shandy: An Essay in Phenomenological Criticism* (New Haven and London: Yale University Press, 1977), 27.

22. Galileo Galilei, *Two New Sciences, Including Centers of Gravity and Force of Percussion,* trans. Stillman Drake (Madison and London: University of Wisconsin Press, 1974), 190.

23. Isaac Newton, *Mathematical Principles of Natural Philosophy,* trans. Andrew Motte, rev. Florian Cajori (Berkeley and Los Angeles: University of California Press, 1934), 398–400. Subsequent references to this edition of *Mathematical Principles* will appear in the body of the essay as *MP,* plus the page number. Having made all sorts of hypotheses concerning divine causation and corpuscular matter in his "Rules of Reasoning in Philosophy," Newton posits the priority of observation and induction over

hypotheses in his fourth and final "Rule," enjoining the reader: "This rule we must follow, that the argument of induction may not be evaded by hypotheses." For a discussion of Newton's evasiveness in claiming to frame no hypotheses, see Turbayne, *The Myth of Metaphor*, 44–45.

24. *Albert Einstein, the Human Side: New Glimpses from His Archives*, ed. Helen Dukas and Banesh Hoffmann (Princeton: Princeton University Press, 1979), 37–38, 43. Subsequent references to this collection will appear in the body of the essay as *HS*, plus the page number. See also Loyd S. Swenson, Jr., *Genesis of Relativity*, Studies in the History of Science, vol. 5 (New York: Burt Franklin, 1979).

25. See Sigmund Freud, "The Antithetical Meaning of Primal Words," in *The Standard Edition of the Complete Psychological Works of Sigmund Freud*, ed. and trans. James Strachey, Anna Freud et al., 24 vols. (London: Hogarth Press, 1957), 11:153–61. See also *Language and Learning: The Debate between Jean Piaget and Noam Chomsky*, ed. Massimo Piatelli-Palmarini (Cambridge: Harvard University Press, 1980). Of special interest in the context of this discussion is the introductory essay by Piatelli-Palmarini, "How Hard Is the 'Hard Core' of a Scientific Program," 1–20. In that essay, Piatelli-Palmarini sees a kind of dynamism that links the language theories of Chomsky and Piaget in such a way as to transcend many of their superficial differences and disagreements. See especially 18–20.

26. See Claude Lévi-Strauss, "The Structural Study of Myth," in *Structural Anthropology*, trans. Claire Jacobson and Brooke Grundfest Schoepf (1958; reprint, New York: Harper and Row, 1963), 206–31; *The Raw and the Cooked (Le cru et le cruit)*, trans. John and Doreen Weightman (1964; reprint, New York: Harper and Row, 1969).

27. See Hofstadter, *Gödel, Escher, Bach*, 17–18.

28. In *Shelley's Prose, or the Trumpet of Prophecy*, ed. David Lee Clark (Albuquerque: University of New Mexico Press, 1954), 279.

29. The labels and distinction are Chomsky's. See Noam Chomsky, *Aspects of a Theory of Syntax* (Cambridge: M.I.T. Press, 1965).

30. See *The New Science of Giambattista Vico*, trans. Thomas Goddard Bergin and Max Harold Fisch, rev. ed. (Ithaca, N.Y.: Cornell University Press, 1968), 116–30. Subsequent references to Vico's *New Science* will appear in the body of the essay as *NS*, plus the page number.

31. For a discussion of Newton's relationship to his God, see Frank E. Manuel, *A Portrait of Isaac Newton* (Cambridge: Harvard University Press, 1968), 23–35, 51–67. The esteemed place of Newtonian thought in the Boyle Lectures has been discussed by Margaret C. Jacob in "Newtonianism and the Origins of the Enlightenment: A Reassessment," *Eighteenth-Century Studies* 11 (1977): 1–25.

32. Einstein's statement of belief is recorded in *Albert Einstein: Creator and Rebel*, ed. Bannesh Hoffmann, with Helen Dukas (New York: Viking, 1972), 95. The repudiation of Heisenberg is discussed by Swenson, *Genesis of Relativity*, 240–41.

33. *The Poetry and Prose of William Blake*, ed. David V. Erdman, comm. Harold Bloom (Garden City, N.Y.: Anchor-Doubleday, 1965) 707. This is the letter to George Cumberland, dated 12 April 1827.

34. Eichner, "The Rise of Modern Science," 24.

35. Kuhn, *The Structure of Scientific Revolutions*, 88.

36. Leon Chai, "Remarks on the Development of Theoretical Structure in Nineteenth-Century Thought," *Theory and History: Studies in the Philosophy of History* 21 (1982): 75–82 (quotation, 80). Stephen Jay Gould, *Ontogeny and Phylogeny* (Cambridge: Harvard University Press, 1977), would obviously disagree, given his view of the

centrality of recapitulation theory to modern science and social science alike, especially in the life sciences.

37. See Thomas Carlyle, *Sartor Resartus,* ed. Frederick William Roe (New York: Macmillan Co., 1927), chap. 15.

38. See Holton, *The Scientific Imagination,* esp. 1–20.

39. For a recent discussion of the discrepancy between Wordsworth's stated intent and the content of *Lyrical Ballads* itself, see Brian Wilkie, "Wordsworth and the Tradition of the Avant Garde," *Journal of English and Germanic Philology* 72 (1973): 194–222.

40. Howard N. Tuttle, "The Epistemological Status of the Cultural World in Vico and Dilthey," in *Giambattista Vico's Science of Humanity,* ed. Giorgio Tagliacozzo and Donald Phillip Verene (Baltimore and London: Johns Hopkins University Press, 1976), 241–50, esp. 244–45.

41. For example, "Structural Study of Myth," in *Structural Anthropology.*

42. Sigmund Freud, *A General Introduction to Psychoanalysis,* trans. Joan Riviere, rev. ed. (New York: Pocket Books, 1953), 174–75.

43. M. H. Abrams, *Natural Supernaturalism: Tradition and Revolution in Romantic Literature* (New York: W. W. Norton, 1971), 96.

44. *Augustine: Confessions and Enchiridion,* trans. Albert C. Outler, Library of Christian Classics, vol. 7 (Philadelphia: Westminster Press, 1955), 10.12.19.

45. See Holton, *The Scientific Imagination,* 229–52, for a discussion of the institutional, self-perpetuated myth of science and scientist.

46. See Manuel, *A Portrait of Isaac Newton,* 23–25, 51–67.

47. I have treated Newton's passage at greater length in "Blake and Newton: Argument as Art, Argument as Science," *Studies in Eighteenth-Century Culture* 10 (1980): 205–26.

48. Holton, *The Scientific Imagination,* 273. For Newton's theory of the Apocalypse, see his *Observations on the Prophecies of Daniel and the Apocalypse of St. John in Two Parts,* 2 vols. (London: J. Roberts, 1733).

49. Isaac Newton, *Opticks, or a Treatise of the Reflections, Refractions, Inflections & Colors of Light,* ed. I. Bernard Cohen (New York: Dover, 1952), 374–405. Subsequent references to this edition of the *Optics* will appear in the body of the essay as *O,* plus the page number.

50. On the notion of a pristine language and the *prisca sapientia,* or pristine wisdom, see J. E. McGuire and P. M. Rattansi, "Newton and the 'Pipes of Pan,' " *Notes and Records of the Royal Society of London* 21 (1966): 108–43.

51. *Albert Einstein,* ed. Hoffmann, 95.

52. Albert Einsten, *The Meaning of Relativity,* trans. Edwin Plimpton Adams and Ernst G. Staus, 2d ed. (1922; rpt. Princeton: Princeton University Press, 1946), 2. Subsequent references to this work will appear in the body of the essay as *MR,* plus the page number.

53. Albert Einstein, *Out of My Later Years* (New York: Philosophical Library, 1950), 123.

54. For a fuller account of Dryden's feelings and their significance for literature after the Renaissance, see Walter Jackson Bate, *The Burden of the Past and the English Poet* (Cambridge: Belknap Press of Harvard University, 1970); and Harold Bloom, *The Anxiety of Influence* (New York: Oxford University Press, 1973).

55. In *Poetry and Prose of Alexander Pope,* ed. Aubrey L. Williams (Boston: Houghton Mifflin, 1969), Ep. II, 1.18.

# Creative Problem-solving in Physics, Philosophy, and Painting: Three Case Studies

DONALD A. CROSBY and RON G. WILLIAMS

*Colorado State University*

In this essay we intend to show that the creative process in the humanities does not differ fundamentally from that in the sciences and, in fact, shares a common structure with it. We also discuss certain views of the relationship of the humanities to the sciences that we believe are called seriously into question by the fact of this common structure of creativity. Our method for proving these points is a close comparison of three case studies of the creative process. The first, from the field of physics, represents the sciences; the other two, one from philosophy and one from painting, epitomize the humanities.

The most striking examples of creativity, from whatever field, seem always to incorporate five major elements, called here *impetus, environment, innovation, justification,* and *regularization.* The impetus for these notable acts of creativity is some problem that requires solution but resists it along conventional lines, some felt incompleteness or incoherence in current outlook, or the gnawing sense that an aspect of a field has reached a dead end and become implausible, tedious, or unproductive. In short, creative breakthroughts in a field are usually spurred by feelings of puzzlement, dissatisfaction, or impasse.

But however radical these breakthroughs may prove to be, they do not occur in a vacuum; that is, they are never purely spontaneous or *ex nihilo.* They always take place against the background of the environment of the field itself, which includes its accomplishments to date, its basic assumptions and

168

approaches (including those that define it as a field), its organizations, and the shared language or sign system that facilitates its investigations and communications. In a television interview just before her death, Margaret Mead observed that "institutions are what make heresy possible." The same can be said of creativity. Factors in the larger environment outside the field may also prove to be important in providing a context for creativity within the field.

Though greatly shaped and influenced by environmental features, the creative act is of course not entirely controlled by them. It exhibits sometimes startling innovations, which propose new contributions to the field, or select certain of its features as essential (relegating the others to the status of the merely accidental and thus dispensable), or draw upon exploited resources in its history, or introduce important revisions into its methodology or sign system—all as ways of responding to the impetus mentioned above. Thus, certain aspects of the environment provided by the field are assumed and continued, while others are made liable to change. The liability to change in the field also creates possibilities for change in the larger environment affected by the field.

It is sometimes thought that a high degree of originality, novelty, or innovation is enough to make an act or proposal creative. But this is by no means true. For an act to be creative, it must satisfy relevant criteria of the field of endeavor it represents, and it must come to be recognized as a creative contribution by a community of persons competent to judge its worth. In other words, a putatively creative act becomes such in fact only when it has undergone a process of justification (or legitimation), however long that process may take. Does it solve the problems it set out to solve, or at least make a decisive advance toward their solution? Does it open up promising new directions for future activity and research? Is it plausible, provocative, exciting? Is it internally coherent or elegant, and is it compatible with well-established methods, assumptions, and practices of the field? Does it come to be frequently noted and made use of by others in the field? Does it stand the test of time and prove to be more than a passing fad? Does it inspire new acts of creativity? These and similar kinds of questions bear on the element of justification and point up an essential difference between mere innovative proposals, however ingenious, and genuine acts of creativity.

Closely allied to the element of justification is regularization. With the passage of time, a creative advance in a field will lose its novelty and become a regular feature of the field, now taken for granted as part of its history of development, list of accomplishments, and standards practices and beliefs. In this way the advance will have helped to produce a new environment to serve as the established context for new acts of creation. The new environment will give impetus to these new acts in the same way the older environment did, by its own stock of problems, perplexities, and frustrations that cry out for creative resolution. The process of creativity thus invariably turns back upon itself and begins afresh, not like the snake eating its tail, but more like Antaeus returned to the earth, there to gain strength and incentive for the battles that always lie ahead.

### A Case From Physics: James Clerk Maxwell's "Physical Lines of Force"

James Clerk Maxwell (1831–79) made many fundamental contributions to physics in his relatively short lifetime. Einstein and Infeld speak of his formulation of his famous field equations as "the most important event in physics since Newton's time."[1] We will focus on one sample of Maxwell's creative genius, namely, his development of a mechanical model for explaining and unifying various phenomena of electricity and magnetism that had come to light in the researches of his predecessors and contemporaries, especially those of his older contemporary, Michael Faraday. The *textus locus* is contained in three of Maxwell's papers published in the *Philosophical Magazine* in 1861 and 1862, jointly entitled "On Physical Lines of Force."[2] Here he presented a theory of "molecular vortices," applying the theory to magnetic phenomena, electric currents, and static electricity, the respective subjects of the three papers. We will outline this mechanical theory and give one illustration of its use, but our principal intent is to show how the development and impact of the theory can be placed in the context of the five phases of the creative process sketched above.

1. *Impetus:* In order to understand the impetus for the papers of 1861 and 1862, we need to recall an earlier paper of Maxwell's, "On Faraday's Lines of Force," delivered before the Cambridge Philosophical Society in late 1855 and early 1856

(*SP*,1:155–299). In this paper Maxwell had endeavored to give exact mathematical form to Faraday's conception of lines of electric and magnetic force "by referring everything to the purely geometrical idea of the motion of an imaginary fluid" (*SP*,1:159). His purpose was not to give a physical explanation of the causes of such forces, but only to analyze and relate them in a purely geometrical manner, using the analogy of a fluid to the extent that it served his purpose.

But Maxwell considered his earlier paper to be lacking in an important respect, although it had made a significant advance toward unifying and simplifying mathematically the various results of Faraday and other researchers in the field of electricity and magnetism. Its deficiency was that it offered only an abstract mathematical analysis and gave little or no recognition to the need to understand in a physical sense how various electromagnetic phenomena work, how they are connected, and how they are caused.[3] In his 1861–62 papers Maxwell proposed to make up for this deficiency by developing an hypothesis of motions and stresses in a physical medium as being the underlying common cause of all electric and magnetic events and their interrelations. Such an hypothesis could give a unifying and simplifying explanation to these events from another, more physical direction. And it could serve as the basis for new mathematical calculations, which could be compared with previous experimental results and established laws, as well as being subjected to the tests of new experiments that the hypothesis itself would suggest. Thus his desire to develop this kind of hypothesis as a complement to the more abstract mathematical treatment of his 1855–56 paper, and as a contribution toward resolution of the deep puzzle about the physical basis of electromagnetism, constitutes the impetus for Maxwell's creative achievements in his 1861–62 papers.

2. *Environment:* In considering the problems and challenges that provide the impetus for creative acts, one must also take into account the context in which those problems and challenges are presented to creative persons. In other words, as already noted, we must understand the environment in which they do their work. Maxwell's environment was of course that of nineteenth-century Newtonian physics. But for our purposes it consisted of accomplishments and problems in the rapidly developing sciences of electromagnetism. People like Cavendish (1731–1810), Coulomb (1738–1806), Volta (1745–

1827), Laplace (1749–1827), Ampère (1775–1836), Oersted (1777–1851), Poisson (1781–1840), Ohm (1787–1854), Faraday (1791–1867), Weber (1804–91), and Thomson, later Lord Kelvin (1824–1907), had all fashioned significant parts of the jigsaw puzzle of trying to comprehend and relate electric and magnetic events, in a tremendous spurt of discovery from the latter part of the eighteenth century up to Maxwell's time. It was Maxwell, more than any other person of his century, who possessed the fecundity of mechanical and mathematical imagination to assemble these scattered pieces into a single pattern.[4]

Another aspect of Maxwell's environment was the debate then going on over the question of action at a distance versus action in a continuous medium. In a paper entitled "Action at a Distance" (SP,2:311–23), Maxwell noted that the idea of action at a distance had stemmed, in a sense, from Newton himself, although the great English physicist very much wanted to find some account of gravitational forces that could explain them in terms of contiguous motions of a medium. In a letter to Bentley (quoted by Maxwell), Newton had stated that he thought it a "great . . . absurdity" that action at a distance should be considered a real fact of nature. Still, he did not publish the speculations in which he tried to account for gravitation by means of the pressures of a medium because he was unable, by experiment and observation, to give a satisfactory account of this medium or of its operations. The editor of Newton's *Principia* in his lifetime, Roger Cotes, had taken it upon himself to assert in his preface to the work that gravitation is an essential property of matter, just like extension, mobility, and solidity, and that action at a distance occurs routinely. Thus the notion of action at a distance came to be associated with Newton's name (SP,2:318).

This notion was assumed by Cavendish, Lagrange (1736–1813), Coulomb, Laplace, Poisson, and others in their studies of gravitational attraction and of the attractions and repulsions of magnetic and electrified bodies. By Faraday's time, action at a distance was the received doctrine in physics. Maxwell granted that these studies had made great strides and led to the discovery of true laws of the forces concerned. But he also considered them to be incomplete because they made no attempt to explain *how* the attractional (or repulsive) forces are transmitted from body to body across intervening space (SP, 2:318–21). He thought that the distribution of iron filings around the poles of magnets gave convincing evidence that the interactions of magnets can be explained as the effects of changes in a contiguous medium, and he was much taken with Faraday's attempts to comprehend electromagnetic events in this manner, with his "lines of force" (*SP*, 1:451–52; 2:319–21).[5] Furthermore, Maxwell believed that the idea of action at a distance, in many of the forms of which it had come to be propounded, violated the law of the conservation of energy (*SP*, 1:208, 488, 526–27).[6]

A number of developments in the environment of nineteenth-century physics anticipated Maxwell's hypothesis that electromagnetic events could be explained by the motions of vortices in a material medium. For example, Oersted had discovered that an electric current acts neither by attraction nor repulsion upon a pivoted magnet, but causes it to position itself at right angles to the plane of the flow of the current. This led him to say that "the electric current acts in a revolving manner" and to surmise that there are material vortices surrounding the current and exerting force on the magnet.[7] Ampère had argued that molecular currents "flow around each of their particles," thus accounting for magnets' attractional and repulsive properties.[8] Helmholtz (1821–94) applied to electromagnetism his precise studies of the actions of vortices in a fluid. Both Maxwell and Thomson drew upon these studies (*SP*, 1:488n., 503; 2:306–7).[9] Thomson had developed a vortex hypothesis in his own investigations of electromagnetism, and Maxwell was greatly influenced by his work (*SP*, 1:209, 453, 505; 2:305–6).[10] Finally, both Maxwell and Thomson were strongly inclined toward the vortex interpretation by Faraday's discovery of the rotation of the plane of a beam of polarized light when it is brought under the influence of a magnetic field (*SP*, 1:504; 2:305–7, 322).[11] So there was much in the environment in which Maxwell worked that set the stage for his creative achievements in the 1861–62 papers.

3. *Innovation:* The numerous innovations in Maxwell's papers were to have revolutionary consequences for the future of physics. However, this sample relates to only four interrelated problems and to the unifying solution Maxwell proposed for these problems. First, what is an electric current? Second, how does an electric current set up an electromagnetic field? Third, what goes on in a permanent magnet? And fourth, when a

magnet is suspended within a circle of wire carrying a current, why does the magnet turn to a position at right angles to the plane of the wire?

Maxwell conceived the idea that when a conductor such as a copper wire is attached at its ends to the positive and negative poles of a battery, small particles within the wire will be set in motion, rolling through it from the positive toward the negative pole of the battery. So long as the battery's chemical action is sustained, this rolling action of the particles will continue, for after passing out of the wire at the negative pole, they will enter it again at the positive pole. The image suggested is something like that of a tube filled with marbles, tilted so that they roll through it, with new marbles continuously being supplied at the high end. This is not quite right, though, for we are talking here of a circuit and of the same supply of particles constantly being cycled through it. Moreover, the particles are not rolling in a tube but along a path among adjoining vortices. As these small rolling particles pass into and out of the molecules of the wire, they will experience resistance, thus generating frictional heat in the wire. In Maxwell's model, therefore, an electric current is constituted by these rolling particles (*SP*, 1:471, 486–87).

But how does such a current produce an electromagnetic field? Maxwell's answer is that the field is created by vortices (or rotating "cells," as he sometimes terms them) adjoining the rolling particles, as the vortices are set in motion by the movement of the particles. These vortices are much larger than the particles, and rows of such particles constitute the boundaries of each vortex. When the particles on one side of a vortex move, as in an electric current, the vortex itself moves and imparts its motion, in turn, to other vortices in the conducting medium and in the surrounding medium (for example, in the air around a wire conducting a current). The motion of one vortex is imparted to another vortex by means of the particles intervening between it and the next vortex. These particles, unlike the ones in an electric current, just revolve in place rather than moving to different places in a molecule of their medium or from molecule to molecule. They function like idler wheels, moving frictionlessly between vortices. The motions of these vortices, first within the conducting medium and then in the medium outside it, are what produce an electromagnetic field. As the vortices spin rapidly, they expand in the direction of their equators by centrifugal force. This produces a pressure in that direction. But it also produces a lessening of pressure, or what Maxwell calls a "tension" along their axes. Since concentric rings of vortices surround the flow of electrical particles at every point, with their axes in a plane at right angles to that of the flow, there will be lines of tension at right angles to the flow. These lines of tension Maxwell associates with Faraday's lines of magnetic force.[12] In order to see how a pivoted magnet will be affected by these lines of tension, we will have to look first at what, according to Maxwell's model, goes on in a magnet.

Like Ampère, Maxwell thought of a magnet as having whirling vortices within it. He reasoned further that these vortices are lined up in such a way that they are mostly spinning in the same direction. He assumed that the direction of motion of the vortices is clockwise when we are looking at them from the south end of the magnet toward its north end. Since the particles in contact with the vortices are not moving through molecular boundaries, there is no friction, and no heat or waste of energy, which explains why a magnet maintains its polarity over long periods of time. Experiments with iron filings had shown that there is a distribution of filings in curves from one pole to the other outside the magnet, and Maxwell pictured the lines of magnetic force as spreading out from the magnet at its north end, to enter it again at its south end. These lines of magnetic force he explained as tensions created by the axes of the rotating vortices of the magnet and then of its surrounding medium, just as with the vortices within and outside of a conducting wire.

When a pivoted magnet is brought within the circle of wire carrying a current, the vortices along the lines of force of the ends of the magnet will either be speeded up or retarded by the vortices of the magnetic field created by the wire, depending on whether the vortices of magnet and field are rotating in the same, and thus mutually reinforcing, or different, and thus mutually impeding, directions in relation to one another. If speeded up, this will cause an increase of tension along the axes of the lines of force on that side of the magnet. If retarded, it will cause a lessening of tension at that side of the magnet. This disequilibrium of tensions will cause the pivoted magnet to be deflected toward the lines of greater tension. In this way, a magnet will orient itself along the lines of tension created by the current-carrying wire, and in such a way that its internal vortices will be rotating in the same direction as the vortices around these lines of tension.[13]

With this physical hypothesis Maxwell sought to account for electromagnetic events and their interrelations in terms of the motions and changes of a contiguous medium, filled with vortices and their bounding particles. It was an attempt to explain electromagnetic events in the spirit of Newton's great dream of explaining gravitational interactions by means of the pressures of an all-surrounding ether. The work of the 1861–62 papers was a tour de force of the creative imagination with crucial import for the subsequent development of physics, despite the fact that the physical hypothesis Maxwell proposed did not gain wide acceptance. He was well aware that in some respect his hypothesis was awkward, and he insisted on its "provisional and temporary character." But he hoped that it would have significant heuristic value for himself and other theorists in their quest for the "true interpretation of the phenomena" (*SP*, 1:486; 2:306). In this hope he was not to be disappointed.

*4. Justification.* There were a number of respects in which the work of the 1861–62 papers was to achieve justification in the judgment of Maxwell's scientific peers. We will mention three of them. First, by working out the mathematical relations suggested by his physical model, Maxwell was able to encompass many known laws and experimental facts,[14] as well as to make new mathematical predictions and discoveries. He here prepared the way for the "General Equations of the Electromagnetic Field," which were to be his greatest single contribution as a physicist. He gave the first complete formulation to these equations in a paper published in 1864 entitled "A Dynamical Theory of the Electromagnetic Field" (*SP*, 1:526–97). Second, Maxwell calculated the velocity of electromagnetic propagations on the basis of his model and found this velocity to be very close to the then current calculations of the velocity of light. He thus concluded that "light consists in the transverse undulations of the same medium which is the cause of electric and magnetic phenomena" (*SP*, 1:500). Or, as he stated in the 1864 paper, light "is an electromagnetic disturbance in the form of waves propagated through the electromagnetic field according to electromagnetic laws" (*SP*, 1:535). This unification of light and electromagnetism was one of the great unifications in the history of science, to be ranked beside the unification of electricity and magnetism. Third, by the time of the publication of Maxwell's *Treatise on Electricity and Magnetism* in 1873, belief in action at a distance had been largely abandoned by physicists in favor of the idea of action in a medium.[15] This change was due in no small part to the work of Maxwell, including the work of his 1861–62 papers. It was a momentous change, for it led to the eventual triumph of field theory, as a third alternative to the two possibilities of action at a distance and action in a physical medium.

5. *Regularization:* Over time, certain ideas, developments, and discoveries that were contained in or presaged by the 1861–62 papers came to be a part of the normal environment of physics and thus to serve as the background for fresh innovations in the future. One of these was the vortex idea, which influenced physicists to think of matter as having an inherently dynamic character, and which was one of the important formative elements leading to the modern concept of the atom. In speculating about the changes of their form whereby spinning vortices might excite the rays of the spectrum, Maxwell commented in a later paper: "It would puzzle one of the old-fashioned little round hard [Newtonian] molecules to execute vibrations at all. There was no music in those spheres" (*SP,* 2:307).

Maxwell's field equations, an early version of which was worked out in the 1861–62 papers, also entered into the settled environment of physics. As these equations came increasingly into use, a surprising thing happened. Although they had been arrived at on the basis of speculations about the properties of a material medium connecting the phenomena of electricity, magnetism, and light, physicists came gradually to think of the field described by these equations as a reality in its own right. Analogies with fluid flow, elastic substances, and whirling vortices had helped to bring the idea of the field into being, but once that idea had been given a firm mathematical description, these particular analogies tended to drop into the background. Maxwell himself, in his 1864 paper, said that mechanical hypotheses, such as the one developed in the 1861–62 papers and still often alluded to in the 1864 paper, were to be considered only as illustrative and as aids to the imagination, and not to be taken literally. He then added a prescient sentence: "In speaking of the Energy of the field, . . . I wish to be understood literally" (*SP,* 1:564). He had not given up the dream of explanation in terms of a physical medium, and he never gave it up in his lifetime. But he already saw that the mathematical descriptions of the field were explanatory in their own right, and that he did not need to be as tentative about them as he had to be about his physical speculations.

In other words a new way of thinking was being opened up by the powerful new language of Maxwell's field equations. It was a new language about changes in the structure of the fields surrounding bodies, not the old language about action at a distance or about motions of hypothetical physical media. Maxwell's papers of 1861–62 were a kind of watershed from the old style of physics to the new. They faced backward to Newton's vision of mechanical interactions in a material medium and forward to belief in the concept of the field. With the passage of time, as Mary Hesse notes, physicists no longer asked how the field assumed by the new language is produced in a mechanical sense; the question itself was coming to be seen as a dubious one, or perhaps as one without any clear meaning.[16] The regularization of Maxwell's idea of the field in the early twentieth century stands out particularly well in a statement from Alfred N. Whitehead's *Science and the Modern World*, first published in 1925: "Mathematical physics presumes in the first place an electromagnetic field of activity pervading space and time."[17]

## A Case from Philosophy: Bertrand Russell's Theory of Descriptions

It is well known that in the two decades surrounding the turn of the century a revolution took place in logical theory, philosophy, and mathematics. From 1900 to 1910 Bertrand Russell and Alfred N. Whitehead completed the bulk of *Principia Mathematica*.[18] Building on the insights of Peano and Fregé, they developed modern predicate logic and sought to ground the axioms of much of mathematics in the axioms of logic.[19] It was an accomplishment of the highest order, which R. B. Braithwaite later characterized as coequal with the Theory of Relativity and one of the two great achievements in this century in the realm of pure thought.[20] A small but significant part of this achievement was Russell's Theory of Descriptions, first published in *Mind* in 1905.[21]

Russell's goal in this paper was to develop what one might now call an illuminating deep-structural description of such statements as "The present King of France is bald."[22] His claim was that though these sentences appear to contain a denoting term (name) as subject, their real grammar is otherwise. On his analysis, the statement is used to assert that there exists one and only one entity such that it is the present King of France and it is bald. In this paraphrase no denoting expression like "the present King of France" occurs; in fact, that phrase now occurs only as part of the predicate, "_____ is a present King of France." Phrases like "the present King of France" are known as definite descriptions, and Russell's paper offered a way to translate sentences containing definite descriptions into the austere artificial language of predicate logic.[23]

Though the paraphrase he offers may seem straightforward or even trivial, its repercussions in philosophy, logic, and the foundations of mathematics can hardly be overemphasized. In asking how he came to his analysis, we are asking what it is to solve a major puzzle in logic.

> A logical theory may be tested by its capacity for dealing with puzzles, and it is a wholesome plan, in thinking about logic, to stock the mind with as many as possible, since these serve much the same purpose as is served by experiments in physical science.
> —Russell, "On Denoting"

*1. Impetus:* When Russell set about the task of giving an adequate analysis of sentences containing definite descriptions, he was haunted, or at least enticed, by certain puzzles to which more traditional treatments of definite descriptions had given rise. He was also intent upon criticizing a then current metaphysical view about what sorts of entities make up the world. Four puzzles to which he responded follow:

A. Russell wanted to find a way out of the following impasse: the following four claims, though plausible, are mutually inconsistent.

(a) A name, or any denoting expression, is meaningless if it lacks a referent. In its crudest form, this is the thesis that the meaning of a denoting expression *is* its referent. If asked what "Frank" means, all we can do is indicate Frank. And one might claim that "Eric Fischer was here last night" is meaningless if there is no such creature as Eric Fischer.

(b) Sentences like (i) "The present King of France is bald" contain as their subjects denoting expressions.

(c) Intuitively (i) is a meaningful sentence; we understand what state of affairs would make it true.

(d) But on the assumption that there is no such king, (i) would be meaningless, because, from (a), it contains a meaningless subject term.

Paradoxically, then, (i) is both meaningful and meaningless, if the king does not exist. Versions of this puzzle had been addressed by metaphysicians before Russell, notably Alexius von Meinong.[24] Meinong sought to escape the contradiction by denying that the definite description could lack a referent. The present king of France might not exist, but in some weaker sense it must have being, because (i) is meaningful and its subject's meaning is its referent. So Meinong was driven to accord being to all that can be talked about using descriptions. A subset of these entities *existed* in the narrower sense. If we say that objects that have being *subsist*, then the present king may not exist but he must subsist.

Russell was revolted by such goings-on:

> For want of the apparatus of propositional functions, many logicians have been driven to the conclusion that there are unreal objects. It is argued, e.g. by Meinong, that we can speak about "the golden mountain," "the round square," and so on; we can make true propositions of which these are the subjects; hence they must have some kind of logical being, since otherwise the propositions in which they occur would be meaningless. In such theories, it seems to me, there is a failure of that feeling for reality which ought to be preserved even in the most abstract studies. Logic, I should maintain, must no more admit a unicorn than zoology can.[25]

Russell, therefore, wanted to find another way out of the contradiction, a way that did not lead to the postulation of strange subsistent entities.

B. Closely related is this puzzle: Necessarily one of the two contradictory sentences "A is B" and "A is not B" must be true. But neither "The present King of France is bald" nor "The present King of France is not bald" appear to be true, given that there is not presently a King of France.

C. Another seeming paradox is related to identity. Russell states it elegantly:

If *a* is identical with *b*, whatever is true of the one is true of the other, and either may be substituted for the other in any proposition without altering the truth or falsehood of that proposition. Now George IV wished to know whether Scott was the author of *Waverley:* and in fact Scott was the author of *Waverley.* Hence we may substitute *Scott* for *the author of "Waverley,"* and thereby prove that George IV wished to know whether Scott was Scott. Yet an interest in the law of identity can hardly be attributed to the first gentleman of Europe.[26]

D. Finally, it is worth noting that even such a simple and true statement as (ii) "The present King of France does not exist" seems unsayable on the credible assumptions that "the present King of France" is a denoting expression lacking a referent and that sentences containing such meaningless expressions are themselves meaningless.

2. *Environment:* So Russell had stocked his mind with such puzzles and was unsatisfied by previously suggested solutions that required subsisting kings and unicorns. In addition, he had inherited certain philosophical axioms and methods that he wished to preserve and use. Put very generally, we can say that from Descartes to Kant to the late nineteenth century, there had been an increasing emphasis on the philosophical study of language and a growing belief that many problems in science, mathematics, and theology, as well as in philosophy, had their origins in misunderstandings about the nature, structure, and limits of language.[27] For example, in 1883, Ernst Mach had raised the fateful issue of whether the concepts of absolute space and time in Newtonian physics were not nonsensical, and for two decades before 1900, Gottlob Frege had been proclaiming that it was a scandal that no mathematician knew what a number was and that the concept of mathematical function was fundamentally unclear.[28] We may add to this Nietzsche's aphoristic and iconoclastic claim that "we are not rid of God, because we still have faith in [traditional] grammar."[29] The point is that it was being widely proclaimed that the most careful studies suffered not simply from falsity but from conceptual confusion and linguistic impropriety.

In the section on descriptions in his *Introduction to Mathematical Philosophy,* Russell says: "Misled by grammar, the great majority of those logicians who have dealt with this question have dealt with it on mistaken lines."[30] He was alluding to the general problem of falling into confusion because we take two sentences to have similar structures when they do not. This subject is nicely illustrated by Kant's warning in his argument against Anselm's Ontological Proof that although *exists* looks like a predicate term, it is not. Russell suspected that some of the puzzles he was trying to solve had their source in this kind of confusion. Kant's remarks about *exist* are part of a long tradition in philosophy according to which the real structures of propositions are believed to be different from their apparent structures. The predicate logic Russell and Whitehead were developing would reveal *real* structure: "The *is* of 'Socrates is human' expresses the relation of subject and predicate; the *is* of 'Socrates is a man' expresses identity. It is a disgrace to the human race that it has chosen the same word 'is' for these two entirely different ideas—a disgrace which a symbolical logical language of course remedies."[31] So Russell had come to share the belief that natural languages contain many pitfalls for the unwary philosopher, and he also realized that the traditional grammars available to him were hopelessly inadequate. One might agree, however, that the deep structures of sentences are not always apparent in their surface forms and that language misleads, without agreeing that formal logic gives a correct account of language. That Russell believed it did was a function of his belief that the new logic had already shown itself to be so impressive that it could not be ignored. And it was (and is) impressive. The logic of *Principia Mathematica* provided for the first time an adequate set of inference rules and an elegant and coherent account of the structures of many of the sentences occurring in mathematics and science. So an obvious constraint to be put on any solution to the puzzles at hand was that they were to be at least compatible with the predicate calculus as it then existed.

3. *Innovation:* Since innovation takes place within an environment, choices must be made about what of the past to preserve and what to change. In the case at hand, Russell particularly wanted to retain two claims, the first of which he shared with Meinong: If a linguistic expression is a name, it is meaningless if it lacks a referent. Russell's second axiom was the ancient proposition that every meaningful sentence capable of expressing a state of affairs is either true or false. Furthermore, as we have seen in the preceding section, he wished to preserve the prevailing attitudes about the role of linguistic theory in philosophy and the necessity for an adequate formal logic.

One other factor must be mentioned. Russell stood in the imposing tradition of British empiricist philosophers from Locke to Mill. Language can be analyzed in any number of ways to further any number of purposes. Russell's empircism dictated what sort of analysis was needed. According to its tenets, human knowledge was based entirely on observation and experiment. Those concepts were meaningful that could be shown to be about observable entities and properties, and those sentences were confirmable or refutable that could be shown to be about the world of our experience. To claim, as Meinong had, that "the present King of France is bald" is about some nonexistent (and thus nonobservable) but nevertheless subsistent entity was for Russell absurd. To be admitted as a legitimate part of an empiricist language, the sentence would have to be shown to be about observable properties and/or entities. If it could be shown in what way such sentences can be tied, not to strange subsistent entities, but to the entities and processes open to inspection, our theory of knowledge and ultimately our scientific theorizing would be that much better understood. We will return to this feature of Russell's program in following sections. Thus the stage was set for Russell's innovation. His insight was that though denoting phrases require referents and though "the present King of France" is the apparent grammatical subject of his example sentence, it is *not* a denoting expression. Sentence subjects need not be names. "But if I say 'the author of *Waverly* was a man,' that is not a statement of the form 'x is a man' and does not have 'the author of *Waverly*' for its [real] subject."[32] In fact, as we have noted, in the logical paraphrase that he offered, "The present King of France" does not occur as a unit at all; rather its function is taken over by predicates and the complex machinery of quantifiers, existence claims, and variables.

*4. Justification:* Sketchy as this account has been, it should be apparent that Russell's theory of descriptions accomplished several tasks at once. First, the puzzles: The paradox of Section 1.A. vanishes because the example sentence rightly analyzed contains no denoting expressions. Further, the apparent contradiction between "The present King of France is bald" and "The present King of France is not bald" disappears as soon as we realize that these sentences are not of the forms "A is B" and "A is not B." They are, according to Rusell, both false, because they both make the same false existence claim. (Similarly, "The present King of France does not exist" becomes simply true rather than meaningless.) Such sentences can be seen to be meaningful even though names lacking a referent are meaningless; the sentences contain no names although they appear to. Finally, since "that author of *Waverly*" is not a name, "Scott" cannot be substituted for it, so the puzzle of identity is dissolved.

In terms of the philosophical claims Russell wished to preserve, he had succeeded in giving a deep-structural description of the sentences in question that removed the philosopher's temptation to be misled by them. He did so in terms of the new logic and in a way compatible with his empiricist predilections. As far as definite descriptions were concerned, the way was now clear to develop an empiricist language containing names only of existing entities—entities of which we could have direct perceptual knowledge. Whatever other entities we wished to talk about were to be talked about by means of descriptions. Of course, sentences containing descriptions were analyzed in such a way that no names occurred in them, only predicates, quantifiers, and variables. Gone were the subsistent but invisible unicorns. In their place was talk of such properties as four-leggedness and animality, properties whose presence could be empirically confirmed or refuted.

Given these remarks, Russell's theory can be seen to be neither obvious nor trivial, and perhaps we can see why it was later hailed by Frank Ramsey as "a paradigm of philosophy."[33] Like other important discoveries in philosophy, mathematics, or science, it was firmly based on the insights of the past and it was also part of a critique of the past. Moreover, the theory was an integral part of the new logic and an early and promising step toward a new method in philosophy.

We have asserted that an innovation is justified in part by its promise, and Russell's theory promised much. As he elaborated it over the next decade, it promised to yield a new method in philosophy. When this century began, philosophy found itself in an acute identity crisis. The success of modern empirical science and the concurrent attack on traditional metaphysics left philosphers wondering just where in the intellectual enterprise their discipline fit. Russell's disagreement with Meinong was part of a general climate of criticism directed at metaphysical thinking, and some philosophers went so far as to claim that virtually the whole of philosophy prior to this century had comprised a series of meaningless claims arising from failure to understand the real structure of language.

In this milieu, Russell saw the task of philosophy to be the analysis of language, particularly the language of science and mathematics, and a new division of labor was envisioned in which it was the job of science to discover new facts and the job of philosophy to analyze the concepts and propositions central to the sciences, logic, and mathematics. Philosophy, then, was to be a purely conceptual undertaking. The philosopher would tell us the real structure of, for example, "The present King of France is bald," and in so doing he would lay to rest a passel of bad metaphysical theories and would further the understanding of our language, our science, and ultimately, ourselves.

5. *Regularization:* In the eighty years since its formulation, the Theory of Descriptions has continued to influence thinking in logic, philosophy of language, and the foundations of philosophy. Not only is it the standard way to analyze definite descriptions in logistic theory, but it has given birth to interesting and productive disputes in the theory of meaning,[34] and it remains the starting point for contemporary discussions of naming and reference. Although the analysis was originally embedded in a purely extensional predicate logic and helped to protect that logic from certain criticisms, it also paved the way for various intensional logistic systems based on the claim that each proper name has a sense equivalent to that of some definite description. More generally, Russell's theory is one of the foundations of the philosophical movement called Linguistic Analysis or Ideal Language Philosophy. The methods Russell and others developed dominated much of Continental and Anglo-American philosophical thinking in the twenties and thirties (until Wittgenstein's critique surfaced in the early thirties). They still survive as an important set of techniques in the philosopher's tool chest.

## A Case from Painting: Robert Rauschenberg's New Grammar of Representation

1. *Impetus:* In 1953, a young Robert Rauschenberg knocked timidly on Willem De Kooning's door to ask if De Kooning would give him a drawing he could erase. De Kooning was skeptical, but he relented. It took a month and forty erasers; it

was shown under the title "Erased De Kooning Drawing."[35] Rauschenberg was responding to a narrow problem: having done some all-white paintings, he wondered how to achieve something similar in drawing. Nevertheless, this provocative artwork came to have larger symbolic value. It stood for the then nascent revolt against the aesthetic of Abstract Expressionism.[36] The world dominance of this movement was about to be challenged.

Not that Rauschenberg saw himself as a rebel. He was quick to point out that "Jasper [Johns] and I were the only two who *admired* Abstract Expressionism so much we decided not to copy it."[37] It was rather that his own predilections and goals left him unable to follow directly in the footsteps of the masters of the "New York School" with whom he was often in contact; besides De Kooning, these included Mark Rothko, Jackson Pollock, Clyfford Still, Barnett Newman, Franz Kline, and others.

The theory of expressionism describes painting as an articulation and communication of feeling. The masterpiece powerfully and specifically communicates profound emotion. Mark Rothko said, "The people who weep before my pictures are having the same religious experience I had when I painted them."[38] In an earlier time, each brushstroke was intended to contribute to the illusion that the frame enclosed a window on reality. For the expressionist, paint is in the service of the evocation of particular emotions. And if those emotions are not evoked, it is a failure of the audience or of the artist and his work.

Rauschenberg felt there were dangers in this expressionist aesthetic, dangers that he at first sensed dimly and largely unconsciously, but that he soon articulated both in paintings and in words. Expressionism is an aesthetic whose roots are in romanticism. Its adherents tended to the grand gesture and displayed the same self-absorption as confessional poets. Expressionism can be concerned almost exclusively with the inner landscape and the individual tortured psyche. At its worst it is precious, overly subjective, and ego-bound. It expects the audience to receive the intended message; to Rauschenberg this seemed too coercive. And last, since it is at least abstract and often nonobjective, representation and represented objects play minor roles; that is, expressionism is a language fit for expression but not for description.

We have been speaking of the negative side of Rauschenberg's motivation—the limitations and dangers he sensed in what we might call the ruling paradigm. On the positive side were his own loves and obsessions. It is a simplification, but true nevertheless, that he was looking out at his environment rather than contemplating his feelings.[39] He had a strong attraction to objects, the more ordinary the better.[40] He wished to enter into a noncoercive cooperation with the common, even banal, objects of our surroundings—from pop cans to magazines to quilts.[41] More and more he began to re-present the urban landscape in its bewildering and inexhaustible complexity.[42] His early white paintings collected and reflected the ambient shadows in the gallery, while his later canvases seemed like magnets attracting every object in their vicinity.

Looking at Rauschenberg's aesthetic in terms of broader social issues, one can say that in the fifties a new postwar and postmodern urban society was coming to birth. He wanted to portray its visual aspects, but the nonobjective and mystical-expressive paintings of the New York School were not designed to mirror it. It is part of Rauschenberg's achievement that he developed a new representational grammar, a sophisticated model of the urban landscape, to show postmodern people the amazing and disturbing society he was creating.

2. *Environment:* "Painting relates to both art and life. Neither can be made. I work in the gap between the two."[43] Rauschenberg's often-quoted remark is on one level a succinct description of his collages, which combine abstract expressionist brushstrokes with bits of the world such as postcards and Coke bottles. On a more abstract level, his claim is a recognition of the importance of "environment." The world is already in place. So are language, the elaborate conventions of art, and the stock of actual images and things and their histories. At the moment of artistic creation, all these systems form the background to the action and cannot themselves be made. In our surprise at the audacity of a tradition-shattering work, we may forget that no matter how iconoclastic the painting, it is fundamentally rooted in that tradition. Rauschenberg is an interesting example of such rootedness because his knowledge of the environment was not based on schooling. He successfully resisted the academy, spending only a few months at a midwestern art school and later at Black Mountain College, where he immersed himself in photography but remained distant from Joseph Alber's strictly disciplined classes. Further, al-

though his collages, begun in the middle 1950s, are similar to the cubist or dadaist collages of the 1920s, he apparently was not aware of these earlier works. So perhaps one should say he reinvented collage. Thus, what looks most like a dependence on the earlier history of his craft is not; his debt to his tradition is broader and more general. It depends on the artists he listened to, rather than on the more usual academic study of art and its history. The major influences on his work are:

A. *Pictures re-present objects:* The most obvious feature of Rauschenberg's work when contrasted with abstract expressionism is that he was one of those who brought the object back into painting. Many of the pieces in a Rauschenberg collage are themselves representational paintings or photographs or reproductions of paintings. Although the formalistic aesthetic theory that dominates this century downgrades the role of representation, emphasizing instead abstract features of form, color, and texture, by far the majority of the world's artworks are representational. Rauschenberg reached back to an earlier emphasis on paintings as mirrors of nature, breaking one immediate tradition by reclaiming an older, more venerable one.

B. *The New York expressionists:* But of course representation cannot be the same after cubism, surrealism, and abstract expressionism. We have mentioned Rauschenberg's critique of the latter, but he drew from it as well. Abstract expressionism is part of the general movement in present-day art that frees the canvas to be itself, an opaque surface, not a transparent, illusionistic window on the world. An expressionist canvas is clearly a flat, thickly painted piece of cloth. It is a real object in its own right, not a copy of something else. As we will see, Rauschenberg and Jasper Johns carried this perception to its logical conclusion.

There is yet another feature of expressionism worth mentioning: Mark Rothko and others believed strongly in the mission of art and saw themselves as part of an avant-garde elite. Only during the last century have artists been given the mandate to go forth and create more or less free of censorship and official patronage. It becomes possible, then, for the artist to view himself as seer, cultural hero, and prophet. Though Rauschenberg rejected some of the posturing and overseriousness of the expressionists, he still evinces the stance of a member of the avant-garde when he says: "What I do is not for my sake nor for the sake of art, but for the sake of change."[44]

C. *Art about art:* Throughout the late fifties, Rauschenberg worked closely with Jasper Johns. Johns's approach is more overtly theoretical. He is, for example, a careful reader of the works of Ludwig Wittgenstein. Like René Magritte's paintings, Johns's work is a sustained look at art itself and what we might call art's semantics. The very language of art becomes the subject of these artworks, just as philosophers, scientists, playwrights, and mathematicians have made the languages and methodologies of their disciplines part of their subject matters.[45]

D. *Marcel Duchamp:* Duchamp produced few artworks during the last decades of his life, but his influence is remarkable. It was he who first centered aesthetic attention on the most common objects in the environment by signing and bringing into museums everything from bicycle wheels to urinals. As one critic put it: "Duchamp reduced the creative art to choice . . . its irreducible requirement."[46]

E. *The gallery:* But common objects, like children, can only be baptized (as artworks) if the institution for baptism exists. Duchamp's banal objects were transformable into artworks because the art museum existed and made such magical transmutations possible. There they could be put before us purely for aesthetic appreciation. The modern gallery is a historically recent invention, and it brings with it many conventions that make modern art possible.

F. *Photography:* As mentioned, Rauschenberg zealously studied photography at Black Mountain College, producing some fine photographs that are distinctively works of photographic technique. He even claims that one of his early ambitions was to photograph all of America a square yard at a time.[47] The artistic conventions available to Rauschenberg allowed photography to be taken seriously as a fine art. At the same time, the urban environment he wished to represent in his paintings contained photographic images at every turn, so it was possible, within the conventions, to mirror photos using photographic printing techniques.

G. *Gertrude Stein and John Cage:* Gertrude Stein said that what changes from age to age is not who we are but what we meet on the road. The composition of our surroundings changes.[48] Art must from time to time change its grammar to be able to depict new landscapes. Stein praised those artists who treated every part of the canvas equally, who lavished as much care on a fold of cloth as on a face. In her writing she went beyond this principle, not only treating equally everything that was in the picture, but trying to get everything into the picture. John Cage shared this urge, and in his compositions he not only makes room for the quarter-tones between the piano keys, but also brings into music the very sounds the concert hall is designed to keep out, those of traffic, conversations, and electronic devices.[49] Cage and Rauschenberg met at Black Mountain and they have often collaborated since. Rauschenberg clearly shares the desire to get everything into the picture. It is a peculiarly American urge, a democratic inclusiveness reminiscent of Walt Whitman's poetry.

Further, Cage had pioneered in music the use of chance processes and random tone generators to defeat his own biases and widen his choices of what to include. Rauschenberg took over this aspect of Cage's work in his collages, as we will see.

3. *Innovation:* We have taken a rather detailed look at the environment to dispel the temptation to believe that it may not be as important in art as in science, that the master artist creates something entirely new and will probably do better for not being schooled in art history or too mindful of what others are doing, or that if a scientist did not do *Newtonian* physics in the nineteenth century, he did not do physics, whereas a painter can draw on the art tradition in any number of ways. For example, in the 1950s he need not be an abstract expressionist to be an artist. Although there is some truth in these claims, it should be noted that for all Rauschenberg's shunning of the academy, he was in close touch with the major movement in art in his time and privy to discussions about the nature of art that drew ideas from many central figures of this century, such as Stein, Duchamp, Cage, Wittgenstein, and Johns. Those traditions revealed certain tendencies to be resisted or furthered and certain problems to be considered, for example, about the status of the artwork as an object and about how best to represent the new urban environment. In a biography of Gertrude Stein, John Brinnin says:

> If Gertrude Stein had never lived, sooner or later works very much like those she produced would have been written by

someone else. Once a particular set of conditions was present, her arrival was inevitable—like an event in Chemistry.[50]

This claim stresses the contribution of environment at the expense of giving just due to creativity and accident. Innovation enters the picture in ways probably not predictable, but usually quite explicable after the fact. With this in mind, we turn now to Rauschenberg's innovations.

A. *Paint as an object:* Throughout the first half of this century, the painting was becoming more obviously a physical object in its own right—paint on canvas. Rauschenberg extended the process, perhaps as far as it can go. Until Rauschenberg, paint was still in the service of something else: the representational illusion or the expression of feeling. What he wanted was that paint just be itself and that the objects and images appearing in his dense collages should also be separate entities rather than mere contributors to the overall effect. In 1981, now fully conscious of the importance of this step, he said:

> Jasper and I thought of what we were working with as materials. They were not intended as something else. Red was not to be translated into an emotion. No, red is a color. We meant what we did. It was a breakthrough in Art's history![51]

He thus introduced a form of "combine" (his word) different from early cubist collages, for the real objects were no longer part of a larger object, as Picasso's newspaper bits were part of a fruit bowl image, for example. He and Johns introduced a more complex pictorial semantics involving objects and images that in addition to traditional sorts of reference related also to themselves.[52]

B. *Choiceless selection:* But it was not just that there were to be objects in his combines. Like Stein and Cage, he wanted everything to be there, as wide a selection of ordinary things as possible (from paint to junk to postcards and magazine pages).[53] To that end, he began to pursue ways to defeat even his unconscious biases about what to incorporate into his collages; these included buying unlabeled cans of paint and painting with whatever color he opened. He also instituted a house rule that he could walk around one square block near his New York apartment to collect street junk for his next work. He collaborated extensively with artists, engineers, and scientists to create partly spontaneous happenings and concerts with the expressed purpose of "defeating his ego." And like Duchamp, he selected ordinary objects that he transformed into artworks by bringing them into the gallery as parts of his combines. Yet there is a difference. Rauschenberg is not looking for a particularly striking object to set before us for aesthetic contemplation; instead, for him, every object is potentially worthy of attention.

C. *A new kind of model:* By 1960, Rauschenberg had perfected the necessary techniques for embedding things and photographic images of things in cloths, cardboards, and canvases to produce combines with an unrivaled density, with complex visual metaphors built up from atomic images and generating indefinitely many meanings. Like the cityscapes they mirror, they need to be seen in several different ways at once, since viewers both read them—combining simple images into complex meanings—and take them in instantaneously as formally integrated wholes.

But most important, because of the artist's ability to choose widely, these combines seem to be random collections while at the same time are formally elegant, purposeful artifacts. Thus, they are representations of the urban landscape at yet another and deeper level: they mirror the fact that many purposes collide in a city, giving rise to what look like purely accidental juxtapositions of elements. As Rauschenberg himself says, describing images on passing trucks in the city,

> With . . . insistency trucks mobilize words and broadside our culture by a combination of *law* and *local motivation* which produces an extremely complex random order that cannot be described as accidental.[54]

This feature of the composition of cities could not be well represented by a traditional realistic perspectival painting because such paintings impose an order on the scene that is now lacking. It is an order appropriate to another time and a different landscape. To solve his representational problem, Rauschenberg has created in his combines a new kind of visual model of some of the salient visual aspects of the contemporary urban environment. It is a revelatory model that helps us see with fresh eyes.[55]

D. *The audience:* A new way of representing requires a new

audience. One of Rauschenberg's objections to abstract expressionism was that each painting dictated the response of the viewer; for the communication to be successful, the viewer was supposed to get the intended and unique message. In contrast, Rauschenberg's combines are radically incomplete, requiring that the viewer approach them actively, responding to their density and actualizing some of the possibilities for meaning which they contain. In the process, he hopes, the viewer will be changed; he will see (and thus respond) differently.[56]

4. *Justification:* In 1964, a bare decade after the erased De Kooning, Rauschenberg received the Grand Prize for Painting at the Venice Biennale in recognition of his preeminence among painters. He had found a way to reflect the "random but not accidental order" of the new environment, and in doing so he had greatly extended the range of materials appropriate for art, devised new techniques for their combination, and had created a new representational grammar. Like other creative problem-solvers in the humanities and sciences, his accomplishment afforded the promise of the simultaneous satisfaction of several goals and solution to several problems.

Rauschenberg's ascendancy was not the product of luck, nor was it the result of the profit-motivated machinations of the art marketplace. Instead, it was well-deserved recognition from the community of artists, collectors, and scholars, a recognition based on good reasons. This community, the "Artworld," acts in ways similar to the community of scientists (or of philosophers) to legitimize, define, explain, and further articulate important innovations.[57]

A succinct theory of scientific justification advanced by Heinrich Hertz in 1894 helps demonstrate the similarities between this process and the process of justification in science.[58] Hertz claimed that we should subject a proposed scientific theory to three kinds of tests: it should be logically coherent, correct, and compatible. By *correct* he meant that it allow us to make true predictions, that it correspond in that sense with reality. And under the heading of *compatibility* he included the aesthetic criteria of elegance and simplicity, as well as the requirement that the theory be compatible with our metaphysical and evaluative presuppositions.

Rauschenberg's achievement fares well under a similar set of requirements. We have argued that he provides a new way of correctly modeling certain aspects of the landscape, and of course his visual grammar meets aesthetic requirements since it is formally elegant. In the language of contemporary aesthetic theory, his works display "significant form."[59] Hertz's criterion of logical coherence does not directly apply here, since artworks are not sets of propositions. However, a broader notion of coherence applies, for the grammar Rauschenberg developed for his many-tiered visual models would not be effective if its various aspects could not be coherently integrated. From one perspective he wedded techniques, subject matters, materials, and style in what can be viewed as the visual equivalent of the logician's demand for consistency.

Last, we can require of great artworks that they be compatible with overarching metaphysical and evaluative presuppositions. Rauschenberg was one of those persons who in the late 1950s turned our attention outward to our society, to its methods of mass communication and its emphasis on consumption. It was the art for its time.

At a deeper level, Rauschenberg's art, like Cage's, is based in part on chance, one of the concepts that dominates the physics and metaphysics of this era. Closely related to this concept is their advocacy of a kind of choiceless selection of the elements of an artwork or composition. This nonjudgmental acceptance has affinities with Zen Buddhism, as Cage has pointed out. But it is also closely allied with something central to the American psyche: the desire to include everything, which we have claimed informs the works of Whitman, Stein, Cage, and Rauschenberg. It is an expression of one version of the dream of American democracy as a melting pot of cultures, with toleration of diverse outlooks. Rauschenberg's vision connects him as well with the American seer and photographer Alfred Stieglitz, who in his photographs, particularly his cloud series, sought not to present extraordinary objects, but ordinary objects in an extraordinary light, thus underscoring the value of each thing and person.[60] In this and other ways, Rauschenberg's art is a uniquely American expression firmly rooted in some of the underlying axioms of the culture he has sought to mirror.

5. *Regularization:* Rauschenberg and Jasper Johns so dominated the art of the 1960s and 1970s that almost every major artist working in America during those decades acknowledges debts to them. First, Rauschenberg created a new way of depiction, a new way of seeing. Such a breakthrough becomes a permanent feature of art; henceforth, new potentials not pre-

viously existing are available to artists. For example; the practice of including real objects in artworks, begun by Duchamp and Picasso, was developed by Rauschenberg to the point that any visible object can now be considered a candidate for inclusion in a painting or sculpture. Even the sky and mountains can be part of an artwork, as they are in Christo's "Valley Curtain," installed near Rifle, Colorado, in 1972. The curtain remained up for only a few hours, but the artist insists that most of the artwork is still there.

Second, Rauschenberg refocused attention on realistic representation in a century that had seen its apparent demise in favor of nonobjective expressionism. From pop art to neo-realism, the last two decades in American art have been dominated by naturalistic depiction. In fact, American Pop Art was made possible by Rauschenberg's concentration on banal objects, including images from the mass media. Rauschenberg's solution to the problem of representation opened the way for Warhol, Lichtenstein, Rosenquist, and others to turn their full attention to the visual languages of the mass culture, the languages of advertising and mass communications.

Third, since form and technique go hand in hand, one might expect that Rauschenberg would have developed new techniques to fit his new grammar, and such is the case. He and Johns reestablished the importance of the print as an independent medium rather than merely a means of reproduction for wider distribution. He also pioneered new methods of embedding images and materials in canvas and other cloths. Most important, this created new forms of collaboration among artists, printmakers, and technicians. All this is part of Rauschenberg's insistence on collaboration as a way of defeating personal biases, as, for example, allowing a wider choice of subject matter. This rationale explains as well Rauschenberg's extensive collaboration with John Cage and the Merce Cunningham dancers in the production of concerts exhibiting an unprecedented reliance on chance processes and improvisation.

Last, Rauschenberg has a distaste for any artist who tries to "dictate the responses" to his work. Besides recognizing that inevitably each viewer will respond subjectively to a painting, Rauschenberg has also introduced a new kind of intention in art—the intention to confront the viewer with a mysterious object that is radically incomplete, needing the active response of the audience to give it meaning. That artworks communicate like open-ended metaphors rather than by conveying a definite idea or feeling has become a dominant belief among artists.

## Some Stereotypical Views

These three case studies make the point that a common structure of creativity underlies the three fields of physics, philosophy, and painting. Establishment of this critical point was the first objective of this essay. The second objective is to discover the implications of this common structure of creativity for a further understanding of the natures and relations of these three fields and, by extension, of the sciences and the humanities as a whole. The focus of the discussion will be certain widely held views of these natures and relations that we can show to be stereotypes by the evidence of the case studies.

*1. Physics:* Physics is frequently viewed as the hardest of the hard sciences, bound by a single rigorous method to the point of near automism.[61] Sometimes its processes of discovery are seen as being so strictly controlled by method and so purely descriptive that they leave little need or room for the contributions of the creative imagination. Or alternatively, these processes are in effect excluded from the province of physics proper and shunted to the domains of history and psychology. In this second view, physics proper is defined largely in terms of stage four of the structure of creativity outlined earlier, namely as a set of exact logical and empirical procedures to be used in justifying or rejecting theories, and in the body of theories so justified. Nonformal, variable elements of community expectation, assumption, and decision are not stressed.[62]

The stage of regularization also enters into this stereotypical description of physics, but only in a restricted sense. For physics supposedly exhibits constant linear progress in disclosing the facts of nature, each generation of physicists adding new plateaus of achievement and understanding to the ones previously laid down, with no need to criticize or alter in any fundamental sense what has gone before. The great figures of physics are portrayed as producing a steady stream of rationally deduced discoveries that compel ready acceptance from their peers. The background of dissent, shortsightedness,

prejudice, accident, trial-and-error, serendipity, sheer speculation, and frequent failure is filtered out.

These stereotypical ideas are reinforced by the way physics is
commonly taught in schools. Little notice is given to the unset-
tled, hectic periods of active research, either in the past or in the
present, and instead most attention focuses on finished results.[63] Physics is presented in textbook and lecture as a body
of polished theories, precise formulae, and stock exercises,
their facticity unquestioned and their origins ignored. The impression conveyed is that of a seamless web of truth, with no
heed paid to the changing environments, shifting concepts, or
deep controversies that gave birth to the theories of physics and
that continue to mark their active development. The outcome is
that physics has come to be seen by many as the sole bright
paradigm of true rationality, in comparison with which all other
disciplines must inevitably pale, unless they can somehow
emulate its exact methods and enviable record of ever-ac-
cumulating objective results. When measured against the standard of this stereotypical paradigm, such fields as philosophy
and painting are usually relegated to the role of subjective
disciplines, lacking rigor and precision and telling nothing important about the real world.

2. *Philosophy:* A widespread conception of philosophy is that
it is an endless milling around with the same set of problems
that engaged the earliest philosophers of the West, with no
agreed-upon method, no consensus about basic assumptions,
no justification procedures to speak of, and no evident progress
in problem-solving. In other words, the field of philosophy
appears stuck mainly at the first level of the structure of
creativity, that of impetus, with problems aplenty and a lot of
conceptual wheel-spinning about them, but with no notable
regularization or progress. Some philosophers of the twentieth
century have attributed this alleged impasse to the environment philosophy inherited from the past, arguing that the
problems presented by that environment have been, for the
most part, bogus and ill-conceived, based largely on miscon-
ceptions created by unconscious misuses of language. But however the matter may be explained, justification among contending theories and systems is thought to be almost entirely
lacking by those who look at philosophy along the lines of the
stereotype we are now discussing. Philosophy is certainly inno-

vative, for its history has undeniably given rise to a great variety of highly original schemes of thought, but these schemes are viewed as being analogous to science fiction; that is, products of the imagination with no firm foothold in fact.

This stereotypical conception of philosophy also is supported, albeit unwittingly, by the manner in which it is frequently taught. Students are presented either with a problems approach or with an historical approach to the subject matter. In the problems approach, a particular philosophical problem, say free will versus determinism, is set up through readings representing various sides of the issue. The teacher helps the students understand the claims and arguments for each side and then leaves them to make up their own minds about the controversy. Similarly, in the historical approach, a parade of systems is run out before the students, who are invited to analyze each one briefly before going on to the next. The systems are critically compared with one another, but only in the sense of trying to understand what A would say about B, B about A, A and B about C, and so on. Neither the problems nor the historical approach tries to assess, on independent grounds, which of the baffling array of options comes closest to being the right one or why it does. Neither approach shows the progress that has been made over time in resolving some of the problems of the field. The impression students get of philosophy, therefore, and one that they carry into their later lives, is exactly the stereotypical one presented here. Philosophy is a budget of paradoxes, a stock of perennial questions to be debated endlessly, all impetus and innovation adding up to a very confusing environment, but with no reliable procedures for adjudicating among proposed answers and with no genuine progress. It is hardly surprising that philosophy tends to be dismissed as a kind of professional dilettantism or "glass-bead game" of the mind and is considered a highly dispensable luxury of a leisured society.

3. *Painting:* We often think of art as the primary example of pure creativity. In the public mind, art is the result of unfettered imagination and free invention, and what is invented is held to be purely fictional. Since it is unfettered, little attention need be paid to impetus and environment. Since it is fictional, justification is not in question. Accordingly, this stereotype of art, a legacy of romanticism, emphasizes innovation, unconstrained

expression, and play; it minimizes the other features of the creative process that we have discussed.

Artists and critics sometimes speak of responding to problems, but in the common view these problems are discussed piecemeal and are not seen to be fundamental. The fact that today each artist of note develops his own style is seen as proof of free invention rather than being akin to the replacement of one paradigm with another, whereby perceived limitations of previous artistic grammars are corrected or transcended.

In this age the importance of tradition is less important than rapid progress and continual invention. Art seems blithely to deny its past and to seek to reinvent itself from moment to moment. Art students already speak of Rauschenberg as passé. Currently art history is based on the idea that what art owes to the past it owes only to the art of the past, so that at most, art history deals with former schools of art rather than with broader issues appropriate to intellectual history. At worst, it is a concentration on the techniques for identifying past works instead of analyzing or evaluating them.

Formalistic aesthetic theory, which has contributed significantly to modern art and art criticism, reinforces the stereotype by denying that anything other than formal properties is aesthetically relevant. This cuts off discussion of the artist's intention and of the work's connections with larger social, ethical, or religious issues.

Further, it is fashionable to deny the efficacy of all talk about art. Barnett Newman's wonderful one-liner, "Aesthetics is for artists as ornithology is for the birds," is taken as evidence for the widely shared attitude that theoretical issues are irrelevant to art.[64] Again, art must be the result of unfettered imagination. The trick is to disarm one's biases and to see anew, which seems to mean that environment should play a minor role. Even an artist's obvious reference to the past in his works is taken as merely the result of his unconstrained choice among the infinite variety of past works now available in museums or photographically reproduced.

There is a similar set of claims for justification. If art is free invention and owes little to tradition or perceived puzzles, then there will be no criteria of the type present in science for justifying, explaining, or evaluating artworks. In the current jargon, it's all a matter of taste, and responses to art are characterized in terms of gut feeling and intuition only. Again, to the public the concept of truth in art seems inappropriate, and to students of art, Plato's insistence that art yield knowledge seems quaintly naive.

Finally, if evaluation of art is a matter of taste, the plausible way to account for the success of a Rauschenberg is to stress luck or to claim that there are tastemakers, usually viewed as wealthy collectors whose unfounded choices dictate public acceptance of an artist. Tom Wolfe, in *The Painted Word*, comes close to this position with his strong emphasis on some of the complex social factors at work in the Artworld.[65] Significantly, he does not ask Socrates' question: Is the work good because certain people collect it, or do they collect it because it is good? The stereotype would choose the former answer to this question. This discussion of Rauschenberg's contribution has argued for the second answer, a position we will develop further in the remaining section.

## The Structure of Creativity and the Stereotypical Views

*1. Physics:* One fact that is quite obvious about Maxwell's vortex theory is that it was not arrived at through a strictly deductive process of reasoning, nor was it simply read out of the facts of experience in an automatic, impersonal manner. Rather, it was the product of the free play of Maxwell's creative imagination, influenced but not determined by the current state of theories, researches, assumptions, and problems in his environment. Furthermore, not all factors in his environment were favorable to his kind of theorizing; many researchers espoused the concept of action at a distance and, as a consequence, saw no need for Maxwell's hypothesis of mechanically linked motions in a medium. So his theory was developed and presented in an atmosphere of basic dissent. It is also notable that the specific physical hypothesis he so carefully worked out in his 1861–62 papers, far from commanding immediate acceptance from his peers, was rejected by them. This happened despite the fact that his mathematical equations of the field, created initially on the basis of the physical model and then developed further in subsequent writings, did come to be accepted.

Some would claim that Maxwell's electromagnetic theory is

just these equations, and that it essentially has nothing to do with the story of their development or with physical analogies of any type, including those that stimulated their discovery and that may continue to color their interpretation. According to this view, a theory in physics is nothing more than an instrument of prediction, an abstract mathematical calculus that can be correlated with and tested by experience. The explanatory import and very nature of such theories lie entirely in their predictive success or in their correlations with observational language. Whatever role physical models or acts of creative imagination may have had in their discovery is irrelevant, once the abstract calculus has been given its final form.

This interpretation of physical theories suggests a character of pure formalism or automism in their justification and tends to conceive their nature almost exclusively in terms of their justification, rather than in terms of other aspects of the creative process like impetus, environment, or innovation. To see whether an abstract mathematical calculus like Maxwell's equations is justified, one has merely to assess in a purely formal manner its empirical entailments and then to put these to the test of experience, again in a purely formal manner. It is a procedure that a computer could carry out as well as a person, and probably better. Given the identification of the essential theory with its predictive capacity, the formalism or automism is carried over into the very nature of the theories themselves, making them appear completely objective—that is, entirely independent of contextual, fallible elements of human history, judgment, and decision.

But this conception of the nature and confirmation of physical theories, a conception that looms large in the stereotypical view of physics presented in the previous section, breaks down at a number of important points. One of these is its failure to take into account the fact that rules or procedures must be devised (or assumed) for connecting the mathematical variables with aspects of experience; that is, an empirical interpretation must be given to the abstract mathematical forms. This act of interpretation is an informal act of judgment. An example of such an act of judgment is the way Helmholtz's mathematical studies of vortices in a fluid medium were extended by him, Thomson, and Maxwell to electromagnetic phenomena.

Second, successful prediction through use of an abstract calculus is not quite the same thing as understanding, and it would seem that physicists are intent upon understanding the phenomena of the natural world that they study. Maxwell himself appreciated this distinction between prediction and understanding and insisted, as we have noted, on the importance of supplementing the development of predictive calculi with the development of explanatory analogies and models. Stephen Toulmin emphasizes this distinction by citing the fact that the Babylonians could predict eclipses with some precision but could offer no explanation for their occurrence. Hence, they could hardly be said to scientifically understand eclipses.[66] Physical models and analogies often constitute an important part of such understanding, even though their explanatory role cannot be formally assessed and their correlations with experience cannot be directly confirmed.

Third, the analogies implicit in the mathematical formulations of a theory, or offered as supplementary to them, frequently serve as guides for further research and often lead to valuable, though unpredictable, results. In the case of Maxwell's electromagnetic theory, the physical analogies of the 1861–62 papers, and those which continued to underlie or to be associated with the formal field equations, helped lead to the later concept of the electromagnetic field, which retains some affinities with Faraday's and Maxwell's ideal of physical lines of force. The vortex idea is still recognizable in such features of later atomic theory as the concept of electrons moving in orbits about their nuclei. There are, of course, important differences between these two later conceptions and the mechanical models of people like Faraday, Thomson, and Maxwell. But the point is that there are important continuities as well.

Fourth, the view of theories and theory-confirmation in physics that we are now criticizing assumes that a hard-and-fast distinction can be made between theories, taken as predictive calculi, and empirical facts, regarded as an entirely independent basis for decisive, final testing of their truth. But Whitehead reminds us that there is no such thing as pure, uninterpreted experience: "If we desire a record of uninterpreted experience, we must ask a stone to record its autobiography. Every scientific memoir in its record of the 'facts' is shot through and through with interpretation."[67] Many philosophers of science of recent decades have agreed with him, arguing that theories and facts cannot be radically distinguished because they are dialectically related to one another.

As Harold Brown puts it, there is an ongoing "interplay" or "transaction" between theory and observation, "where theory determines what observations are worth making and how they are to be understood, and observation provides challenges to accepted theoretical structures."[68] Even Israel Scheffler, despite his complete lack of sympathy with subjectivist views of science, recognizes that observation statements "are not isolated certainties, but must be accommodated with other beliefs in a process during which they may themselves be overridden."[69] So once again, fallible elements of human assumption, expectation, and judgment cannot be eliminated from the investigatory act. Justification comes down in the final analysis, even in so exact a discipline as physics, to the consensus of people in a position to judge. And the firm consensus of one time may well be overturned at a later time. Such a fundamental change in consensus took place shortly after Maxwell's time, overturning the Newtonian assumptions that he and his contemporaries took so much for granted. Maxwell himself unwittingly made important contributions toward the eventual overthrow of those same assumptions. The role of the ironic, the unpredictable, and the surprising in the history of physics is thus made readily apparent.

The lesson, then, is that physics is not so much a body of fixed theories and final formulations as an active, never-ending program of research.[70] The direction and character of that research undergo some fundamental changes over time as new theories are created in response to the impetus of new problems or of old problems seen in a new way. To identify physics with fixed theories established by indisputable facts, and to dismiss as irrelevant its ongoing processes of innovation and discovery, is a much too static and after-the-fact way of looking at it. Physics is, after all, a human undertaking, both suffering and benefiting from changes in human imagination, habituation, and perspective, manifesting themselves over time. The world portrayed by physics is, to a significant extent, the product of the inventiveness and creative imagination of physicists. Creation, discovery, and description go hand in hand.

To be sure, physics does exhibit a bright paradigm of rationality and accomplishment in which we can rightly take pride. But it is not the only such paradigm, nor is its rationality one of unchanging certitude, unbroken progress, or total objectivity. It is essential to remember, moreover, that the methods of physics, like those of other disciplines, gain much of their distinctive value and degree of precision at the price of abstraction; they pay close attention to some aspects of experience and ways of responding to it at the expense of others. As William James observed, "We have so many different businesses with nature that no one of them yields us an all-embracing clasp." Another of his dicta is equally cogent and apropos: "There is no possible point of view from which the world can appear as an absolutely single fact."[71] The rationality of physics, therefore, needs to be complemented with the methods and approaches of many other perspectives, including those of the traditional humanistic disciplines, if we are to begin to do justice to the complexity and concreteness of our experience. For example, physics has helped to get us to the moon, but we need to draw extensively on the resources of such disciplines as poetry, philosophy, and religion in order to comprehend fully the significance of having gotten there and to weigh the consequences of this and similar feats for the future of humankind.

2. *Philosophy:* The stereotype of philosophy portrays it as being lodged mainly at the first stage of the structure of creativity, the stage of impetus, all problems and no resolutions. Its innovations, though impressive and many, do not quite count as creative ones (in our sense of the term) because they never get anywhere, so far as justification and regularization are concerned. It follows that the environment of philosophy seems to be hopeless confusion, marked by endless debate among seemingly incommensurable perspectives and systems, by glaring lack of consensus on any important issues, and by absence of recognized accomplishments that have served or can serve as stepping stones to progress.

What was Bertrand Russell's environment like? Was it really as chaotic and confused as the stereotype would have us believe? It hardly seems so, for as we have pointed out, there was an emerging consensus, from the time of Descartes, through Kant, up to the turn of the twentieth century, about the importance of the careful study of language as it relates to problems in philosophy. And progress had already been made in distinguishing the surface grammar of language from its deep structure, as with Kant's crucial insistence that *exists*, though it may occupy the place of a predicate, does not refer to a property in the way that predicates ordinarily do. One important feature of the predicate calculus, worked out by Russell and Whitehead, was that it was able to symbolize clearly the distinction between property aspects and existence aspects of our statements.

Both Kant's insight and the development of the predicate calculus were genuine milestones in the history of philosophy,[72] which Russell was able to take into account when devising his theory of descriptions. Just as Kant had seen that *exists* used as a predicate does not function as a predicate, so Russell was able to realize that sentence subjects need not be names. He was also anxious to maintain five important features of his environment in developing his theory of descriptions, a fact that clearly militates against the idea that every new theory of philosophy is developed in a "vacuum," oblivious to its environment. This is not to say that Russell agreed with everything in his environment. He strongly disagreed, for example, with one aspect of Meinong's theory (though he agreed with another). It is in the nature of an innovation that it adds new elements or new emphases to the environment, and it is likely that the new perspectives it opens up will be in tension with some features of the environment. But Russell's disagreement with Meinong was in the interest of maintaining certain traits of the environment, as for example, the long-standing stress on empirical tests of meaning and truth, which Meinong's theory had tended to neglect.

Turning now to justification, one may find that not only are there contending philosophical schools, but that philosophers (like artists) can only establish themselves professionally by developing a unique vision at odds with all other positions, and that given such a field of contending views there could be no justification, since what would count as justification would also be forever under contention. But the case studies argue otherwise. First, science, the paradigm of justified research, is the result of contending views among its practitioners. Maxwell's physical model was widely disputed and ultimately ignored, but such disputes do not show that scientific theories lack evidential support.[73]

Furthermore, the discussion of Russell's theory of descriptions shows that there were many good reasons for accepting it as a justified analysis. It solved specific and long-standing puzzles, removed a temptation to an otherwise suspect ontology (Meinong's), and played an important role in advancing both formal logic and empiricist epistemology. More could hardly be asked of a proposal. In addition, it promised a new avenue of philosophical research that soon became a major movement, Ideal Language Analysis. This movement dominated Anglo-American thought for over a decade and still is basic to philosophers in the broad tradition of linguistic analysis. Linguistic philosophy provides one set of answers to the question What is the role of philosophy in a scientific age? These answers attempt to delineate philosophy's unique mission among intellectual disciplines, while at the same time placing philosophy in close cooperation with science, mathematics, and logic.

There is also meaningful progress in philosophy. To take one example from the case study, Meinong's argument for the subsistence of the Golden Mountain was thoroughly discredited by Russell's theory. This does not mean we might not want someday to distinguish, say, possible from actual entities and argue that both possess some sort of existence (as some contemporary modal logics seem to do). But we will not invoke Meinong's reasons for such a move, for it is now obvious that at least two of his presuppositions are suspect, and so we need not be driven to his conclusion by a naive trust in those principles.[74] That we might return to a view similar to one of Meinong's conclusions no more argues lack of progress in philosophy than a return in some future physical theory to a concept of action-at-a-distance would show that science fails to progress.

Given that we can speak meaningfully of environment, progress, and justification in philosophy, it is no surprise that what we have called regularization can be found there as well. Indeed, it is presupposed by the idea of progress: today's innovation becomes tomorrow's basis for future research. It remains only to add a word about agreement in philosophy. There are two aspects of Russell's achievement to note in this regard. First, his analysis became the standard in predicate logic and his method of logical paraphrase became a widely employed philosophical tool. So to that considerable extent there was agreement among a large group of professionals about the importance and correctness of his view. But also, Russell's arguments attained a clarity that allows us to know what sort of claims will count against it. This precision permits a rational debate about his conclusions, which is another aspect of agreement. A professional community not only agrees about goals and presuppositions, but agrees to disagree in certain established ways.

There are, of course, competing schools of philosophy that disagree fundamentally with Russell's most basic presuppositions about correct method in philosophy. Those who deny that there is agreement and progress in philosophy have in mind such basic disagreement. But it should also be pointed out how few such paradigms there are at a given time, and that some rational conversation is possible even across such chasms. Science is thought to lack such widely divergent schools of thought, and perhaps it does. But whether scientists ought to confine themselves to one paradigm at a time is hotly debated among philosophers of science, so this purported difference between philosophy and science may not be fundamental.

3. *Painting:* Discussions about art are still often influenced by positivist dichotomies according to which science describes the facts, whereas art expresses feeling. In part, the fact that the sciences possess rather well-defined confirmation procedures tempts us to portray the arts, in contrast, as resting on taste rather than judgment, as concerned only with values (read feelings), as lacking intelligence, and as having no methodology that would make appropriate the word *research.*

Even the best of these claims are misleading half-truths. But unfortunately, they are reinforced by much that visual artists themselves say about the nature of their craft. Artists lead an embattled existence, often surrounded by aesthetically illiterate viewers who attend more to the content of the work than to its formal and expressive qualities and who tend to overly intellectualized responses. Furthermore, as so many visual artists claim, it *is* one of art's special powers to help viewers articulate and express feelings. Artists rightly perceive that paintings are not theories and cannot be verbally paraphrased. Not surprisingly, they sometimes try to express this set of ideas in slogans that emphasize subjectivity, taste, intuition, invention, and feeling at the expense of reasoned judgment, justification, thought, discovery, and truth.

Nevertheless, as the case study illustrates, the institution of painting is a highly intelligent and complex set of activities that cannot be reduced either to the mere display of formal qualities or to the simple expression of feeling. Painting is surrounded by sophisticated discussion and theory, and necessarily so.[75] Philosophy of art, criticism, and art history play roles vis-à-vis art quite similar to those played by the philosophy and history of science with respect to science. Such meta-theoretical and methodological concerns are well exemplified by Rauschenberg's accomplishment and his discussion of it, in which, as we have shown, he displays a sensitivity to ontological, metaphysical, and historical issues.

In discussing the stereotype we have mentioned formalist aesthetic theory. Like positivist theories of science, formalist aesthetics is both the glory and the misery of modern art. It has made possible a productive and revelatory concentration on the formal properties of paintings such as color, balance, line, and texture, and it has provided a conceptual framework for viewing art autonomously, so that artists can concentrate on their own purely aesthetic ends apart from the intrusion of extrinsic religious, political, and ethical issues. For formalist theory comprises two claims: that what makes paintings unique among objects are just these formal features (such as line, color, and texture, which all and only artworks have in common); and that since these properties are unique to art, they alone must be relevant to understanding and evaluating artworks. Good artworks display significant form; bad ones lack it.

The structure of creativity for which we are arguing can fit purely formalist artistic intentions, since there are innovations in form made in a context of, and as responses to, formal problems. But in general, formalist doctrine claims to be irrelevant many features of artworks, attention to which makes even more plausible the model of the creative process. The discussion of Rauschenberg's work indicates that he was accomplishing several things at once, only one of which was the creation of formally sound artworks. His paintings were highly plausible, sophisticated models of the urban environment that introduced a new ontology and a new grammar and that were intended as politically and even spiritually instrumental. All such considerations are ruled out as aesthetically irrelevant on the formalist account, but all of them are relevant to seeing the work in context and evaluating its full value as a cultural artifact to be judged in part by its truthfulness, social efficacy, and utility. The meanings of Rauschenberg's works go beyond the formal properties themselves; indeed, these properties are in the service of the communication of these meanings. It is in terms of such meanings that the work is to be justified in the sense of justification discussed in the case study.

Classical formalism, as developed by Clive Bell, for example, rests on an intuitionist theory of value akin to G.E. Moore's ethical intuitionism.[76] Significant form is claimed to be in effect a nonnatural property which we can intuit that a painting lacks or possesses. This is an interesting theory, but it is easily confused with the more misleading claim that judgments of aesthetic worth are completely subjective expressions of taste, and are hence nonrational.

This brings us to the question of evaluation. Emphasis on innovation at the expense of the other features of the creative process leads to the simple-minded view that the artist creates and the audience likes or dislikes the creation. "It's all a matter of taste," "There are tastemakers who control the artworld," and "There is no art history, only a history of taste" are often-heard claims among artists and nonartists alike. Again, these claims are half-truths, and again our concern here is to expose their shortcomings.

It is worthwhile to remember the distinction between questions of taste and questions of judgment celebrated in introductory logic texts. "I like it" is about me; "It is good" is about the artwork and implies that reasons can be given in its support. The case study indicates that there are indeed many and varied justificatory reasons for praising Rauschenberg's achievement. The critical process, when seriously carried out, is never merely an expression of taste, for it requires literacy in the visual languages of art, careful and true description, imaginative analysis, and educated interpretation.[77] It is a matter of theorizing about the meaning of the work and its place in the context of the problems and concerns of the time.

Such judgments are fallible and controversial, of course; but to make that point by invoking talk of taste leaves us unable to discuss adequately the potential profundity of paintings and the nature of serious attempts at interpretation and evaluation. To try to characterize aesthetic evaluations in terms of taste is, in fact, to fail to take evaluative questions seriously.

The stereotype, emphasizing as it does creation *ex nihilo* and skill in one's craft, leaves no room for the discussion of research in the arts. Indeed, that term may seem strangely out of place, in spite of the fact that use of the phrase *scientific research* implies that there could be nonscientific research. Research in art usually applies to work in art history.

But on the account we are developing here, one could speak meaningfully of the painter's research activity, so we argue that this important word should not be uncritically narrowed to apply only in scientific contexts. On the contrary, in showing that an artistic accomplishment like Rauschenberg's fits our model of creativity, we have shown in fact that the term *research* is appropriate, at least if we take seriously its etymology. For the *re* in *research* comes from a particular use in Latin referring to activities undertaken (a) in response to a stimulus and (b) with intensive force. Thus, the word as a whole connotes intensive searching or investigation undertaken in response to a stimulus and directed towards discovery.[78]

We, of course, understand "in response to a stimulus" in terms of what we have called impetus. Further, we have emphasized that directed and intensive investigation is best accomplished in the context of institutions, meta-theoretical discussions, and the judgments of a peer community— whether the investigation is that of painter, physicist, or philosopher. Last, though the stereotypes dictate that discovery belongs primarily to science, we have tried to indicate by our case studies that the distinction between discovery and creation does not mark a difference between science and painting and that in each of our example disciplines the two are inextricably mixed. It would thus be appropriate and revealing to speak of Robert Rauschenberg as a leading researcher in art, and to characterize the combined efforts of Rauschenberg, Johns, and the pop artists who followed them as research into certain visual aspects of our culture and the visual media that dominate it.

## NOTES

1. Albert Einstein and Leopold Infeld, *The Evolution of Physics* (Cambridge: At the University Press, 1938), 148.

2. *The Scientific Papers of James Clerk Maxwell*, ed. W. D. Niven, 2 vols. (Cambridge: At the University Press, 1980), 1:451–513; hereafter referred to as *SP*.

3. For an interesting discussion of Maxwell's views on the complementary relations of mathematical descriptions and physical analogies in science, see *SP*, 1:155–56.

4. Useful portrayals of the environment for Maxwell's work, and of its development, can be found in *Science in the Nineteenth Century*, ed. René Taton and trans. A. J. Pomerans, vol. 4 of *History of Science*, ed. René Taton (New York: Basic Books, 1965), 178–211; R. A. R. Tricker, *The Contributions of Faraday and Maxwell to Electrical Science* (Oxford: Pergamon Press, 1966), 3–12.

5. See also Maxwell, *A Treatise on Electricity and Magnetism*, 2d ed. (Oxford: Clarendon Press, 1892), 1:ix.

6. See also ibid., 2:483–84, 487, 492–93.

7. Quoted in *SP*, 2:317. See also Mary Hesse, *Forces and Fields* (New York: Philosophical Library, 1961), 216.

8. Ampère, *Reply to Van Beek,* October 1821, quoted in Taton, *Science in the Nineteenth Century,* 188.

9. See also Maxwell, *Treatise,* 2:492; Taton, *Science in the Nineteenth Century,* 207–210; Harold I. Sharlin, *Lord Kelvin: The Dynamic Victorian* (University Park: Pennsylvania State University Press, 1979), 212–13.

10. See also Maxwell, *Treatise,* 2:468–70.

11. Ibid., 2:460–61; Sharlin, *Lord Kelvin,* 69–71, 86–88.

12. See fig. 1 in *SP,* 1:488, for a pictorial representation of the production of an electromagnetic field by an electric current. And see p. 468 for Maxwell's introduction of the "idler wheels" analogy.

13. See *SP,* 1:460, for a diagram portraying the deflection of the north and south poles of a magnet in a magnetic field, and for Maxwell's explanation of this effect in terms of the interplay of the vortices of the magnet and the field.

14. Lenz's Law is one example. See Lewis Campbell and William Garnett, *The Life of James Clerk Maxwell* (1882; reprint, New York and London: Johnson Reprint Corporation, 1969), 526, 540.

15. Hesse, *Forces and Fields,* 221.

16. Ibid., 210.

17. A. N. Whitehead, *Science and the Modern World* (Cambridge: At the University Press, 1926), 189–90.

18. The first volume was published in 1910 (Cambridge: At the University Press). Volumes 2 and 3 were published in 1912 and 1913, respectively.

19. *The Autobiography of Bertrand Russell* (New York: Bantam Books, 1951). Russell credits Peano more than Fregé. See pp. 191–93, where he describes his meeting with Peano at the Paris International Congress of Philosophy in 1900. In contrast, Russell had been reading Fregé since 1893, but he claims he did not understand the latter's work until he himself had had the same thoughts (pp. 82–83).

20. See the cover notes to *Principia Mathematica to \*56* by Whitehead and Russell (Cambridge: At the University Press, 1962).

21. Russell, "On Denoting," *Mind,* n.s., 19 (1905): 530–38. Reprinted in *Contemporary Readings in Logical Theory,* ed. I. M. Copi and J. A. Gould (New York: Macmillan, 1967), 93–105.

22. These are statements that contain as grammatical subject a definite description: a phrase of the form *the-so-and-so.*

23. The full translation is: "There exists at least one entity, x, and there exists at most one entity, x, such that x is a present King of France, and x is bald." Note that the apparent name ("the present King of France") occurs nowhere in this paraphrase as a denoting expression. Instead it has been spread out over the quantifier expression and the predicate, "x is a present King of France." Since there is nothing of which this predicate is now true, the original proposition becomes simply false rather than meaningless.

24. See J. N. Findlay, *Meinong's Theory of Objects and Values,* 2d ed. (Oxford: Clarendon Press, 1963).

25. Russell, *Introduction to Mathematical Philosophy* (London: George Allen and Unwin, 1919), chap. 16. Reprinted in *20th-Century Philosophy: The Analytic Tradition,* ed. M. Weitz (New York: Free Press, 1966), 146–55. The quote is from p. 147 in the Weitz reprint.

26. Russell, "On Denoting."

27. See, for example, Noam Chomsky's discussion of the distinction between deep and surface structures of sentences in natural language that arose among the

followers of Descartes: *Cartesian Linguistics* (New York: Harper and Row, 1966), 31–51. See also Kant's critique of Anselm's Ontological Proof for the existence of God in *Critique of Pure Reason,* trans. N. K. Smith (New York: St. Martin's Press, 1961), Chap. 3, sec. 4, pp. 500ff.

28. Ernst Mach, "Newton's Views of Time, Space, and Motion," in *Readings in the Philosophy of Science,* ed. H. Feigl and M. Brodbeck (New York: Appleton-Century-Crofts, 1953), 165–70; *Translations from the Philosophical Writings of Gottlob Frege,* ed. Peter Geach and Max Black (Oxford: Basil Blackwell, 1960), particularly "Function and Concept," 21–41.

29. Friedrich Nietzsche, *Twilight of the Idols,* in *The Portable Nietzsche,* ed. W. Kaufmann (New York: Viking Press, 1954), 483.

30. Russell, *Introduction to Mathematical Philosophy,* ed. Weitz, 147.

31. Ibid., 149.

32. Russell, "On Denoting," 101.

33. Ramsey is quoted in the introduction to the reprint of Russell's "Descriptions," in *Classics of Analytic Philosophy,* ed. Robert Ammerman (New York: McGraw-Hill, 1965), 15.

34. The most fruitful of these disputes is the one between Russell and P. F. Strawson. See ibid., pt. 3, 315–40.

35. Calvin Tomkins, *Off the Wall: The Art World of Our Time* (Garden City, N.Y.: Doubleday & Co. 1980), 96.

36. Actually, there were two ruling aesthetics, often combined: abstract expressionism and what we might call nonobjective formalism. Many expressionist paintings were nonobjective (they did not represent objects at all, even abstractly). And often the discussion centered around their formal properties as well as their expressive characteristics.

37. From videotaped remarks at Colorado State University, March 1981. Our italics.

38. Selden Rodman, *Conversations with Artists* (New York: Devin-Adaro, 1957). Quoted in Tomkins, *Off the Wall,* 37.

39. In a videotaped interview at Colorado State University, March 1981, Rauschenberg said in response to the question whether his works were autobiographical that "I do not editorialize. . . . My private horror is my own."

40. Before entering art school, Rauschenberg changed his name from Milton to Robert choosing the latter because it belonged to more of his Navy buddies than any other name. Later, when people began sending him exotic objects for his collages, he refused to include them. This predilection for the unobtrusive, ordinary object runs through his work.

41. Lawrence Alloway, "Rauschenberg's Development," in Alloway, *Robert Rauschenberg* (Washington, D.C.: Smithsonian Institution, 1976).

42. See Alloway, *Robert Rauschenberg,* 5, and Ron G. Williams, "Public Image: A Philosopher's Homage to Rauschenberg," in the exhibition catalogue *Rauschenberg in the Rockies* (Fort Collins: Colorado State University, 1981).

43. This remark is often quoted but rarely footnoted. See Robert Hughes's informative article on Rauschenberg in *Time,* 29 November 1976, 59.

44. Informal remarks, Colorado State University, March 1981. For a similar point see Philip Smith, "To and About Robert Rauschenberg," *Arts Magazine* 51 (1977): 120–21. In context, "change" refers to the changes that take place in persons and ultimately in society when we learn to see with "fresh eyes," eyes less constrained by habit and preconception.

45. Ron G. Williams, "Talking Picture, Silent Sentences: A Philosopher's View of 'Bent Blue,'" in the exhibition catalogue *Jasper Johns Prints* (Fort Collins: Colorado State University, 1979).

46. Lawrence Alloway, *Systemic Painting* (New York: Solomon R. Guggenheim Museum Catalog, 1966), quoted in Jonas Mekas, "Notes After Reseeing the Movies of Andy Warhol," in *Andy Warhol*, ed. John Coplans (New York: New York Graphic Society, 1970), 140.

47. In videotaped remarks at Colorado State University, March 1981.

48. *Gertrude Stein on Picasso*, ed. Edward Burns (New York: Liveright, 1970), 18.

49. John Cage, *Silence* (Middletown, Conn.: Wesleyan University Press, 1961). See also Tomkins, *Off the Wall*, chap. 4.

50. John Malcolm Brinnin, *The Third Rose: Gertrude Stein and Her World* (New York: Grove Press, 1959), xiii.

51. In videotaped remarks at Colorado State University, March 1981.

52. Since the resulting artworks display paradoxes of self reference, only an elaborate, probably intensional semantic theory could do them justice. See Williams, "Talking Picture, Silent Sentences," for a discussion of some connections among contemporary painting, logic, and the philosophy of language.

53. For reproductions of Rauschenberg's major combines, see Alloway, *Robert Rauschenberg*.

54. Rauschenberg, quoted in ibid., 7.

55. John Cage often speaks of his music as intended to help the listener have "fresh ears." Rauschenberg takes this idea over into his own work by declaring that it should help us have fresh eyes. And like Cage, Rauschenberg insists that if his work were successful, "there would be no need for art," for we would be able to respond aesthetically to our environment. See Smith, "To and About Robert Rauschenberg," 121.

56. Rauschenberg, in videotaped remarks, March 1981: "I wouldn't make art if I thought there was no person who was changing," and "I crave your [the audience's] participation."

57. Arthur Danto, "The Artistic Enfranchisement of Real Objects: The Artworld," *Journal of Philosophy* 61 (1964): 571–84.

58. Heinrich Hertz, *The Principles of Mechanics Presented in a New Form* (New York: Dover Publications, 1956), particularly the introduction.

59. Clive Bell, "Art as Significant Form: The Aesthetic Hypothesis," reprinted in *Aesthetics: A Critical Anthology*, ed. G. Dickie and R. Sclafani (New York: St. Martin's Press, 1977), 36–48.

60. Dorothy Norman, *Alfred Stieglitz* (Millerton, N.Y.: Aperture, 1976), 12.

61. We refer here to a stereotype that dominates much of the field, the teaching of the field, and attitudes of many outside the field, despite the fact of twenty years of criticism by such philosophers of science as Thomas Kuhn, Norwood Hanson, and Paul Feyerabend. There are, of course, physicists who do not endorse this view, especially those actively involved in basic, vanguard research.

62. This stereotype has been given some support by the distinction, made by Hans Reichenbach and others, between the "context of discovery" and the "context of justification," with an accompanying tendency to emphasize the latter and to neglect the former, at least so far as the idea of philosophy of science as a "rational reconstruction" of science is concerned. See Reichenbach, *Experience and Prediction* (Chicago: University of Chicago Press, 1938), chap. 1, sec. 1. The work of the philosophers of science mentioned in the previous note has helped to correct this exaggerated emphasis

on logic and method in physics. Another work of this sort, which especially emphasizes the role of nonformal community consensus and judgment in science, is Harold I.
Brown's *Perception, Theory and Commitment* (Chicago: University of Chicago Press, 1979).

63. Norwood Hanson, *Patterns of Discovery* (Cambridge: At the University Press,
1958), 1. Hanson's book is an admirable attempt to focus on one such period, namely,
that of current work in microphysics.

64. Tomkins, *Off the Wall*, 59.

65. Tom Wolfe, *The Painted Word* (New York: Farrar, Strauss, and Giroux, 1975).

66. Stephen Toulmin, *Foresight and Understanding* (Bloomington: Indiana University Press, 1961). This example is also cited in Ian G. Barbour, *Myths, Models and
Paradigms: A Comparative Study in Science and Religion* (New York: Harper and Row, 1974),
41. Barbour's book has a more extensive discussion of some of the points made in this
subsection. See esp. 34–42, 92–98.

67. A. N. Whitehead, *Process and Reality* (New York: Macmillan Co., 1929), 22.

68. Brown, *Perception, Theory and Commitment*, 167.

69. Israel Scheffler, *Science and Subjectivity* (Indianapolis: Bobbs-Merrill, 1967),
119.

70. This point is made particularly well by Harold Brown and is the central
theme of his *Perception, Theory and Commitment*. See the summary of his position on
166–67. His book contains many useful historical illustrations for some of the arguments and claims of this subsection.

71. William James, *A Pluralistic Universe; The Will to Believe and Other Essays in
Popular Philosophy*. Excerpted in *William James: A Comprehensive Edition*, ed. John J.
McDermott (Chicago: University of Chicago Press, 1977), 493, 135.

72. The development of the predicate calculus was as monumental a mark of
progress in logic and philosophy as was the discovery of the infinitesimal calculus by
Newton and Leibniz in the fields of mathematics and mathematical physics.

73. Similarly, the fact that there is disagreement about certain formulations or
features of Neo-Darwinian evolutionary theory among its contemporary advocates is
no significant reason for rejecting the theory as a whole, despite the claims of some
creationists.

74. The principles in question are (a) that definite descriptions (and sentence
subjects generally) are always denoting expressions, and (b) that denoting expressions
lacking referents are meaningless. The first, of course, was challenged by Russell. The
second has been questioned by more recent philosophers of language.

75. For the claim that the Artworld and meta-theory make art possible, see
Danto, "Artistic Enfranchisement of Real Objects," 572.

76. Clive Bell, *Art* (London: Chatto and Windus, 1914), and G. E. Moore, *Principia Ethica* (Cambridge: At the University Press, 1903). Bell's intuitionism is indirect
compared to that of his friend Moore, but it is there.

77. For a succinct outline of the various phases of the critical process, see
Edmund Burke Feldman, *Varieties of Visual Experience* (Englewood Cliffs, N.J.: Prentice-
Hall, 1973), 466–84.

78. *The Oxford Dictionary of English Etymology*, s.v. "re" and "research."

# Notes on Contributors

STEPHEN BRUSH is a professor of history at the Institute for Physical Science and Technology at the University of Maryland, College Park. He has edited the principal writings on kinetic theory (*Kinetic Theory*, 3 vols., 1965, 1966, 1972) and published *The Kind of Motion We Call Heat: A History of the Kinetic Theory of Gases in the 19th Century* (1976) and *The Temperature of History: Phases of Science and Culture in the Nineteenth Century* (1978).

DONALD A. CROSBY has published *Horace Bushnell's Theory of Language, in the Context of Other Nineteenth-Century Philosophies of Language* (1975) and *Interpretive Theories of Religion* (1981). He is professor of philosophy at Colorado State University, Fort Collins.

LEONARD ISAACS is professor of humanities in the Lyman Briggs School, Michigan State University, East Lansing.

GLENN W. MOST is presently writing about the poetic career, with reference to Virgil, and about the theory of allegorical interpretation of the Greek gods. Professor Most teaches classics at Princeton University.

GEORGE OVITT, JR., is professor of English at Drexel University, Philadelphia. Currently he is writing about the relations between technology, the liberal arts curriculum, and science in the fourteenth century.

STUART PETERFREUND, who teaches English at Northeastern University, Boston, is the editor of *Romanticism Past and Present* and has written and published extensively on eighteenth- and nineteenth-century aesthetics, romantic literature, and critical theory.

RON G. WILLIAMS is professor of philosophy at Colorado State University, Fort Collins. He coauthored with Samuel Gorovitz *Philosophical Analysis: An Introduction to Its Language and Techniques* (1965; 3d ed., 1979) and has written introductions and notes for shows by contemporary artists such as Jasper Johns, Shelby Adams, Robert Rauschenberg, Andy Warhol, and Roy Lichtenstein.

# Index

Aristotle, 11–33; *De Interpretatione*, 16–18; on homonymy, 11–15; on language and signification, 15–19; on metaphor, 19–23, 29–30; on *phantasia* and sense perception, 11, 27–30; *Poetics*, 15–16, 18–22; *Rhetoric*, 11–12, 22; *Sophistical Refutations*, 13; *Topics*, 14

Astronomy: Isidore of Seville on, 35, 37–38; medieval views on, 35–40

Augustine, Saint: on philosophy of language, 152–53

Bacon, Sir Francis, 135, 136; on Aristotle, 50–51, 138; on language and science, 141–43

Baltimore, David, 91–92

Blake, William, 147

Bronowski, Jacob, 134, 135

Cage, John: and modern art, 189–91, 194

Campbell, Joseph: on myth, 77

Chargaff, Erwin, 85, 89

Chaucer, Geoffrey: *Treatise on the Astrolabe*, 34–58; and "Masha'allah's" *De compositione*, 42–50, 52; and use of vernacular in science writing, 41–42

Creative process: definition of elements of, 168–70; stereotypical views of, 196–200

Darwin, Charles, 122

Davis, Nuel, 72, 73

Duhem, Pierre, 51

Eichner, Hans: on science and romanticism, 135, 136, 147, 148

Einstein, Albert, 144; and relation between science and religion, 156–61

Elie de Beaumont, Leonce, 120

Fourier, J. B. J., 120–21

Frankenstein: as public myth, 59–104. *See also* Shelley, Mary

"Frankenstein scenario," 59–104; and atomic bomb research, 63–73; and recombinant DNA research, 80–98

Freud, Sigmund: on language and creativity, 145, 150–51

Galileo, 39, 138, 143

Geikie, Archibald, 112, 114, 124–27

Geology: in nineteenth century, 119–27

Hegel, Georg Wilhelm Friedrich, 109

Historiography: in nineteenth century, 107–19, 126–27

Holton, Gerald: on language and science, 134–35

Jungk, Robert, 67

Kuhn, Thomas S.: and history and philosophy of science, 118, 134, 147–48

Lyell, Charles, 107, 109–14, 119–24

Maxwell, James Clerk: creative process of, 200–204; and mechanical theory of electromagnetism, 170–78

Meinong, Alexius von, 180, 205–6

Metaphor in science, 7–8, 112–13, 134–36, 158–59, 161–64

Mislow, Kurt, 97–98

Myth, 59–60, 77–80, 98–101, 137–38, 144–45, 163

Newton, Sir Isaac, 146; on scientific language, 143–44, 152–56

Oppenheimer, J. Robert, 63–73

Plato: *Cratylus*, 139–41; on *phantasia*, 28
Prague School: on ordinary and poetic language, 137
Popper, Karl: on philosophy of science, 110, 148–49

Ranke, Leopold von, 107–13; and history of English Civil War, 115–19
Rauschenberg, Robert: creative process of, 207–10; and Willem De Kooning, 185–86, 193; and Jasper Johns, 186, 188–89, 194–95; and modern art, 185–96
Recombinant DNA research, 80–98; and Watson and Crick, 82–84
Rifkin, Jeremy, 93; *Who Shall Play God?*, 86
Russell, Bertrand: creative process of, 204–7; and empiricism, 183–84; and Ideal Language Philosophy, 185; and Theory of Descriptions, 178–85

Sacrobosco, Johannes de: *De Sphaera*, 45–46
Schrödinger, Erwin, 81
Scientific language, 7–8, 134–48, 152–56, 156–61
Shelley, Mary: *Frankenstein*, 60–62, 66–68, 71–72, 74–76
Singer, Maxine, 86
Sinsheimer, Robert, 84, 85, 89
Stein, Gertrude, 89–90
Suess, Eduard, 112

Teller, Edward, 69, 70
Thomson, William, 123–24
Trevelyan, George Macaulay: and history of the English Civil War, 113–119

Vico, Giambattista, 111; on language and myth, 150–51, 162–63
Vulcanism: nineteenth-century account of, 119–26

Wald, George, 90
Werner, Abraham, 112
Wordsworth, William, 149; *The Prelude* (Book 5: The Dream of the Arab), 23–26